AF560855

THE NOVELS OF ANITA DESAI

A CRITICAL STUDY

THE NOVELS OF ANITA DESAI

A CRITICAL STUDY

Edited by
Manmohan K. Bhatnagar
M. Rajeshwar

Published by

ATLANTIC

PUBLISHERS & DISTRIBUTORS (P) LTD

7/22, Ansari Road, Darya Ganj,
New Delhi-110002
Phones : +91-11-40775252, 23273880, 23275880, 23280451
Fax : +91-11-23285873
Web : www.atlanticbooks.com
E-mail : orders@atlanticbooks.com

Branch Office
5, Nallathambi Street, Wallajah Road,
Chennai-600002
Phones : +91-44-64611085, 32413319
E-mail : chennai@atlanticbooks.com

Printed in India at Glorious Printers, A-13, D.S.I.D.C., Jhilmil Industrial Area, Delhi-110095

PREFACE

Anita Desai has incontrovertibly added a few rich dimensions to the thematic spectrum of Indian English fiction. Her novels are deeply moving stories of individuals on the horns of a socio-cultural and existential dilemma. Her novels also constitute an artistic success formally through deft deployment of images, symbols and other poetic devices. Applying sociological, psychoanalytic, structural and other approaches of close textual analysis, the essays in the present anthology take a fresh look at established works, exploring thematic as well as stylistic dimensions of her novels, hitherto left unexplored. The contributors to the present volume of the anthology, have specially worked out their studies from the chosen perspective for this collection, for which they deserve sincere thanks. A special word of indebtedness to the publisher, Dr. K.R. Gupta — a fellow academic, whose immense help and moral support made all the difference.

M.K. BHATNAGAR

CONTENTS

1

"Cry the Perturbed Self" — A Note on Anita Desai

PROF. M.K. BHATNAGAR*

Bereft of the revolting excesses of the ideologue feminists, Anita Desai has silently but steadily and certainly made the marginal move to the centre stage. Gently shaking off the paternalistic and at times condescending liberalism of a Bhattacharya, the abstraction-mongering of a Raja Rao, the propagandist tokenism of an M.R. Anand, Anita Desai in both the form and content of her writings leaves unmistakably the feminine imprint without pausing to define 'a female sentence', 'female time' or some other such inartistic formulation. Her women are quintessential seekers, hankering after what has since long been routine pursuits for their male counterparts but what appears preposterous and appalling in their case. One must hasten to add that the questing protagonists of Desai include a couple of males too. What these protagonists strive for is self-realization, self-fulfilment, carving out an identity, a true image of their individual beings, literal and figurative space to be themselves, to define themselves, to make a foray into the outward, to make their own mistakes and retrace their steps if the need be, rather than being chaperoned everywhere. To ask whether they all succeed or not in doing what they endeavour to do is to belittle the enormity of their situation. The singular most distinction of the novelist is in suggesting in quite a few of her novels, at times overtly, at times covertly, the small but significant change wrought in the perceptions of the other characters in the wake of the strivings of the central

*Department of English, Maharshi Dayanand University, Rohtak (Haryana).

characters. Even where the note on which the novels end is stark and devoid of any tangible sign of complacence, they do seem to succeed in jolting one into a new perception of reality. While Sita in *Where Shall we Go This Summer*? does have a sort of family reunion and 'where shall we go this summer' is no more a disquieting question left hanging in the air, her other artistic siblings — Maya (*Cry, the Peacock*); Monisha and Amla (*Voices in the City*); Sarah Sen (*Bye Bye Blackbird*); Nanda and Raka (*Fire on the Mountain*) and Bim and Tara (*Clear Light of Day*) — are poised tentalizingly at different junctures of the philosophic spectrum. Even the travails of male protagonists in Desai in characters like Devan Sharma (*In Custody*) and Baumgartner (*Baumgartner's Bombay*) have been sympathetically attended to.

Anita Desai's novels have excited both lay readers and critics alike. The central concerns in both the cases have not been very much dissimilar : alienation, the 'inscape' of a guest for the elusive self, existentialist yearnings in claustrophobic environs, the interaction between the old and the new, the dilemma of choosing between the instinct to conform and the urge to rebel. The essays on different novels of Anita Desai touch these vital issues in a precise and systematic manner. Dr. S.S. Rengachari in "Fate and Fatalism in Anita Desai's *Cry, the Peacock*" attempts a nimble tight-rope walking sorting out how far the protagonist wills her fate in the novel. Dr. Inamdar's article, "Treatment of Neurosis in *Cry, the Peacock*" focuses on the state of mind of the protagonist. Dr. M. Rajeshwar in "Superstition and Psyche in Anita Desai's *Cry, the Peacock*" offers a psychoanalytic perspective. It is from the same angle that Dr. M. Mani Meitei approaches the novelist in "Anita Desai's *Where Shall we go this Summer*? — A Psychoanalytic Study." The theme of immigration and its human fallout, as dealt with in the novelist's works, has been brought out in Dr. Sumitra Kukreti's "Love Hate Relationship of Expatriates in Anita Desai's *Bye Bye Blackbird*." Dr. S.P. Swain in "The Alienated Self — A study of Anita Desai's *Clear Light of Day*" focuses on the novelist's capturing of the individual's plight. How the characters and the setting around them contribute to each other to queer the pitch has been gauged by Dr. K. Ratna Shiela Mani in "Character and Setting in Anita Desai's *In Custody*." Carmen Concilio in "Anita Desai's

Fire On the Mountain and the Iconography of the Crone" deals with the artistic rendering of her theme in the novel. Another critique of the novel, viz., Dr. Brahmananda Chary's "Raka as a Metaphor for Ruined Childhood in Anita Desai's *Fire on the Mountain*" isolates some particular dimensions of the novel for detailed analysis.

The latter essays in the anthology take ahead the discussion by taking up later novels by Desai or focusing on her whole cropus. B. Vyaghreswarudu's "A Focus on Anita Desai's "Games at Twilight" is another sustained critical exercise in thematic and formal analysis. Dr. S.P. Swain takes a broad, generalising look at the novelist's works in "Tradition and Deviation — A Study of Anita Desai's Novels" to focus on the contrary pulls in her novels. The same critic's other over-all study is innovative insofar as it works out the rendering of a theme through formal, poetic devices, *viz.*, "Images of Alienation — A Study of Anita Desai's Novels." The special travails of the female psyche is under focus in Dr. C.V. George's "Alienation of Women Characters in Anita Desai's Novels." Moving beyond alienation, Dr. S.P. Swain isolates the philosophic dimensions in literature in his article "Note of Existentialism in the Novels of Anita Desai." Dr. O.J. Thomas in "Anita Desai : A Grain of Sand in an Oyster'" has similar critical inclinations. Dr. Sandhyarani Dash lays bare the cosmic design in "The Ironic Presence of Nature in the Novels of Anita Desai." Moving from matter to manner Ms. Jayita Sengupta probes into the novelist's narrative strategy in "Time As Narrative Device in the Novels of Anita Desai." The exploitation of the evocative dimensions of time as a sequential factor get rendered effectively in the study.

The analysis of themes, characters and formal strategies in Anita Desai's novels in different essays of the anthology bears an unmistakable testimony to the obvious success of the novelist in capturing the quintessential dilemma of the modern psyche in a form which gives her works perennial artistic significance, independent of the time and the clime.

2

Fate and Fatalism in Anita Desai's *Cry, the Peacock*

DR. (MRS.) S. S. RENGACHARI*

"Writing is to me process of discovering the truth — the truth that is, nine-tenth of the iceberg that lies submerged beneath the one-tenth visible portion we call Reality. Writing is my way of plunging to the depths and exploring this underlying truth. All my writing is an effort to discover, to underline and convey the true significance of things."[1] This is precisely what Anita Desai has attempted in her first novel *Cry, the Peacock*. As is true of most of her novels, the major themes in *Cry, the Peacock* (CTP) are marital disharmony, less of identity, escapism and a sense of the meaninglessness of life. Much has been written on the themes and style of Anita Desai's novels. This article takes into consideration of the different attitudes to fate and fatalism presented in the novel.

The Novel has three parts to it. The first and the third can be considered as the prologue and the epilogue of the novel. In the prologue the author describes the agony and depression suffered by Maya on the death of her pet dog Toto. The atmosphere of gloom reminds her of the albino astrologer's prediction that in the fourth year of her marriage there will be a death, either hers or her husband's.

The novel is mostly in the first person narrative, told by Maya the heroine. She relates her own story and often gives details of her own happy days as a child. The author uses the stream of consciousness technique to explain the cause and growth of her

* Head, Department of English, St. Mary's College, Tuticorin.

despair. To quote Vinod Bhushan Gulati, "The present and the past are juxtaposed to highlight the temperamental incompatibility"[2] between Maya and her husband Gautama.

The second section of the novel reveals the gradual stages by which Maya moves from sanity to insanity. But even here there are occasional flashes of sanity. She makes use of the technique of the stream of consciousness along with the first and third person narratives. She provides full length pictures of the hero as well as the heroine although the central theme revolves round Maya. The section comes to a close with the death of Gautama. The final section which acts as the epilogue provides a powerful picture of the effect of the calamity on the important characters and concludes suggesting some possible endings for the novel.

Maya reveals the first kind of attitude to fate. She believes the albino astrologer's warning regarding her future. She lives a life of horror and fear at the prospect of the astrologer's prophecy being fulfilled. Her heart craves for love and understanding, solace and support from her husband. Gautama tries to lay his finger on the exact problem that bothers her but Maya is too secretive to allow him to learn the cause. He is a normal gentleman interested in his profession of an advocate, perhaps too practical and materialistic to allot time for expressing his love. Maya does not tell him about the albino's prophecy for fear of hurting him. At the same time she is unable to bear the oppressive burden of the secret.

Gautama is the representative of the second attitude to fate in the novel. He does not believe in fate at all and he is of the view that no educated person ought to believe in such things. Pom, a close friend of Maya is anti-theatrical to her in character. She has no thought of fate or tradition or superstition in her life. She enjoys life and is a source of relief to the highly strung Maya.

Maya goes through very strange experiences in her life. Her hallucinations and the repetitions rearing to and from sanity and insanity are responsible for her unhappiness. She feels frightened because she recognises a demoniac creature dancing to the deafening rear of silent drums. She thinks it is the mad demon of Kathakali Ballets. Then she identifies the white body of the dancer. She concludes that it is the "limpid appellation of the noon. It was, I remembered it new, Fate.'' (CTP 28). The strange part of it is that her hallucinations are essentially solipsistic and consequently she cannot share her thoughts with any one.

She visualises fate thus. She remembers his eyes that were pale, opaque, and gave him a look of morbidity. She recalls the experience of her childhood when she met an astrologer who was an albino. She went with her ayah (nurse) and she held the lady's hand in her trembling fingers afraid of being left alone. She avers, "Just as the shadow spread and spread, a stain edging towards me who stood, clutching my ayah's hand, in paralysed terror and even fiercer fascination, my toes curling away from oil, from his shadow, 'Not only here, but in your horoscope also,' he said, tapping the long chart the ayah had made for me, 'and there, on your forehead too,' he smiled, and laying down the paper, he raised his hand, a plump, oiled hand with dyed nails, bringing it close to my face so that I felt as though a bat were caught in the same room with me, and shrank involuntarily. But he lowered it without touching me and turned to finger the horoscope instead, its minute figures and designs. 'Just as it is prophesied here, I see it there,' he smiled. 'Unmistakably.'...Sometimes he grew emphatic, and creased his brow, and raised his arms, his voice. 'Death,' he finally admitted, in one such moment, 'to one of you. When you are married and you shall be married young.'....'Death — an early one — by unnatural causes''(CTP 28-29).

The ayah and the child trembled in terror at the prediction but the albino continued, 'Listen to me, women,' noticing the terrors struck customers he allayed their fears saying, '....[There] is only a faint possibility that her life should take this path. The sign is there. The stars prophesy it. But we are in the hands of God....God guides us all. He may guide you on to another path, if you pray for it to be so, offer sacrifices in order that it may be so.'

It is four years since Maya and Gautama were married and Maya feels certain that one of them has to die. She never thinks of the possibility of averting the calamity by accepting the advice of the albino and seeking the grace of the all-merciful God Almighty. She dare not speak of it to Gautama and there were no friends with whom she could share her fears. The albino becomes a nightmare and his prophesy haunts her repeatedly. 'It seemed real, I could recall each detail, and yet — God, Gautama, father, surely it is nothing but an hallucination. surely not, I sobbed' (CTP 64).

Maya and Gautama go out one evening to attend a dinner party. She feels wretched because the party, the host as well as the guests, did not measure up to her conception of refinement. This reaction, Gautama observes, is the result of her excessive involvement in the party. Mr. Lal, the Sikh friend of Gautama was also his classmate once. He made a reference to the word 'fate' saying he had wanted to meet the brilliant lawyer Gautama but "it was not written in our fate to meet again, till tonight" (CTP 74). The word triggered off a valley of experience from the past for Maya. The word had actually been banned from Maya's household.

To Gautama who was no traditionalist, 'fate' was an alien word right from birth. Maya recalls, "Sitting at the uncovered table under the naked electric bulb, how he had his brothers and sisters would heat with derision at the mention of superstition, with pity and scorn for those who allowed their lives to be ruled by them. and ruined by them. Gautama's father would ask, 'Fate? What is that? I don't know of it — only of work' " (CTP 75). Maya could not bring herself to confide her fears regarding the prediction in her in-laws who seemed to be dead against such notions.

The Sikh offered to read Maya's palm but she became nervous on hearing it. At the same time there was a lurking desire in her to get his opinion regarding her future. She confesses, "I know danger was close now, very close, and the Sikh was no ally of mine, but of that magician of the underworld, the albino, his shadow" (CTP 79). She dare not ask him to prophesy her days ahead lest the prognosis of the albino should get confirmed.

Maya had always believed in the perfection of her world but after learning Gautama's views on astrology and fate she felt that her life was tainted with Fate-fatality. The mental conflict that resulted gets reflected in her physical condition as well. She feels very hot in her bed as she turns over in her mind the experiences of childhood. She avers, "Upon this bed of hot, itching sand, I summoned up again the vision of the tenebrific albino who had cast his shadow like a net across me as I fled down the corridor of years..."(CTP 94/5). She remembered the astrologer's words again.

"Do you not hear the peacocks call in the wilds? 'Pia, pia,' they cry, meaning 'lever, lever....' 'Mie, mie — I die, I die.' The peacocks tear each other to strips before they mate. 'Living they are aware of death. Dying, they are in love with life' " (CTP 96). Maya heard the peacocks and imagined that she could feel the mortal agony of their cry for lever and for death. She is afraid that she will also die like the peacocks. She weeps for the lot of the peacocks and also her pathetic conditions.

During day time she manages to forget the Damocles sword that she believes, hangs above her head and sets it aside as hallucination. But the night are unbearable and she starts wondering whether she had lost her sanity. She raves, "Am I gone insane? Father! brother! Husband! Who is my saviour? I am in need of one" (CTP 98).

Maya associates Gautama with a different world, a world scented with jasmine, resounding with poetry and amiability. She yearned to be part of this world. But she was certain she could never become part of it because her own world was "...hell. Torture, guilt, dread, imprisonment — these were the four walls of my private hell, one that no one could survive in long. Death was certain..." (CTP 102). She is convinced that Gautama is the one fated to live in the world that she loved more and more as days passed and she was the one to die. It never occurs to her to allay her fears through prayers to the Almighty.

Maya loved not only the world but also her husband. She loved the very presence of Gautama, the very thought of being with him. She loves him too much to leave him, separate from him even in death. She tries to locate the mark on her forehead that prophesied what the albino detected, *i.e*, "a relentless and fatal competition between myself and Gautama" (CTP 106). She never thinks of carrying out the final injunctions of the astrologer.

Maya becomes aware of the fact that she is gradually going insane. She avers, "I am moving further and further from all wisdom, all calm, and I shall be seen mad, if I am not that already..." (CTP 108). Her brother Arjuna's letter comes as a reminder of what she wanted to forget. It refers to "the absurd fuss over a horoscope that, I remember was once cast for you..." (CTP 141). Gautama wants to knew the significance of her brother's words. With great effort she restrains herself and says that she does not remember the incident.

A poetry session is arranged in Gautama's house where several poets and lovers of poetry gather together. Maya wishes to join them as she has done in her father's house during such occasions. But Gautama does not seem to relish her entry and therefore she quickly quits the place. Later on when "she comes in after the session is over, Maya complains, "You did not want me..." and he retorts, "Not want you? Did I say so? Did anyone say so? Why all this melodrama?" (CTP 111). She explains to him that all she wanted was to be with him but he had failed to recognise her presence. His indifference literally forced her to rush inside. Gautama tries to clarify things by quoting from the Bhagavad Gita. He says, "Listen, Thinking of sense objects, man becomes attached thereto. From attachment arises longing and from longing anger is born. From anger arises delusion, from delusion, loss of memory is caused. From loss of memory the discriminative faculty is ruined and from the ruin of discrimination, he perishes" (CTP 112). The words "he perishes" remind Maya of death and the prophesy. She wonders whether Gautama may be the target of fate.

As they have tea together, he waits for Maya to pour out his tea. When she does not come forward to do it, he pours it himself. Maya consoles herself on the ground that it is better he learns to do it himself because, she says, "One of us would be left alone to always pour out his or her tea in loneliness..." (CTP 142). Gautama asks her whether she has replied Arjuna's letter and Maya says that she had forgotten the whole thing. Gautama does not pursue it further. In a passage that was perhaps included after the calamity, she says, "(Had you noticed more, Gautama, been more aware, and spoken of what you saw and sensed — the world might revolve still — coloured and alive)". Maya alternates between moments of sanity and insanity. She prays to the Almighty:

I might, after all, have achieved the way to grace
Had you granted me a few years more, O Lord

(CTP 177)

Maya and Gautama go out for a stroll. Their cat crosses them and it appears disturbed. They come up to the terraced end. She watches the moon's vast, pure surface, touched only faintly with petals of shadow, "as though brushed by luna moth's wings, so that it appeared a great multifoliato rose, waxen white, virginal, chaste and absolute white, casting a light that was holy in its purity, a soft, suffusing glow of its chastity, casting its reflection upon the night with a vast, tender mother love" (CTP 208).

At this juncture Gautama moves over to the front of Maya and hides the view of the moon. She thrusts out her arms towards him to push him aside so that she could enjoy the beautiful sight of the moon. She saw him fell then, down to the bottom and that was the end of Gautama.

Maya is taken to her father's house. She gets lost in the joy of getting back home perhaps because her temporary insanity made her forget the death of her husband whom she loved with all her heart. Her mother-in-law and her sister-in-law Nila had gone with her. Nila insisted on treating her brother's death as an accident, not a murder. For, Maya had said in all playfulness, "So then I pushed him, hard, and he fell. And when I went down the stairs to the terrace he was lying there — don't you like your tea?" (CTP 214). Even in such a mental condition Maya explains all that had happened and ends, "You see, so Gautama it didn't really matter. He didn't care and I did" (CTP 216).

Suddenly they hear Maya's frightened voice from the balcony. Perhaps it was a moment of sanity when she realized that she had caused her husband's death and committed suicide. Much critical ink has been spilt on this issue. The questions asked are, whether Maya committed suicide or was sent to a lunatic asylum. *Cry, the Peacock* is an open ended novel leaving the readers free to form their conjectures. Anita Desai has admitted, "I know the creative act is a secret one. To make it public, to scrutinise it in the cold light of reason is to commit an act of violence, possibly murder."

Gautama represents the second attitude to fate and fatalism. He does not believe in fate or astrology. He attributes Maya's unusual behaviour to her being a neurotic and a spoilt child. He avers, "...she can't bear one adverse word. Everyone must bring a present for little Maya — that is what her father taught her" (CTP 115).

He accepts the existence of rebirth and says that the little incident that in life is just a flash-in-the-pan. He points out, ‘‘How insignificant and trivial it appears compared with the immortal cycle to which all humanity is bound, living or dying, and which turns without stop, without point, you might say...’’ (CTP 122). This, he says, is *Fatalism*. He explains the logic of it saying, one incarnation acts upon the other and the action done in one bears fruit in the next. This is as certain as the seasons that follow one another in regular succession. ‘‘Knowing this, knowing that our deeds have significance, meaning, our lives develop an impetus without which life would be one amorphous darkness (CTP 123).

He asks Maya about the horoscope mentioned in her brother’s letter but Maya evades his question. During the party, when they meet Gautama’s friend and classmate Lal, she wants to know the Sikh’s opinion regarding her future. But Gautama has no faith in it. He asks, ‘‘What can you find out?’’ He is of the view that no ‘‘educated adult can seriously be expected to believe that the patterns or the movements of the astral bodies — solids, after all, of earth and ice and rock — or the lines in the palms of your hands, and in those of monkeys and gorillas as well have the remotest influence upon our deeds and actions in our everyday lives — or those of the apes. Can you — seriously?’’ (CTP 79).

The third attitude to the theme is presented through the ‘‘pink, plump, pretty pen’’ who never spoke of fate and was always gay and cheerful. She complained against her in-laws in her usual casual fashion and decided to shift to a flat with her husband Kailash. But all was said in a happy-go-lucky tone. Even the high-strung Maya avers that it was easy to laugh with her and a let of fun to tease her. She kept chatting ‘‘glibly and gaily all day long, jumping up now and then to bring out a new pair of shoes, a new set of rings to show one, talking with eagerness and animation of anything that was new and bright, and never, never referring to family, tradition, custom, superstition...’’ (CTP 61). Maya is surprised when she invites her to accompany her to Birla Mandir. Pom was not the type to take trips to temples seriously. The greater surprise is that the suggestion has come from her mother-in-law and Pom and willingly accepted it. Pom is in the family way and wants a son. Her husband has three brothers and her mother-in-law has told her that she will also get a son if she prays regularly at Birla Mandir. Pom accepts beliefs that are a sources of joy to her and ignores the rest.

Can anyone claim to be greater or more powerful or more loving than the great God Almighty? If Maya had accepted the albino astrologer's advice asking her to seek God's blessings instead of getting worked up over the prediction, she might have averted the agony of hallucinations and terrifying fears. If, she had shared her thoughts with a friend like Pom and sought her advice, the tragedy might not have occurred. But then, any tragedy is almost invariably caused by the "ifs' that are ignored.

REFERENCES

1. Anita Desai's comments in *Contemporary Novelists*, ed. James Vinson (New York : St. Martin's Press, 1972), p. 348.
2. Vinod Bhushen Gulati, "Structure in the Novels of Anita Desai," *Perspectives on Anita Desai*, ed. Ramesh K. Srivastava (Ghaziabad : Vimal Prakashan, 1984), p. 105.
3. Quoted in Anita Desai, Exploration in *Indo-English Fiction* ed. R.K. Dhawan (New Delhi : Bahri, 1982), p. 223.

3

Superstition and Psyche in Anita Desai's *Cry, The Peacock*

DR. M. RAJESHWAR*

Maya, the central character of Anita Desai's *Cry, the Peacock,* is obsessed almost from the beginning of the novel with the gloomy prophecy of an albino astrologer. According to the prophecy she or her husband would die during the fourth year of her marriage. Her father dismisses the prophecy as nonsense and orders that it should be forgotten. Obeying his wish Maya keeps the prophecy rigorously repressed in her unconscious until her marriage with Gautama enters the fourth year. Now triggered off by the death of her pet dog, Toto, it assumes during the course of the novel the shape of an obsessional neurosis and keeps gnawing at the core of her being like an oversized pest feeding on a tender leaf.

It is strange that Maya should so superstitiously believe in the veracity of the prophecy although she knows that Gautama and his family "hoot with derision at the mention of superstition."[1] In the beginning of her neurotic affliction she frequently tells herself that it was she herself who was fated to die. But she is in ardent love with life and so she soon begins to wonder whether it was not "Gautama's life that was threatened" (164). Taking this line of reasoning further she fears for her life and would keep the secret for herself at any cost.

> He must not know, not even guess. Never, never, never. If he guessed, new dangers would arise like sudden fires out of the cracked earth.... Ah, if

* Senior Lecturer and Associate Editor, Kakatiya Journal of English Studies, Department of English, Kakatiya University, Warangal.

> Gautama found out, would he, might he not put me in peril of my life? Did he not love life too...(151).

Not very long after she is almost convinced that Gautama is certainly fated to die and the thought makes her more and more secretive.

> I glanced at him now, slyly, for sly I had grown with such a load of secrets that had to be hidden from him, such evil and awful secrets (165).

It has been suggested in the novel and later harped on by critics that Maya is obsessed with the prophecy because of the romance involved in it. But the knowledge of depth psychology holds the promise of examining her irrational and superstitious belief from an entirely new angle. Freud attributes superstitious beliefs to suppressed hostility.

> It can be recognized most clearly in neurotics suffering from obsessional thinking...that superstition derives from suppressed hostile and cruel impulses. Superstition is in large part the expectation of trouble; and a person who has harboured frequent evil wishes against others, but has been brought up to be good and has therefore repressed such wishes into the unconscious, will be especially ready to expect punishment for his unconscious wickedness in the form of trouble threatening him from without.[2]

Does Maya's superstition too originate in her suppressed hostile and cruel impulses? To all appearances she has been an absolutely submissive and obedient daughter, sister and wife and so it may sound outrageous to accuse her of harbouring cruel impulses. But probing into her unconscious would reveal that there is immense suppressed hostility in her unconscious against her husband and to an extent against her father.[3] Being a "creature of instinct" (16) she seems to hold Gautama responsible for her unfulfilled instinctuality in the marital relationship. She is also angry with him because after four years of life together she is compelled to come to the sad conclusion that she would soon lose her already rudimentary self. She grows anxious on account of the threats to her self-preservation and neurotically perceives Gautama's death as a solution. The prophecy comes as a convenient external justification to her unconscious wish and for that reason she tenaciously clings to it. I will dwell at some length on Maya's reasons for wishing Gautama dead and then return to her superstitious belief.

Maya is extremely faithful to her instincts which, as is their nature, crave for unqualified and wild satisfaction. According to Freudian tenets normal people in her circumstances would have effected a withdrawal by influencing the instinctual urges at the psychic level. But tragically for Maya, her very life appears to be intricately woven with and highly dependent on her instincts. Given her instinctuality Maya expects some emotional and physical satisfaction in married life but both of them are denied her, one by Gautama's cold intellectuality and the other by his age. Maya's longing for the sensuous enjoyment of life is dampened by liberal doses of the *Gita* philosophy of non-attachment. Her effusive emotionality is always counter-balanced by Gautama's analytical mind. While he views "nothing subjectively, nothing with passion" (150) she is "flooded with tenderness and gratitude"(11) when he merely touches her hair, falls "into the soft, velvet well of the primordium of original instinct, of first-formed love" (11) when he draws a finger down her cheek, and takes to hating her own pretty face for failing to make any impact on him. She has to thus continually contend with unreciprocated emotionality and feels terrible on that score.

Sex is not only an intensely and intrinsically pleasurable experience but it can act as a revitalising force in an otherwise sterile life. Freud, in fact, views sex as the prototype of all pleasurable experiences of life. Maya's earth-bound nature makes her well-inclined to derive the fullest satisfaction from this intimate experience. It is difficult to conjecture what course her psyche would have taken if she were married to a much younger man and has been satisfied sexually. But because of Gautama's age and attitude to sex she remains a much disappointed woman. Even when they do make love the act is utterly devoid of passion. Several passages in the novel have been devoted to the portrayal of her disillusionment in sex. At the beginning of the novel itself Maya makes a frank admission of her sexual dissatisfaction born of Gautama's unpardonable negligence.

> Telling me to go to sleep while he worked at his papers, he did not give another thought to me, to either the soft, willing body or the lonely, wanting mind that waited near his bed (9).

Frustrated by his coldness she gives herself up to a fit of pillow-beating! As her disillusionment becomes a routine experience she increasingly sexualises her surroundings, perhaps by way of displacement. The papaya trees in the courtyard, for example, assume a new sexual significance for her.

> I contemplated that, smiling with pleasure at the thought of those long streamers of bridal flowers that flow out of the core of the female papaya tree and twine about her slim trunk, and the firm, wax-petalled blossoms that leap directly out of the solid trunk of the male...(92).

As her grip over herself begins to slacken she begins to experience hallucinatory visions of lizards and birds coupulating in weird settings.

> Of lizards, the lizards that come upon you, stalking you silently, upon clawed toes, slipping their clublike tongues in and out, in and out with an audible hiss ... they have struck you to a pillar of salt which, when it is motionless they will mount and lash with their slime-dripping tongues, lash and lash again, as they grip you with curled claws, rubbing their cold bellies upon yours, rubbing and grinding, rubbing and grinding (127).

What Maya experiences here seems to be a symbolic gratification of the sexual desire which remains unfulfilled in actual life.

The image of fighting and mating peacocks, apart from being the central motif of the novel, underlines Maya's sexual frustration too. The memory of her innocent enjoyment of their call in her childhood becomes a foil to her present over-crowded mind, full of bird and animal imagery.

> But sleep was rent by the frenzied cries of peacocks pacing the rocks at night — peacocks searching

> for mates, peacocks tearing themselves to bleeding shreds in the act of love, peacocks screaming with agony at the death of love. The night sky turned to a flurry of peacocks' tails, each star a staring eye (175).

In spite of her total frustration, Maya's moral scrupulosity does not allow her to cross the bounds of marital morality. Nor is she able to sublimate this powerful biological urge in the manner of her friend Leila who selflessly serves her tuberculous husband. Her married life ends up being emotionally and socially sterile.

A continuous frustration of the body's sexual needs can be disastrous to somebody like Maya, given her fierce instinctuality. A healthy emotional and sexual life would have given her a sense of security and stopped her psyche from decaying. This view acquires validation from Freud's observation :

> experience shows .... that women, who, as being the actual vehicles of the sexual interests of mankind, are only endowed in a small measure, with the gift of sublimating their instincts, and who ... when they are subjected to the disillusionments of marriage, fall ill of severe neuroses which permanently darken their lives.[4]

Freud attributes neurosis of women to sexual dissatisfaction resulting from the rigours of civilized sexual morality. Biologically speaking, marital unfaithfulness could be a viable cure for the ailment. However, such a thing entails perhaps the most severe indictment in the rigidly organised Indian society. Freud continues :

> the more strictly a woman has been brought up and the more sternly she has submitted to the demands of civilization, the more she is afraid of taking this way out; and in the conflict between her desires and her sense of duty, she once more seeks refuge in a neurosis. Nothing protects her virtue as securely as illness.[5]

Maya too seeks a neurotic solution but only to find it inadequate. Something more drastic than neurosis needs to be considered by her psyche.

Secondly, Maya perceives that eventually she will lose her self as a result of a long experience of eventlessness. Her life appears to her as an endless tedium with nothing significant taking place at any time. She is never the centre of importance nor is she instrumental in any event. The sphere of her social activities is so severely restricted that she seems to feel suffocated within it. But by Indian standards her life situation appears to be ideal. She has a secure home, earning husband and well-defined future. These seemingly ideal external conditions are however not acceptable to her unconscious where her desire for unbridled freedom is hidden.

The novel abounds in incidents that show how her longing for outdoor life is constantly frustrated mainly by Gautama. As a child she had enjoyed the scenic beauty and cool weather of Darjeeling and now she longs to go there with Gautama. When she timidly suggests the possibility to Gautama he replies in a cold astringent tone, "Why don't you?... Your father would take you wherever you wanted to go. He *can*" (40). The Kathakali ballets performed at night in parts of South India, hold great attraction to Maya.

> 'I want — I want,' ... 'to see the Kathakali dances. I have heard of the ballets they have in their villages.... And the dancers are all men,....' The masks they wear — you must have seen them? And their costumes. And the special kind of music. And it is all out in the open, at night, by starlight — and perhaps they have torches (42-3).

To her imploration to take her to the South, Gautama coolly suggests that she wait till a Kathakali troupe comes to Delhi. He apparently sees no strong reason to undertake a tiresome journey down South in the sweltering summer.

The fact of Maya's constricted life comes most vividly alive in the scene of Gautama's all male party. Charmed by the vibratingly rich Urdu poetry recited by these cultured wine-drinking gentlemen, Maya breaks an age old rule and joins them. While the other men politely, but uneasily, respond to her presence Gautama not only shatters her hope of participating in the pulsating and poetry-charged atmosphere but also subtly drives home to her the truth that she does not belong there.

> Turning his back to me, he stood talking to a friend, a glass in his hand, and his voice rose, in order that I might hear, when he said, 'Blissful, yes, because it is unrelated to our day, unclouded by the vulgarity of ill-educated men, or of overbearing women...' (104).

To add to her problems stemming from inactivity she remains childless. The birth of a child would have given her a sense of achievement and her creative urge would have got focussed on a helplessly dependent human being instead of getting diffused over nature and spread outside human interest.

Three plus years of married life and the prospect of a passionless and unchallenging life for the next forty or fifty years, during which she would continue to be obedient to her husband and face neither choices nor challenges, comes as a shocking revelation to her hyper-active mind. Her repeated confession that she or Gautama will surely die, in a way, indicates that the opposite would be true — that especially Gautama will not die before her. So according to this logic if she is to live and find the happiness that is her due Gautama will have to go. And the focal point of her thought, day in and day out, becomes the albino's prophecy which appears to justify and dramatise her wish. But she allows herself considerable time before she does anything drastic. All through the novel she keeps her wish hidden in her unconscious and the prophecy itself shrouded in secrecy. This is because as a neurotic she is still aware of the moral sanctions against such wishes. Indoctrinated to be faithful to her husband, she feels her hand held back by an invisible force. The neurotic defence mechanisms such as sleep rituals, hallucinatory visions and nightmares (where her secret longings come alive to her), experience of split personality, adverse somatic symptoms and religious avoidance of violence woefully fail to blunt the edge of her unconscious wish. At most places she appears to reel under the pressure and break to pieces as a result of the struggle within. Yet she hesitates. She is aware of the unseemly consequences and she is scared of not only society but her own conscience. In order to be done with Gautama without antagonising the social imperatives and her own super-ego the only way that is still open to her is psychosis. Once a human organism is entrusted to psychosis nature takes its own course. The preservation of its physical integrity becomes more important than the protection of its social image. In fact, in psychotics the super-ego, the moral agency, becomes completely inactive. Psychosis would thus help Maya to carry out her wish without earning disapproval. She therefore progressively moves towards a psychotic solution to her struggle.

Her transition from neurosis to psychosis is powerfully underscored in the scene of the dust-storm in which she is shown as running "on and on, from room to room, laughing as maniacs laugh once the world gives them up and surrenders them to their freedom" (190). Maya's shutting herself in as a measure of protection from the raging dust-storm is symbolic of her total withdrawal from the world of purposeful action and meaningful relationships. The exact point of her plunging into the abysmal depths of psychosis, however, is her act of violence itself. Maya's pushing Gautama off the parapet of their house is not fortuitous. There are simply no accidents in psychic life. Behind Maya's final indulgence in violence there has been a prolonged psychic struggle which she has not known herself. Having done the deed and having taken recourse to psychosis she relaxes and openly declares that unlike her, Gautama has not been in love with life and so according to the prophecy he had to die.

> 'It had to be one of us, you see, and it was so clear that it was I who was meant to live. You see, to Gautama it didn't really matter. He didn't care, and I did' (215-16).

Governed by the primary process thinking she does not camouflage her thoughts by drawing on her linguistic resources any more. Her adult life with all its responsibilities and anxieties has become a sealed book for her. She is faithful to herself and the social and moral consequences of her actions do not matter to her any more now.

Her superstitious belief thus helped her immensely in the process of unconsciously identifying her problems and their source. From a shadowy figure the albino sprang to life and has come to mean much to her during her neurotic struggle. After she embraced psychosis what the charlatan said years ago has become gospel truth to her. But for him she would not have perceived Gautama as her foremost enemy and would not have considered the possibility of violently working out her equation with him.

REFERENCES

1. Anita Desai, *Cry, the Peacock* (Delhi : Orient Paperbacks, 1980, rpt. 1988), pp. 75-6.
2. Sigmund Freud, "Determinism, Belief in Chance and Superstition — Some Points of View, "*The Psychopathology of Everyday Life*, tr. Alan Tyson (Harmondsworth : Penguin, 1960), p. 232.
3. In an earlier article while playing down the father fixation theory I argued that Maya nursed a grouse against her father Raisahib for impeding the development of her individuality with his over-protective attitude all through her childhood and adolescence, then for throwing her into the fetters of marriage with a passionless and cold intellectual and finally for callously neglecting her thereafter. I concluded that Maya unconsciously took her revenge against him by creating a scandal which she knew he dreaded. But in psychological life things are 'over determined.' Every significant psychological event in a person's life has a multiplicity of reasons. Maya's wish to avenge herself on her father could be only one of the many reasons for her to want to kill Gautama.

   "Anita Desai's *Cry, the Peacock* : The Father's Unconscious," *Indian English Literature Since Independence*. IAES Golden Jubilee Volume, ed. Ayyappa Paniker (New Delhi : The Indian Association for English Studies, 1991), pp. 44-8.
4. Sigmund Freud, *Civilized Sexual Morality and Modern Nervous Illness*, tr. James Strachey (Harmondsworth : Penguin, 1985), p. 47.
5. *Ibid*.

4

Treatment of Neurosis in *Cry, The Peacock*

Q.F. INAMDAR

Madhusudhan Prasad in his *Anita Desai : The Novelist* briefly alludes to Maya as a neurotic figure :

> In *Cry, The Peacock*, Desai explores the turbulent emotional world of the neurotic protagonist, Maya, who smarts under an acute alienation, stemming from marital discord, and verges on a curious insanity.[1]

I partially agree with his discovery of Maya's neurosis in the novel based on "marital discord" arising out of her "morbid preoccupation with death" and it shatters the very identity of "woman in our contemporary society dominated by man in which woman longing for love is driven mad or compelled to commit suicide." In my opinion the blame should not be squarely put on Gautama's shoulders. Maya's neurosis does not entirely arise out of "marital discord" in which Gautama is entirely to be blamed. On the contrary, he desperately tries to understand her problem. Moreover, in her hours of tension he is very much concerned about her perturbed mind and acts as a nurse. Therefore, she admits that he is "her guardian and protector".[2] The marital discord arises out of her neurotic personality in the face of which she is herself helplessly struggling to extricate. The novel dramatizes life and death struggle of Maya with her neurotic personality. Ultimately, Maya succumbs to her schizophrenic self which takes the toll of her husband and herself.

Madhusudan Prasad has overstated the fact that Maya's struggle is a representation of contemporary woman's longing for love in which man is responsible for driving her mad and compelling her to commit suicide.

The thematic nexus of the novel is in Maya's neurosis arising out of various reasons, such as her growth and development without maternal love. The heartbreak house in which she grows up under the care of her father which develops in her a sense of loneliness. Moreover, her neurosis increases as a result of her father's conflict with her brother, Arjun. As a child, she does not play with the children of her age group. This also adds to her neurosis. Added to these, the basic factor of her neurosis is her encounter with the albino in the temple and his horoscope about the marriage. After her marriage with Gautama, she finds her life empty without children. She aspires for love and life. Toto has been substituted for children in her life. Therefore, Gautama says, "As for death Toto's dying... a matter of missing the games you played with him, finding empty time heavy on your hands and, ultimately, a search for a replacement." (18)

My aim in this paper is to explore Maya's neurosis arising out of her arguments with Gautama. Her neurosis is explored by the novelist through the summer, the dust-storm, the moon, the mirror, the zoological images, the light and the sea.

I

Maya's neurosis arises out of her need for Gautama's concern for either her "soft willing body or the lonely wanting mind that waited near his bed" (8), but he is not bothered about either of these. Yet, as a husband, he tries to help her avoid worrying. But her mind always finds something to worry about. Her helplessness arising out of neurosis is gnawing her. Therefore, she says :

> So, rambling, he drew me away from my thoughts of anguish which rose, every now and then, like birds that awake from dreams and rise out of their trees amidst great commotion, circle a while, then settle again, on other branches. (19)

Moreover, she is certain that in Gautama's family "one did not speak of love far less of affection" (40). This makes her lonely and dejected. She craves for her father and his consoling words.

Similar consolation she tries to get from her husband, but he is unable to give her these. Therefore, her neurotic behaviour heightens. As a result of this she says, "...I wish I could see father again. It always helps.... In his words, 'It must be so'...he said to me, Come now, we mustn't fret. If it must be so, we must learn to accept" (46-47). But Gautama can only express his annoyance for her sad mood by asking her " 'Help what ? whom'", he asked puzzled..." (46). Maya is schizophrenic as she displays the qualities of one catalogued by Thomas J. Scheff who says that one of its qualities is "...bizarre behaviour (*e.g.*, delusions and hallucinations)[3] Maya's world is one of delusions and hallucinations. In her world along with the albino there emerge the lives of the women such as Pom and Lila. She thinks that her neurosis has intensified as a result of her recalling the episodes connected with these women. She is unable to give up the thoughts of the albino. Therefore, she consoles herself by bursting out : "God, Gautama, father, surely it is nothing but an hallucination" (55). After this she hopes to be "same again" thinking that it is "nothing but a flagrant nightmare"(56).

For Gautama the previous evening and the party and his guests were boring. But these incidents make her life horrible. She is wretched. The height of her agony is evoked by the drop of the ruby from the ring which was presented by her father (56).

The significant cause for the mal-adjustment of their married life is that they converse without communicating. Gautama does not understand Maya's internal trouble. She is vocal about it :

> 'You were bored ?... Didn't you feel anything more ?... You weren't stifled in that house ? You didn't weep when you saw that pregnant woman ?...' (56).

This agony is felt only by her. She craves to be understood. But Gautama is ignorant of Maya's mind.

For Gautama, Maya's psychic trouble is too strong to be handled. We hear not replies to his practical reactions but Maya's physical outbursts. His sensible suggestion that the sight of pregnancy should not reduce one to tears (56-57) makes her "jump to lean over the bedstead" (57), and throws back her head to scream at his. She appears to him as if she is preparing to plunge off a cliff. Then only he is able to realize his mistake. Therefore, he says, "I don't even understand what you are working yourself up over" (57). Through this Anita Desai is unique in probing the depth of the 'mind diseased'.

As a neurotic she momentarily calms down, realizes her mistake and sees herself in the mirror : "Like a foolish baby...a round-faced child in a white petticoat" (57). Gautama pacifies her as does a father figure :

" 'You are a grown woman now, Maya, no light-headed child. You mustn't allow yourself to grow so upset... What if they live in a grubby house ? What if she is pregnant again ?' " (58).

According to Maya the cause of her neurosis is her getting "too involved" in others. This is exactly the agony of a neurotic. Therefore, her doctor's orders are that she must be kept free from anxieties and excitements (77). Gautama rightly puts the blame of her neurosis at her father's door.

" 'Neurotic', he said, 'Neurotic, that's what you are. A spoilt baby, so spoilt she can't bear one adverse word. Everyone must bring a present for little Maya — that is what her father taught her' " (99). Gautama's diagnosis of her neurosis is correct. He says "From a passion of wonder and excitement you are led surely to a passion of unhappiness in its loss, depression and disillusionment" (103). From Gita he could advise her to remain detached. Gautama detects the physical symptoms of Maya's neurosis. She has temperature and a damp hand. Moreover, her meaningless waiting for the postman confirms Gautama's conviction about her neurosis. He says, " 'Why? Who is going to write to you?' ". As it is expected of a neurotic, she shouts in reply : " 'Nobody' " (111). When Gautama goes to office, her comfortable house appears to her no more than "a tomb"(111). This feeling of Maya is a major achievement of Anita Desai as a psychic protraiture of Neurotics. For a neurotic, an ice-cream bar during summer night appears no less than a hell full of demons drinking blood. The neurotic prefers to run away from that place. The morbid thoughts crowd in upon her leisure hours as when Gautama is with her. When he returns home from office in the evening, her thoughts dwell on their lonely future existence :

> One of us would be left alone to always pour out
> his or her tea, in loneliness, and I felt the shroud
> of death blur my vision,... (122).

This fear of Maya is another corner in the region of fear of a neurotic's heart. Neurotics always fear death, loneliness, poverty, destruction. From time to time realization dawns on Maya that her actions are one of an insane person. Convinced of this, she says, "There is something weired about me now, wherever go, whatever I see, whatever I listen to has this' unnaturalness to it. This is insanity. But who, what is insane ? I myself ? Or the world around me?" (125). Maya's abnormality is best understood through Freud's psychoanalytic theory in which he classified the ideas of the original undifferentiated mind, "the repository of inherited urges and instinctual energy. It contained the instincts of Eros the life or sexual instinct, and Thanatos — the death instinct."[4] Maya is quided by death instinct as a result of the astrologer's horoscope. Therefore, she lives in the present as if she were living in the past. Gautama pertinently remarks : "If you knew your Freud it would all be very straightforward.... You have a very obvious father-obession...the reason why you married me, a man so much older than yourself. It is a complex that, unless you mature rapidly, you will not be able to deal with,..." (126). She destroys of course, not her neurosis but 'Gautama and herself.'

The episode of the laboratory monkeys increases her uneasiness. She identifies herself with their plight as the cages contain a bowl of water eventhough they were thirsty and hungry. Therefore, she appeals to Gautama; "'Let me out ! I want to live, Gautama, I want to live !'" (134).

A simple thing like walking home from station makes her loose control over herself. Ultimately, she cries out : "You have left me deserted," (135). She does not feel like staying with her husband after her mother-in-law decides to go with her daughter. She says, "God, to be alone with him again, my unknowing, unsuspecting and steel-hard adversary in this oneiric battle, all night, all day;" (140). This ultimate aim of a woman's existence, for maya, turns out to be hell. Thus, the neurotics find hell in heaven; turn a bed of roses into nails of torture.

She surprises Gautam by a new trend in her by her obsession with death : "Though why you should give thought to such a subject mystifies me-" (144), he says this in despair. When she gets intensely disturbed, Gautam sits by her side, nursing her as best he can (146). But a mere word to describe her activity lands her in one of her tantrums : "How dare you ? My outraged heart pounded against my ribs, till I chocked, till I saw night about us and began to cry hysterically" (154).

II

Maya's mid-summer madness heightens during the month of May. The heat glues her hair to the skin with perspiration. The heat oozes into the room and pours like thick warm, oil. It swells and expands till it becomes physical, a presence that presses against her body. This external heat relates itself with her psychic state which causes Gautam's fall. The outside heat is revealed as a parallel to the inside heat (156-157).

Similarly, the dust-cloud cloaks her vision. It predicts her future death and destruction. It becomes for Maya the final vision of her final fate. It is the inside insanity objectified. It makes Maya burst into a rhetorical flourish encompassing the events of her life. Her encounter with dust presages her violent act of killing Gautam (160).

It is a common belief that neurotic people loose control over themselves under full moon. Maya behaves madly when the summer moon is full. Under its influence, she becomes poetic and hurls down Gautama from the roof (179).

The mirror for Maya becomes a window to see the world outside : "...the mirror that reflects the window, I saw no rain, no clouded sky, no promise, no sweetness, but only the summer heat, the summer sky..." (149). It also images their future death and destruction : "...the world was tilted upside down, insanely, unnaturally,

> So that our faces appeared bloated, as though
> they were the faces of corpses..." (126).

The zoological images in the novel are used to explore the psychic state of Maya. A bat evokes Maya's imprisoned self : "I felt as though a bat were caught in the same room with me, and shrank involuntarily''(25). For Maya, the lizard Gautam becomes an insect to be swallowed : 'The lizard, with glazed eyes, glared sullenly. The tail no longer twitched, but it had done so once. That was the warning, the threat''(159). The dog image is central to the novel. It brings back the idea of the astrologer and his horoscope, ultimately leading to the couple's death. It also images one's child — the pet. The owl, an image of death is insistent in the novel. Before Maya pushes Gautama, she significantly draws her attention to the owl : '''Listen', I said, stopping at a sound.''' '''Do you hear that ? It's an owl' '' (178). With similar implication, the peacock is used. Its cry is the image of her yearning for love. Born out of this urge, she tears Gautam as peacocks do in love making. Moreover, its cry evokes the death wish in Maya :

> ''It was I. I who screamed with the peacocks, screamed at the sight of the rainclouds, screamed at their disappearance, screamed in mute horror'' (151).

Maya is confused by the horoscope. The close and suffocating psychic state does not help her to see the meaning of life. Therefore, even the light blinds her : ''The light from the open window was too bright : it hurt my eyes like a giant, red thumb pressed into the sockets of my eyes, and lit up Gautam's face luridly'' (124).

Her neurosis evokes Maya as a spent swimmer in the sea. The sea leaves her flabby and loose : ''...the sea yes, it was as though I had been bathing too long in a high and hectic ocean''(13). It evokes her fight with her innerself.

The window for Maya becomes her journey back into the past. Ultimately, she gives up hunting for the windows :

> ''I gave up my hunting of the windows — not even a ghost was left there...'' (159).

To conclude, the essence of the novel's development is to be found not in the gradual unfolding of the protagonist's consciousness, but of her neurosis. Out of this arises an encounter of the self and the world outside. The novel deals with the problematical rather than the comfortable answer to the question of neurosis, nightmare and the subconscious world. Maya's attempt to liberate herself from fear of death becomes a writing down of the stars this week, horoscopes, blind superstitions, that many of us make a hell of our lives. In the ultimate analysis Maya's fear is for death, and so her choice of flight and consequently, that leads to death and destruction of life.

At the heart of the story fear exists by virtue of concrete facts of consciousness. This consciousness, as depicted by Anita Desai, is dependent upon the Look, through which conflict in human relationships and domination of the object are also brought out in bold relief. Death as a theme has been one of her concerns. Since fear of death is also fear of the unknown, the reflective emotional awareness of it is brilliantly dramatized in this story.

REFERENCES

1. Madhusudan Prasad, *Anita Desai : The Novelist* (Allahabad : New Horizon, 1981), p. 3.
2. Anita Desai, *Cry, The Peacock* (London : Peter Owen, 1963) p. 10. Subsequent references are to this edition, page numbers are included parenthetically.
3. Richard J. Morris (ed.), "Schizophrenia as Ideology", Thomas J. Scheff (New York : Pugamion Press Inc., 1974), p. 14.
4. *Ibid.*, Richard J. Morris (ed.), p. 55.

5

Anita Desai's *Where Shall We Go This Summer*? A Psychoanalytical Study

DR. M. MANI MEITEI*

In her fourth novel, *Where Shall We Go This Summer?* (1975), Anita Desai presents an intense identity crisis of the central character Sita, a sensitive woman in her early forties. Unable to live in the strife-torn present she is in the throes of identifying herself with the past, represented by her childhood on Manori island twenty years ago. The past becomes a psychic residue in her "personal unconscious", the backdrop of her life, and her obsessive preoccupation with it gives her the strength to leave her home, husband, two children and the urbanized life of Bombay for Manori island, where she thinks she would be able to live under a magic spell :

> She saw that island illusion as a refuge, a protection. It would hold her baby safely unborn, by magic [for she is in her advance stage of pregnancy]. Then there would be the sea — it would wash the frenzy out of her, drown it. Perhaps the tides would lull the children, too, into smoother, softer beings. The grove of trees would shade them and protect them.[1]

This vision is the motivating force that urges Sita's leaving her home, much to the dismay of her husband Raman, who sees the

* Associate Professor of English, Manipur University, Canchipur, Imphal.

absurdity of the plan — a pregnant woman leaving for an unreal place as if she were bewitched :

> She had escaped from duties and responsibilities, from order and routine, from life and the city, to the unlivable island. She had refused to give birth to a child in a world not fit to receive the child. She had the imagination of offer it an alternative — a life bewitched (139).

Sita's problem seems to be due to maladjustment with her husband; the home life and surrounding atmosphere nauseating her. She is fed up with her husband, a businessman, whose complete lack of feeling brings her to the verge of insanity. And a deep change takes place in Sita, from a proud mother of four children, "sensual, emotional, Freudian" (31) to a woman of "rage, fear, and revolt", for "Control...had slipped out of her hold" (32). A close examination of the whole situation, however will reveal that Sita's is more a psychological problem than being external, as resulting from unfulfilled wishes. Tragically, her dreams of getting love and affection from her husband end in a nightmare. The point at issue is that her husband ignores her instincts, and what she likes him to treat her in a gentle and tender way is what he cannot do. As a result, in the long run the husband-wife relationship is dragged into difficulties that come out in the form of identity crisis, for both Raman and Sita stand for binary oppositions. Raman is a creature of society, more or less an extrovert, more accommodative, apathetic whereas Sita is hypersensitive, an introverted personality and a pessimist. She not only hates Raman for his lack of feeling but also derides the "subhuman placidity, calmness and sluggishness" and the routine manner of her husband's family. As a reaction against these, when she speaks she speaks with rage and anguish, and with "sudden rushes of emotion" (48). In order to seek a means of escape she takes to smoking, abuses her children for trifles, and flies into a rage when the servants talk in the kitchen because she thinks they are quarrelling. Finally, she, like Stephen Dedalus in *A Portrait of the Artist as a Young Man*, chooses three things — exile, silence, and cunning. All this is the ultimate rejection of the values her husband represents, and she has resolved to go to Manori island as a kind of self-exile in her search for identity in silence and in her revival of the past, away from home, and civilization, thus reminding one of Billy Biswas in Arun Joshi's *The Strange Case of Billy Biswas*. She has her vision to fulfil on the island as one sees it in the early part of the novel :

> .She had come here in order not to give birth.... Wasn't this Manori, the island of miracles? Her father had made it an island of magic once, worked miracles of a kind. His legend was still here in this house...and he might work another miracle posthumously. She had come on a pilgrimage to beg for the miracle of keeping her baby unborn (31).

The clash of identities between Sita and Raman that takes an unhappy dimension has other interesting points of focus. At the root of the husband-wife conflict there is the theme of tradition *versus* modernism. By temperament and upbringing Sita's root is in tradition represented by her father and Manori island. Her sudden encounter with Bomay following a hasty marriage to Raman threatens her very root of existence, for Raman and Bomay stand for modernism. *Where Shall We Go This Summer*? is a faithful record of the post-war state of reality, charactrerized by a sense of muddle, confusion, meaninglessness, pervasive horror and fear. The only thing that represents tradition is Sita's memory of the past; and her conviction that the past still continues to exist in its full form is countered by the debris of the past itself. The present, however, is not religious enough to retain the glory of the past, hence her isolation, loss of identity and breakdown of her relationship with her husband and others in the family. In *Where Shall We Go This Summer*? the suffering of Sita is caused by factors psychical in origin. The betrayal of her unconscious inclination to preserve and uphold traditional values of an integrated life in face of the chaotic values of modern city civilization is at root of her unhappiness and loss of identity. The values she represents are rejected in modern waste-land because there is all round degradation. Life turns out to be "a tale told by an idiot", as Shakespeare says in *Macbeth*, when the world is faced with tendencies of the "lost generation". There is no concentric focus in the present century so as to ensure a common term of reference in all spheres of life.

The world presented in *Where Shall We Go This Summer*? deviates from the institutional values, dogmas and old certainties, nor is it surrounded by either magic or illusion, as Sita thought earlier. The characteristic meaninglessness of absurd literature has become the meaning sought for. Anita Desai's world in the novel is the present age which "has shrunk in spirit languishing in confusion, frustration, disintegration, disillusionment, meaninglessness and rootlessness", as R.S. Pathak suggests in his study of "The Alienated Protagonist in the Indo-English Novel".[2]

One of the aims of Anita Desai in her novels is to display how this characteristic spirit of the age has loosened the bond of husband-wife relationship. It will be interesting to account for the obsessive preoccupation of the novelist with this theme of broken family when she lightly touches upon the relationship of Sita's father and mother. Their relationship was one of estrangement, for her mother deserted her father before she had headed for Benares from where she did not return. Even her father, who had been a saint to his chelas (disciples), a charleton to his critics and a wizard to the villagers, led a strange life so far as his relationship with women was concerned. He had an affair with a mistress and his relationship with Rekha, Sita's step-sister, seemed to have been coloured by Electra Complex. Sita's escape to the island is an unfailing echo of the earlier husband-desertion motif in her identification with her mother, a "ghost in white" (87), which cannot be exorcized by her. But this side of the story has other interesting points to note.

Going back to history will reveal some facts about Sita's enigmatic and mysterious nature as having been a symptom of her want of care and sympathy of a mother or a real sister — a healthy ground for lack of confidence in her later life. In her moments of joy and sorrow she has none to share, hence she keeps herself to herself. That becomes her character trait quite unpalatable to others, and it has its origin in her childhood life and experience. The seeing of her father's unusual tenderness towards her step-sister Rekha confuses her with internal questions which never became articulate and were kept repressed. Usha Bande rightly comments : "This experience breeds feelings of worthlessness, and its consequent strategy is rebelliousness. Sita cannot corroborate her father's dubious ways. It seeps down her psyche as a bad human experience."[3] Childhood experience is of vital importance in the study of mind's behaviour, for that lies embedded in the individual consciousness as latent content that appears and reappears as drives and urges in the individual's unguarded moments. If the person is fully or partially under the control of this aberrant mental process he is subject to neurosis or hysteria according to the degree of the force of drama that is inside the mind. Sita in the novel is a case in point. Lack of a mother, an elder sister of a girl companion further worsens Sita's condition. She suffers from nervous disorder being herself faced with this void, emptiness, irreparably continuing to exist even after her marriage resulting in her loss of identity, self-confidence and inability to reassure love and security to her children. This is aggravated by her husband's mechanical and matter-of-fact attitude towards her with no warmth of feeling, understanding and attachment. No wonder, Sita is completely alienated from the world around her and starts living in a world of dream and fantasy and "make believe" under the strain to "a serious psychological confusion".[4]

The central issue of the novel, that is, identity crisis as a result of husband and wife polarity, is also a predominant theme of the other novels of Anita Desai. Together with this the cultural and racial conflicts as evident in *Bye Bye Blackbird* may have originated from the writer's own family background directly or indirectly, consciously or unconsciously, for she is an offspring of parents of different cultural backgrounds. Though little material is available as to how far the subject in question is true or not, in psychoanalysis this is a matter of immense significance. Through the study of symbols used by a writer, his or her personal life as mirrored in the work can be divined. This suggests that the writer and his work are inseparable. The truth of this platitude may be seen in proper perspective if one recalls what Lawrence once said : "But one sheds one's sickness in books — repeats and presents again one's emotions, to be master of them."[5] What Lawrence says is that a creative writer is a neurotic and his book is a symptom of his neurosis. In other words, the relationship between the author and the work is analogous to that of the patient and his dream. This, however, is in the center of the psychoanalytic study of a work of art. The relevance of this critical acumen to the study of the book in question is further hinted at by the presence of a number of psychological elements like obsession, love-hate relation hysteria, phantasy, memories, perceptions, reveries, drives and complexes.

In order to psychoanalyze the book as a whole and Sita's mind in particular, some situations may be discussed. One such is the eagle-crows fight, which testifies to Sita's conflict with her husband and her struggle for supremacy at a deeper psychological level. The symbolic situation of the eagle-crows fight reveals very subtle personality clash between Sita and Raman. Sita is the eagle and Raman is symbolized by the crows that attack the helpless eagle "on the ledge that jutted out below their balcony" (38).Sita's desparate effort to save the eagle from the attack of the crows whose "scimitar beaks" pierce the eagle is her fight against the masculine values represented by her husband. Again the "scimitar beaks" are a symbol of phallus, and the attack of the crows with them is suggestive of male chauvinism unleashed against the feminine instinct. To fend herself off she resorts to a kind of penis-envy by summoning the strength of her sons, who supply her with a "long handled brush" and a "toy gun"(39), symbols of mother-son incestuous relationship, and also the collusion of the mother with her sons against the father. There is a strong does of Oedipus Complex in his episode. And the last scene of the fight or aftermath of the fight, blood stains, and the feathers sticking out of a crow's beak (41) and the disappearance of the eagle are an added meaning to the entire strength of the novel. The blood symbolizes rape, further suggesting Sita's state of utter defeat. It further symbolizes sexual conflict in the husband-wife relationship : Sita's momentary inmpulse to kill her child inside the womb, a kind of her deathwish. In cultural psychology falling hair is a symbol of castration. In the novel the drift of feathers in the beak of a crow is a psychological situation in which the triumph of the father — Raman — over his sons who fight on the side of his wife — is strongly suggested. His triumph is associated with castration motif — castration of his sons. Despite everything in the novel it is Raman who is victorious in the worldly sense. Defeated Sita's weak defence "perhaps it flew away?" against her husband's caustic remark that her eagle has been eaten by the crows, suggests the future course of her action following her defeat and loss of identity. She hurriedly packs up and leaves for Manori island in complete defiance of her husband's hostile and hypocritical world. Like a *chela* she returns to her father's island, charmed by him. This is, indeed, her last effort to try to save her identity by showing her faith in her father's magic world. Perhaps she is searching for a great revelation or a miracle to happen.

In order to cast a cultural colour over Sita's exile Anita Desai captures the great exile motif of the Indian epic *The Ramayana*. Through the use of the paradigmatic pattern of Indian culture the underlying theme and structure of the novel are made more significant. Even the choice of names, Sita and Raman, is highly purposeful. The mythical Rama is in the caricatured in the character of Raman. Both Ram and Raman rarely show emotion and love for their wives which they face the reality of life. This is one of the reasons why both the Sitas suffer. Besides, the bringing of *The Ramayana* theme is to impose an artisitc unity on the form of the novel in the mode of Joyce and Eliot. For Sita in *Where Shall We Go This Summer*? escape seems almost inevitable or she has to face a life of slow suicide without her identity and self. To her, her father is her all, a wizard, who still casts a spell over her : "He had been a wizard, she accepted that now, her father. He had cast an illusion as a fisherman casts a net...upon a flock of fish in the sea" (100). He is a picture of her personal myth, a personal dream, to which her childhood belongs and future still gnaws at for refuge and for self-identification.

Where Shall We Go This Summer? is a subtle psychological study of human personalities which are at war. At a deeper psychological level Sita's quest for her identity is an outcome of the husband-wife conflict. The strange and overtly insensitive nature of Raman causes serious libidinous problems to the mental life of Sita. The whole situation is to aggravate her introverted nature, that finds a kind of wish fulfilment in the following evocative manner. In her state of perversion Sita gets pleasure out of the sight of strangers. First, the sight of a foreign tourist, who wants to go to Ajanta without knowing which direction he has to go attracts her attention much to the annoyance of Raman. To her the foreigner is an example of courage Raman lacks. Another such situation is presented by the sight of a young Muslim woman in the lap of an old man in the Hanging Gardens, an unworldly sight, a perfect work of art. This can be singled out as a situation having intense psychological pressure on Sita, who is torn between a desire to have that husband-wife intimacy and a shocking lack of it. A psychological clue to this particular fascination of Sita for strangers is three-fold. Firstly, to her such encounters are uncommon, and are not a dull repetition of her routine life. Hence they are vigorously stimulating to her. Secondly, they are a source of aesthetic pleasure, a means of diversion from boredom and ugliness; and thirdly, these two situations, being associated with courage and beauty respectively, give her emotional satisfaction. All together the subtle irrational working of Sita's mind at such moments is governed by "Pleasure-Principle" by lessening or extinguishing the amount of stimulation that resides in her mental apparatus in the form of excitement, hunger, drives, etc. About the attainment of pleasure Freud says : "It seems that our entire psychical activity is bent upon *procuring pleasure* and *avoiding pain*, that it is automatically regulated by the PLEASURE-PRINCIPLE."[6]

To her husband these are irrational and unintelligible freaks. He wonders why the happiest memory of his wife is "strangers, seen for a moment, some lovers in a park"(147) and bot her own children. "Children only mean anxiety, concern-pessimism. Not happiness", says Sita. The whole situation can be interpreted in terms of her repressed feelings at violent eruption. It is a general symptom for a psychologically repressed person to release his or her libidinous drives particularly when they are active, fully "unchecked by any inhibition", as Freud observes.[7] And for such a person it is natural to hate or wish somebody who is very near and dear death. Freud once more adds : "Hate, too, rages unrestrainedly; wishes for revenge, and death-wishes, against those who in life are nearest and dearest — parents, brothers and sisters, husband or wife, the dreamer's own children — are by no means uncommon."[8]

Anita Desai's creation of Sita is an example of repressed person. She hates her husband for not understanding her, dislikes her children for they are insensitive, so on. During the journey on the sea Karan excitedly calls the sea weds "Snakes", which enrages her. Of all the children she dislikes Menaka most because the latter cuts flower buds, tears her Sunday water colours, wants to pursue medical science instead of literature, and, above all, calls her father onto the island to fetch her, save her from the boredom and void of the island. Sita feels she is betrayed by her children who turn to their father. At heart she also recognizes her husband, his disposition, his courage :

> He never hesitated — everything was so clear to him, and simple : life must be continued and all its business....That was why the children turned to him, sensing him to be the superior in courage, in leadership (138-39).

But even then her unhappiness is that her husband comes there to take Menaka on receiving her letter, and not to take her. She loves him when she sees him for the first time after her escapade : "She felt so weak, she wanted to lay down her head and weep, 'My father's dead — look after me," ' (131). All her life she has been searching for a father-figure, and Raman is far from being so. In her present state of defeat on the island the desire for security, tenderness and gentleness grows all the more increasing. But her agony is that her insensitive husband remains unchanged, dull and impotent so far as his response to her is concerned. On his second coming to the island this is evident :

> ...he had nothing more to give her, or he was just unaware of her needs and demands. He raised his hand and stroked Karan's hair with a gentleness she herself ached to attract, and she stared at him, bored into him with her eyes, wanting and not being given what she wanted (132).

No doubt, Raman is impotent. A sudden sense of his getting old and grey and not wanting to have another child mark his unattractive role as a husband sexually, physically and emotionally (134). Sexually repressed Sita remains isolated in the background while her children and husband share their life and experience together. Her realization that hers was a "farce marriage" makes her unnerved because her husband does not know the "basic fact of her existence" (145) her soul's existence, her instinct's existence. The more she thinks the greater is her shock. Once more she becomes hysterical, and to an introverted person this is bound to happen. She lives in a world of phantasies, incongruities and violent outbursts as a means of escape from reality. Her entire life is woven in this strange manner inscrutably. It is at such a moment that her mind recaptures the image of the two lovers in a park. This may truly be characteristic symptom of introversion as put by Freud :

> ...introversion describes the deflection of the libido away from the possibilities of real satisfaction and its excessive accumulation upon phantasies previously tolerated as harmless. An introverted person...is in an unstable condition; the next disturbance of the shifting forces will cause symptoms to develop, unless he can yet find other outlets for his pent-up libid.[9]

But at the height of her frustration and self-defeat things come round. The island is no more hospitable. Both Moses and Miriam are in different to her; the house is dirty, dusty, dark; food is not available on the island; the sea is muddy. It is in the midst of this murky atmosphere that she remembers her Bombay house : "the thought flickered through her the flat in Bombay, white with electric light, the twinkle of china, the meal served by servants in white, the routine to which the children were used, and their beds, smooth cool"(29).

About the change in Sita one will be interested in what Anita Desai says when interviewd by Jasbir Jain. The novelist says that Sita :

> has had an unusual childhood, she is led to expect life to continue to be an extremely unusual, full of large, meaningful happenings, whereas life comes to her as very trivial, full of disappointments, it comes as a tremendous depression to her. Really her entire will is not to give birth to a child in such a world. There is no sense of ontentment at all, it is rebellion right through the last moment. When she realises what she h to live to, she has to compromise.[10]

The concluding part of the novel, however, has a different tone, and this is an essential artistic development in the whole structure of the novel. Sita who has been unable to come out of her egotistical self now gets an apocalyptic vision. Earlier she was unable to compromise with her husband, but now she can see things in a circular form, and ring, making the moment's experience something permanent. She finds that all her life is false, a *maya*, and her immediate experience is real, the still centre, marked by a vision of revelation. As Virginia Woolf says in her *To The Lighthouse*, "there were little daily miracles, illuminations, matches struck unexpectedly in the dark...."[11] In fact, it is the supreme moment of getting self-knowledge in which Sita melts in others melt in her. Now she loves her husband, admires him, his ideas and his self. The reign of chaos is over; there is unity. And like an artist she gathers things, binds things, packs things in complete understanding and harmony. All elements of negation vanish in the thin air, and Sita's journey takes on a positive note. At such a moment she is angry "at the confusion, the muddle of it all" (153). She sees things in terms of oneness : her husband, children, herself, their belongings, and even the sea and sky, which were earlier two antipodes; the "island had seemed a small, dark blot of foreign matter on the pale dun sheet of the sea" (20). But now "Neither sea nor sky were separate or contained — they rushed into each other in a rush of light and shade, impossible to disentangle" (153). As her mind is eddying, whirling round and round, Sita is in full agreement with the natural rhythm of life : she is ready for the birth of her child in the womb; she sees the vision of herself in the nursing home, doctors, nurses, labour pain, garments of the infant in her stream of consciousness with a mixed feeling of pain and pleasure during childbirth.

The novel *Where Shall We Go This Summer*? thus emphasizes the triumph of life over chaos, and of art over life. The three-part structure of the novel, "Monsoon 67", "Winter' 47", and "Monsoon 67", further illustrates the thematic pattern of the novel. The first section "Monsoon 67" presents disintegration, in which the central protagonist Sita is tossed about rootlessly on the waves of a monsoon sea. The island home left for about twenty years becomes, in D.S. Maini's words, "an apt metaphor for her condition''.[12] The second part "Winter 47", which should essentially precede the first section chronologically, stands for integration, and the third and last part "Monsoon 67" is a continuation of the first part of the novel divided by a fixed hinge of the past and is suggestive of reintegration, as in Virginia Woolf's *To The Lighthouse*, integration, disintegration and reintegration form three integral parts of the novel structurally.

The novel presents a deep crisis of identity in the modern world, a crisis which has become a major theme of modern Indian-English fiction. While projecting this the book achieves the status of being a masterpiece in the portraiture of Sita. At the end of her stay of Manori she comes out as a different personality who is no more disturbed by the concept of time, past, present and future; all are melted into one. Now she is supreme commander of life, absorbing all the incongruities of her surrounding, her husband, her children. Looking forward to the future she becomes a benign mother, an understanding and sympathetic wife. Thus, she goes out of hard shell of one individual identity, making herself a complete personality in duality, That, indeed, is the androgynous vision of the novelist. For beauty lies not only in a acceptance but in the adjustment of masculine and feminine principles — the anima and the *animus* in the Jungian concepts. However, it is Sita's triumph not Raman's; the only thing she thinks is that at such a moment should her husband deserve that triumph. She lovingly calls her children "Menaka", "Karan" while putting things together, which is of course a symbolic act, as if she were a player, whose part is well-acted on the stage. And she wants to avoid such questions as what is true and what is false. In the midst of all this confusing, this muddle, she sees a circle. She has seen her childhood, growing up stage, marriage, middle aged life and has yet to give birth to a child, attaining to a full circle of life — *rites the passage*. Here is the vision of Sita :

> ...She...looked out of the window to see him [Karan] running round and round in circles on the terrace, as if warming up his motor for the journey. Giddy from kneeling and bending so long, she felt herself whirling round and round as well, she felt the long, straight, monotonous tract of her life

> whip itself round her in swift circles, perhaps a spiral, whirling around and around till its very lines dissoled and turned to a blur of silver, the blurred silver of the mirror-like-window-panes. All was bright, all was blurred, all was in a whirl. Life had no periods, no stretches. It simply swirled around, muddling and confusing, leading nowhere (154-55).

And at such a moment of illumination life stands still, and all personalities melt into one. Sita's identity crisis is over. Her identity is one of impersonality. This corresponds with life when it is worth living. Life is a continual process of sacrifice, adjustment, and compromise, *Where Shall We Go This Summer*? deep psychological probings into the innermost recesses of mind of modern man in quest of identity in the contemporary world.

REFERENCES

1. Anita Desai, *Where Shall We Go This Summer*? Delhi : Orient Paperbacks, 1982, p. 101. All textual references to this work are from this edition.
2. R.S. Pathak, "The Alienated Protagonist in the Indo-English Novel", in O.P. Saxena, (ed.), *Glimpses of Indo-English Fiction*, Vol. I, New Delhi : Jainsons Publications, 1985, p. 69.
3. Usha Bande, "Childhood in Anita Desai's Novels : A Psychological Interpretation", in R.K. Dhawan (ed.), *Indian Women Novelists*, Set I, Vol. II, New Delhi : Prestige Books, 1919, p. 107.
4. R.S. Pathak, "The Alienated Self in the novels of Anita Desai" in Dhawan R.K. (ed.), *Indian Women Novelists*, Set I, Vol. II, New Delhi : Prestige Books, p. 30.
5. Harry T. Moore (ed.), *The collected letters of D.H. Lawrence*, Vol. I, London : William Heinmann Ltd., 1977, p. 234.
6. Sigmund Freud, *A general introduction to psychoanalysis*, New York : Washington Square Press, Inc. 1968, p. 365.
7. *Ibid.*, p. 149.
8. *Ibid.*, p. 150.
9. *Ibid.*, pp. 382-83.
10. Jasbir Jain, *Stairs to the Attic : The Novel of Anita Desai*, Jaipur : Printwell Publishers, 1987, p. 11.
11. Virginia Woolf, *To The Lighthouse*, Harmondsworth : Penguin Books, 1974, p. 183.
12. Darshan Singh Maini, "The achievement of Anita Desai", in K.K. Sharma (ed.), *Indo-English Literature : A collection of critical essays* Ghaziabad : Vimal Prakashan, 1977, p. 227.

6

Love-Hate Relationship of Expatriates in Anita Desai's *Bye-Bye Blackbird*

DR. SUMITRA KUKRETI*

Expatriation and the problems and complexities prevalent in the life of these expatriates has emerged as a major theme in the novels of the 20th century authors, crossing the barriers of caste, creed and nationality. Rudyard Kipling, E.M. Forster, Bharati Mukherjee, Toni Morrison and Farhana Sheikh have been articulate enough in narrating the complexities of the life of immigrants. Another author in this series is Anita Desai, who dives deep in the unconscious and sub-conscious psyche of the expatriates and reveals their nausea, nostalgia and longingness to their native land. Her depiction of characters and situation is not one-sided and her protagonists seem to be cherishing a strange love-hate relationship with the land of their adoption. With great precision and brilliance, Adit, the chief protagonist is weighing the merits and demerits of this foreign land, but at the close of the novel he comes up with a conclusion when his English self was receiving and fading and dying — that to achieve their real self and to have a "real life"[1] (204) he must go to India, his native place. Anita Desai's *Bye-Bye Blackbird* depicts circular journey of a soul searching for a perfect life, as she feels that all these immigrants are prone to a schizophrenia and predicament to live or not live in England.

Bernard Bergonzi's views that "the best literature — and

* Lecturer in Technical Writing (English), Institute of Engineering and Technology, Rohilkhand University, Bareilly.

specially fiction — is full of contradictions''[2] find great support by the depiction of Adit and Dev's characters in *Bye-Bye Blackbird*. Adit is the chief protagonist in the fiction who has been settled in London, the ''land of opportunities '' (19). He is all praise for London'', being a romantic Oriental in love with cynical West''. While Dev is his friend who have come to England and still cherish hatred for Britain and Britishers who invaded, suppressed and tramplled his country, while ironically, at the close of the fiction, Adit leaves England for good and Dev remains behind. The plot of the novel is tightly well knitted and the story takes some very beautiful and unpredictable twists and turns and at times, the highly imaginative or sensitive readers find himself amidst the Londoners, facing the humiliation of their taunts while enjoying the fresh morning air of country side as well. It is the prodigy of her description that reader is able to empathise himself with the characters.

Adit, the hero in *Bye-Bye Blackbird* is born in a middle class and he had come to England to enjoy the freedom and here he fell in love with an English girl Sarah, and got married to her. Adit was attending a party, where Sarah had also been invited and then it was ''her shyness and rectitude that brought out the protective in Adit whereas all the other guests and the hostess had only made him feel uncertain and possibly even humiliated'' (73). It was love at first sight and in the very first meeting itself, he expresses his love to her, complementing ''you are like the Bengali girl, Bengali women are like that reserved quite. May be you were one in your previous life''. (73) 'Though apparently, it seems to be his fondness of Indianism in her but actually it is just the opposite of it. As he comments'.

These English wives are quite manageable really, you know. Not as fierce as they look — very quiet and hard working as long as you treat them right and roar at them regularly once or twice a week (29).

This is also a part of Adit's fascination for this foreign land to whom everything about London is fascinating and captivating who expresses unreservedly ''I love England. I admire England. I can appreciate her history and poetry as much as any Englishmen''. (164) He has molded and transformed himself entirely up to the expectations of England, he has fully adopted the life style of Britishers. Time and again, he keeps comparing England with his own native land, and openly criticises India for its traditionality and backwardness. Truly, his experiences in India were not very pleasant and he portrays its heart-rending gloomy picture to others as he tells them that during his visit to India he "Only notice the laziness of the clerks and the unpunctuality of the buses and trains and the beggars and the flies and the stench and the boredom of it" (49). When Dev declared that he had come to England to make the right approaches, he at once retorts hatefully and sarcastically "do you think you can get into an English college by sending the principal a basket of mangoes"(8). The aforesaid statement is a testimony of Adit's feelings for his own country, which may be appropriate at that particular instant but at times it goes beyond the limits of tolerance :

> Nothing ever goes right at home — there is famine or flood, there is drought or epidemic, always. Here the rain falls so softly and evenly, never too much and never too short. The sun is mild. The earth is fertile. The rivers are full. The birds are plump. The beasts are fat. Everything so wealthy, so luxuriant so fortunate. (129)

When Dev feels disgusted to see a couple hugging each other under a lamp-post and remarks about the obscenity of these people as, "a bunch of exhibitions"(66), who flaunt themselves to catch a attention of people and retorts disdainfully whether he could imagine an Indian couple behaving like that, Adit made a prompt reply with brisk air of confidence and sarcast, "No... There aren't any. Not unmarried ones, and the married ones aren't in the parks, they're at home, quarreling"(66) and comes up with a concluding remark, "in India, too much goes on in the dark"(67).

Adit is proud of his blind admiration of England. Love, admiration and loyalty, he has so much to offer to England and in return he feels that he has every right to enjoy and celebrate "the Convent Garden Operas and the pub down the road... picnics in the Hyde Park. I have every right to enjoy them — because of my education, my taste, my interests in them. No Englishmen can deny that"(164).

Ironically, notwithstanding all his appraisal, his worship and trust on this land of liberty, eccentricity and individualism, he realizes that England can provide him neither of these. Wherever he goes, he becomes a victim of racial discrimination and apartheid and is constantly regarded as not only a second grade citizen, but also an intruder and consequently to stand in a separate lavatory queue for Asiatics or to be called *Wog* is his irresistible destiny and he has to get on with it as long as he wishes to stay in England. The dialogue between Dev and Adit explains his helplessness.

> "That boy at the bus stop — he called us wogs. You heard him." "I did not."
> "Adit, I saw you turn, I saw your face. You can take that — from a school boy."
> "It is best to ignore those who don't deserve ones' notice." (162)

He knew perfectly well that despite his best efforts he would never reach at the top post in his office because always here will be a Britisher for that and he is an Indian, an unwanted expatriate in this country and his destiny is to listen the taunts and comments of Britishers. Even Sarah had to suffer and face discrimination for getting married to an Indian. These Britishers would not spare her and enjoy every opportunity of teasing her. "Hurry, hurry, Ms. Curry" (32) the group of school children teases her. Even at school, when surrounded by her colleagues, she is always self-conscious, feeling glad if escaped having answer personal questions. They compel her to explain various recipes of cooking curry and to tell them about her future plans, or would enquire regarding the whereabouts of her parent-in-laws, and seeing her reluctant and stammering while trying to answer these questions they would make some very cruel remark, "if she is ashamed of marrying an Indian husband, why did she go and marry him"(37). While Adit is found declaring his choice emphatically, "I love it here, I am so happy here. I hardly notice the few drawbacks" (164), Sarah despise this treatment meted out to her just because she got married to an Indian. And when Adit asks here whether she would be able to go to India leaving the beautiful England with its silent grey Church at the hiltop, Crimson blue rose-vines, tufted grass and nostalgia laden violates, she answers promptly "when I think of all the Millers of England, I could leave at once"(83).

Despite his love and admiration for England, he feels himself as an alien and stranger and at these moments his heart is full with nostalgiac reveries of his native land. He longs for his home and all the things associated with it. On Christmas he would tell Sarah to cook Carat Halwa for him as it reminds him of being at home. And at one such instance he expresses his desire to visit India "I will go. My mother will cook hilsa fish wrapped in banana leaves for me. My sisters will dress Sarah in Saries and gold ornaments. I'll lie in bed till ten every morning and sit up half the night listening to the Shehnai and Sitar. (48) The roots of this nostalgia are hidden in Adit's inward hatred for England and nothing but love for his native country. Another more strong tes.imony of his love to his own country is his effort to raise fund during India's war with Pakistan and it is during the war that he took the major decision that he would go to India alongwith Sarah. Everyone was surprised at his decision, his friend Jasbir makes a comment "I'd like to make sure you actually leave. I cannot believe it otherwise — you, the most *Pukha* sahib of all, going back to India and leaving all the *Kala* sahibs here. " Lastly, with enormous hopes and desires he moves to India, his own land where none would call him a Wog or Asiatic, or look down upon him.

The chapter of Adit is closed, the circle of his migration complete — from India to England and again to India. But here is Dev, another emigrant who had come to England to pursue higher studies, always criticising Britain and Britishers who would laugh at Adit about his love for England, found himself enticed by its did not took admission and college charm and declares that the streets of London are and education so rich that he can't possibly cut it short by entering the stuffy halls of some ancient college"(85). Though in the beginning, he was fully determined that he would not stay in England where he has to bear all the insults and tell vehemently to Adit "I wouldn't live in a country where I was insulted and unwanted"(17). He is not ready to accept the indifferent rather scornful attitude of Britishers and all the time, he is conscious of it. For appreciating England's green and grisly land and life in London, Dev shouts at Adit "If the British were still in India you would be one of those Babus who used to go crawling after them, drooling if they noticed you so far as to give you a kick"(163).

Later on, there was a slow but blatant change in his attitude. Anita Desai gives an opportunity of deep penetration into his psyche :

> The life of an alien appears to be enthrallingly rich and beautiful to him, and that of a homebody too dull, too stale to return to ever. Then he hears a word in the tube or notices an expression on an English face that overturns his latest decision (86).

It was the beginning of his predicament, when he find himself getting lost in the toffee apples in Petticoat Lane, Battersea Power Station, Laurel Lane or Russell Square and he is intoxicated to think long programmes of music, theatre and art exhibitions. And at the close of the fiction one finds him completely bewitched and succumb to the charms and future perspectives of his life in England, when instead of quitting the job and going back to India with Adit, he would stay in England and join the tourist bureau in which Adit was working previously. Instead of realizing that he soon will have to undergo all the insults, pain and mental torture Adit was facing, he felt "exquisite relief of the unemployed at last employed"(230). With his joining in the new job, chances of his return to India have been diminished.

As a corollary, it can be easily evinced that *Bye-Bye Blackbird* depicts the love-hate relationship of the expatriates with England. Anita Desai presents a clear reversal of attitude of these two expatriates. Adit, the man who loves it, leaves it for good and decides to settle down in India contrary to Dev who had come to England with a purpose to pursue higher education and was detriment to go back; settled down here. While staying in London, Adit was constantly staying in London and going through the predicament whether he should go or stay and a constant struggle of emotions used to jeopardize his mental peace : he finally comes over his indecisiveness and decides to return to India. These were the moments when his unconscious nostalgia and longingness for India has suppressed his conscious self or to say that his unconscious and conscious self have become one. Though England would make his career, yet it is India where he belongs to, and may achieve fulfilment, and self-contentment. The beauty of London still captivates him yet at last he admits the fact that there "everything tells you you're an outsider and not entitled to the country" (162) and this realization brought him emancipation from all the mental conflict, pain and predicament he was going through. The symbolic title *Bye Bye Blackbird* seems to come alive.

REFERENCES

1. Bernard Bergonizi, The situation of the Novel (Penguin : 1972), p. 8.
2. Anita Desai, *Bye-Bye Blackbird*, Orient : New Delhi, 1985. (All references to the texts of *Bye-Bye Blackbird* have been taken from this edition and the page numbers are subsequently given in the parentheses.

7

The Alienated Self — A Study of Anita Desai's *Clear Light of Day*

DR. S.P. SWAIN*

From fire to light, *Clear Light of Day* dwells on existentialist theme of time in relation to eternity. Existentialism which is basically concerned with the enduring human predicament in relation to unchanging human destiny has been the sole concern of Anita Desai. Desai quotes on the last page of the novel a very significant line from Eliot's *Four Quartets* : "Time the destroyer is time the preserver". It is 'time' which brings about a change in the lives of the characters in the novel. The childhood intimacy of the four children — Tara, Bim, Raja and Baba is gradually lost as they grow older and become aware of their variegated dreams and aspirations. In their pursuit of individual aims they reckon the loss of a wider-based, socially integrated deep-rootedness. Anita Desai presents their polarities of personalities through images of sounds and silence. The despair and isolation of Bim is projected through the image of the mosquito (zoological image of sound) :

> Tara and Bakul, and behind them the Misras, and somewhere in the distance, Raja and Benazir, only to torment her and mosequito-like sip her blood. All of them fed on her blood.... Now when they were full, they rose in swarms, humming away, turning their backs upon her (153).

The zoological image of a "snail slowly, resignedly making its way from under the flower up a clod of earth only to tumble off the top onto its side — an eternal, miniature Sisyphus" (2),

* Department of English, Rourkela Municipal College, Rourkela.

symbolically stands for the silence of Bim who withdraws herself from the El Dorado of life to shoulder all alone the responsibility of looking after her mentally retarded, dumb brother, Baba, and her widowed Aunt Mira. Then again, we have the image of the morning sun that instead of providing inspiration and zeal for existence shuts Tara out from the general go of life. Tara bows her head to "the morning sun that came slicing down, like a blade of steel onto the back of her neck (1). The morning sun repels and isolates Tara. It is not homely but alien that acquires a brutal and harsh nature which "slices down like a blade of steel" (1). It is not a playful and cheerful sun. It is formidable and intimidating which triggers off the feel of alienation in Tara, who drops the screen and remains isolated from its ghastly sight :

> She actually got up and went to the door and lifted the bamboo screen that hung there, but the blank white glare of afternoon slanted in and slashed at her with its flashing knives so that she quickly dropped the screen (21).

Desai evokes, through Tara's reactions to the light of the full-moon, a sense of the eerie : "...like snow, its touch was cold, marmoreal and made Tara shiver.... She could not free herself of them, of this shabby old house" (158-159). The most striking and powerful image projecting isolation and estrangement in the novel is the image of the cow drowned in the well. The cow can drowned but was never taken out. It becomes the symbol of nausea, nausea generating isolation. Tara "seemed to fly apart in rejection and agitation" (159) from the house that "looked like a tomb in the moonlight, a whitewashed tomb rising in the midst of the inky shadows of trees and hedges, so silent — everyone asleep, or stunned by moonlight" (*Ibid.*). The children continually broke apart into violent eruptions of emotion, seemed rigid, encased in separate silences like larvae in stiff-spun cocoons.

In this fourth dimensional novel, Desai endeavours to fathom the depths of time as destroyer and as preserver, mirroring the vicissitudes, distortions and manifestations that the two realities — past and present — bring about in the identity of the characters. In an interview with Sunil Sethi, Desai elaborates upon the theme of the novel :

> My novel is set in Old Delhi and records the tremendous change that a Hindu family goes through since 1947. Basically my pre-occupation was with recording the passage of time : I was trying to write a four-dimensional piece on how a family's life moves backwards and forwards in a period of time. My novel is about time as a destroyer, as a preserver and about what the bondage of time does to people. I have tried to tunnel under the mundane surface of domesticity (Desai interviewed, *India Today* : 142).

The novel does not have a tangible story in the true sense of the term. There are some sharp, interlinked, episodic splinters of a disrupted family life, discussed or recollected after a long lapse of time by the two leading characters — Bim and Tara. Their recollection forms a new pattern, a transformed design within the old and the common, the unusual and the familiar, thereby revealing an enervating scenario of passions and personal traumas, love and sacrifice, death and betrayal, anger and accusation. The novel revolves round two brothers and two sisters who grew up in a house in old Delhi. The mental agony of a delicate young woman trapped in the pattern of movement and stillness has been musically orchestrated in this novel. Points and counterpoints, to and fro movement of the story bring about a sequential harmony to the entire piece. Thus the novel carries the pattern of a musical composition. It sets off with the song of the koel and concludes with the song of the old master, thus suggesting a fusion of the rhythms of life, both natural and human. Time-bound existence is juxtaposed with timeless existence. Here again there is a creative tension between polarites, between death-themes and life-themes, between creation and destruction. It has the "pattern of a *raga* with harmonious *arohas* (rises) and *avarohas* (falls)" (Sharma 1981 : 131). The four sections of the novel, suggesting "the four dimensions" of time, document the transitions in identity that take place in a New Delhi family. Prof. R.S. Pathak opines that "the novel throws some significant light on discords at various levels" (*The Fiction of Anita Desai* : 44).

The young girls, Bim and Tara, growing up with their callous and disinterested parents have to cope with a diabetic mother, a father who is nothing but "a master of entrance and exist" (131) and a mentally retarded brother. The novel describes the emotional affinity between the two main characters, Bim and her younger sister Tara, who are haunted by the memories of the past. The two epigraphs, one by Emily Dickinson :

> Memory is a strange bell —
> Jubilee and Knell

and other by T.S. Eliot :

> See, now they vanish
> The faces and places, with the self which,
> as it could, loved them, To become
> renewed, transfigured, in another pattern

which preface the novel highlight the theme of the effect of the remembrance of things past on the chief protagonist. While to Tara, the memories are a "jubilee", a source of wistful joy, to Bim, they strike the "knell" of sorrow, thus suggesting their temperamental alienation. The former wants to retain and cling to her past identity and enjoy it, while the latter is wearied of it and is in search of a new identity. Hence the meeting of these two chief characters implies a clash of identities — the past and the present. By delineating their present identity, Anita Desai links it with their past and shows the inherent tie between the two. Here again, she comes back to the theme of polarisation and temperamental disaffinity. The two sisters differ in their attitudes to memories of childhood. The circumstances of their lives differ. The identity of each enacts and articulates the past in its own pattern. Tara, wife of Bakul, a diplomat posted abroad, is home after many years. Her homecoming is a return to the pleasant and unpleasant memories of childhood. Tara is a girl of modest ambitions "physically smaller and weaker than Bim", she lacks Bim's "vigour, her stamina" (123) and is a nonentity at school. Bim has an ambition to shape herself in the image of Florence Nightingale and Joan of Arc. Tara rejoices in the sheltered and cloistered life of her home in the company of Aunt Mira. In fact, Aunt Mira is her other identity. The marriage with Bakul and her stay abroad bring about a great change in the identity of Tara. Her life turns over a new leaf. When Tara returns to old Delhi, her old love for home revives and she wishes to fade away, to dissolve in the reminiscences of the past and to lose herself in order to recover her past identity. She feels "a part of her was sinking languidly down into the passive pleasure of having returned to the familiar" (12). The "old rose walk" (2), the sight of the snail, "an eternal, miniature Sisyphus" (*Ibid.*) kindle her memory ablaze. But "I had not meant to go anywhere", she exclaims, when her husband invites her to his uncle's house, "I only wanted to stay at home". Tara opts for a home-bound life. Bakul is annoyed at her relapse into her childhood frivolities. On the other hand, Bim's reactions to her adolescent days have nothing of the romantic glamour of Tara's passionate musings about them. Bim is a victim of circumstances. Contrary to Bakul's expectations, she leads a different life. Usable to take decisions, face challenges and be strong, she revels in her childhood fancies. The abrupt change in the circumstances of her life and her family not only poses a threat to her high aspirations but simultaneously breeds identity crisis. She is unable to reconcile her aspirations to the circumstantial changes around her. After her parents' death and Tara's marriage, she is left alone to nurse her ailing brother Raja, attend to the aged, alcoholic and invalid aunt and look after her mentally retarded brother, Baba. It is these burdens and responsibilities that shatter her marital bliss and destory her conjugal identity. With the passing away of Aunt Mira, she feels forlorn. She is left alone in the company of her helpless younger brother. The said and dismal experiences she passed through and the alienation from those she so foundly cherished, drain all her enthusiasm for the past.

Tara was fed on romances, and in reading them she would be "dragged helplessly into the underworld of semi-consciousness of the romances", while "Bim was often irritated and would toss them aside in dissatisfaction" (121). The polarities of temperament and imagination between Tara and Bim has been very lucidly portrayed by Anita Desai :

> Physically smaller and weaker than Bim, Tara lacked her vigour, her stamina. The noise, the dense populace, the hustle and jostle of school made her shrink into a still smaller, paler creature...

> Whereas school brought out Bim's natural energy and vivacity that was kept damped down at home, school to Tara was a terror, a blight.... To Bim, school and its teachers and lessons were a challenge to her natural intelligence and mental curiosity. Tara, on the other hand, wilted when confronted by a challenge, shrank back into a knot of horrified stupor...(123).

Both Tara and Bim realise the tremendous transformation brought about by time, altering their relations and attitudes. They recall the period of childhood as an age of love and intimacy with each other, the four of them forming a complete whole. But cracks begin to appear as they grow up and acquire more individual personalities. The Partition of India and Pakistan creates a fissure in their familial ties. It distintegrates their family, becoming a powerful image of their feeling of estrangement. The Partition brought barriers between people who had lived together for centuries in an atmosphere of mutual social and cultural understanding. Tara, Bim and Raja face a severe identity crisis. They are unable to relate their present to the past — their adulthood to childhood. Santosh Gupta observes :

> The period that lies inbetween — the growing consciousness and search for individuality of adolescence — fails to provide a continuity from the early period of childhood to the later stage of adulthood, causing deep psychological trauma and stress (*The Fiction of Anita Desai* : 122).

Tara wistfully yearns for her childhood days, but all in vain. She is unable to resurrect the past. Her old home — the abandoned and moribund house symbolises the frustrated life of the aging Bim. The house is her identity. She too, is abandoned and in decay. Her realisation of her suffering, her dedication for others and her self-sacrifice intensify her feeling of loneliness. She thinks all her relations — Tara, Bakul, Raja and Benazir ... came brutal invaders into her life only to torture her. In this cantankerous mood of agony, she wishes to get rid of the responsibility of her helpless brother Baba : "... but I might have to send you to live with Raja. I come to ask you ... what would you think of that? Are you willing to go and live with Raja in Hyderabad" (183). But Bim is not without the milk of human kindness. As her rage is spent, she feels sorry for having chosen "Baba to vent her heart and pain and frustration on" (*Ibid.*). She gradually regains her calm, and her heart is filled with love for "Raja and Tara and all of them who had lived in the house with her". So far she was living in a dark, dismal world where she could hardly get a glimpse of the clear light of day, where she experienced again and again, "the spider fear that lurked at the centre of the web-world" (135). But with her redeeming realisation and penitence, she is able to see this clear light :

> Although it was shadowy and dark, Bim could see as well as by the clear light of day that she felt only love and yearning for them all, and if there were hurts, these gashes and wounds in her side that bled, then it was only because her love was imperfect and did not encompass them thoroughly enough, and because it had flaws and inadequacies and did not extend to all equally (165).

The vision of childhood dominates the novel. The adult world of the characters is seen as a projection of their childhood identity. The contrast between time past and time present, between childhood and adulthood is crucial to the aesthetic get-up of the novel. The moonlit dream-world of childhood is seen against the passage of time. Thus the adult life of the characters is beclouded and bedimmed by their childhood identity. The novelist visualises the reality of childhood with a feminine and poetic-sensibility. The pestilent-stricken, violent world of the adults is contrasted with the boisterous and carefree world of the children. The images of sickness, disease and violence suggest the adult world, whereas images of joy, enthusiasm, curiosity and carelessness characterise childhood. This is the only Desai novel in which the domestic drama of absurdity is harmoniously juxtaposed against the backdrop of the partition of the country. Tara discovers her tender sensibility and her feminine identity in her adolescent infatuation with her teacher and even Baba is able to decipher the identity of his inarticulate world in the sounds of the gramophone he had collected from the abandoned house of Hyder Ali. The children in this novel pass through different levels of awareness. They are alienated from the external world which intrudes upon their consciousness, breeding anguish in their unruffled existence. Lost in their fairy world, they are attracted by forces, beyond their control, which bring about a change in their identity. Time acts as a catalytic agent in their lives. Tara seems to have lost her identity in marriage. But she gains in terms of family and motherhood. She assumes a new identity with her marriage, the identity of a mother and a housewife. Raja, too, seems to have lost his own. He relinquishes his Byronic longings in marriage, but experiences a new kind of freedom and a new kind of awareness linked with his marital and conjugal life. Both Bim and Tara admire Raja but Bim alone is able to keep pace with him. Tara finds it difficult to learn passages of poetry and recite them. She feels left out of the orbit of the companionship in which Raja and Bim stood together. Raja, Bim and Tara realise the dullness of their household and the strange distance between the world of adults and children. The adults, with their separate world of club and card-games, remain away from the children who are very close to each other in search of love and security.

Bim seems to have lost love, marriage and domesticity and is eagerly waiting for new experiences, new livers and new roots. Bim symbolises forces that have strengthened the foundation of all family life. She is the archetypal mother, a metaphor that Anita Desai subtly employs to reaffirm and reassert the life-themes in the novel. The sustaining presence of the maternal identity has been referred to in a number of ways. Mira Masi acts as a mother substitute and when she is gone, Bim plays the foster mother to her brothers and sisters. Thus the three facets of the mother identity have been fictionalised in the novel — the mother who bears, the mother who cares and the mother who shares. But not the mother who destroys, as in *Voice in the City*. Bim is a mother and a housewife. She embodies not only the katabolic impulses but also the forces which ensure permanence and continuity in a dynamic and transient world. Bim reflects Desai's vision of the identity of the new Indian woman, the dim stirrings of which we see in her desire to dress and smoke like men. She revolts against the traditional image of the Indian woman in words and deeds. Unlike most Indian girls, she opts out of marriage for the life of a spinster. She is reluctant to play the conventional role of a sex-object and a yoked-wife. In a sense, she is the symbol of the emancipated woman, the forerunner of the emerging Indian woman with her liberated womanhood.

Both Bim and Tara represent two aspects of the maternal identity — begetting and upbringing, breeding and nursing. Characters are brought together by the marriage of Moyna, Raja's daughter. Thus marriage which, in Desai's earlier novels, was a destructive institution, breeding alienation assumes a positive significance. It is a source of movement in stillness, of continuity in change, of permanence in transience. Desai discovers the ultimate truth of life in an intuitive apprehension and a human acceptance of the polarities and paradoxes of life. The existential angst acquires a new dimension. Bim achieves her 'feminine self' in fusion, not in fission, in association, not in alienation, in affirmation, not in negation. Her deep commitment to her past as a maternal symbol, a feminine principle sustains her against the ravages of time. Her quest, positively affiliated to others, goes beyond her introvert self. Both Bim and Tara admire Raja's love for Urdu poetry but Bim alone is able to keep pace with him. "Tara finds it difficult to learn passages of poetry and recite them. She feels left out of the circle of companionship in which Raja and Bim stand together" [Gupta, *The Fiction of Anita Desai,* (ed.) Dhawan 1989 : 119].

Unable to communicated and conceptualise, Baba lives in a vacuum of silence. Forced to live on the margins of the lives of others, he becomes a centrifugal force moving on the periphery of the lives of Tara and Bim. His withdrawal from the world of human Voices to the artificial sounds of the gramophone records makes him an eerie presence in the Mishra household. In the shaded darkness of the house "silence had the quality of a looming dragon" (13) and Baba overcomes this oppressive and oneirodynic silence by playing the records on the gramphone "so endlessly, so obsessively" (*Ibid.*). In associating himself with the world of the gramphones, Baba moves from a state of alienation to a state of identification. But Baba's fondness for music is confined to the traditional music, that of the 1940s. He dislikes contemporary music. Even the musical notes of the birds calling out in the garden and the sounds of the life outside his window do not move him.

He finds solace in mechanical music : "... a mechanical bird had replaced the koels and pigeons of daylight" (30).

The theme of movement and stillness which figures prominently in *Fire on the Mountain*, is suggested in this novel through metaphors of the stagnant pool and the ever-growing tree. The theme of fusion or contact is indicated through reiterative allusions to the balustrade, the supporting railing. The balustrade exists only in relation to the individual balusters supporting it. After this revealing realisation, Bim forgets all her bitterness — she forgets the objects that had alienated her from Raja and Tara. She is gradually relieved of the trauma of alienation.

The alienated anguish of a thwarted motherhood and the searing pangs of a widowed existence are most powerfully evoked in Mira Masi. The anguish of Bim's marital life is transformed beyond the limitations of traditional motherhood so as to give a new form to her marital identity. Her presence is a 'maternal presence', and it is this aspect of her character that renders a new dimension to her personal identity. She is the consummate symbol of a mother. Patterns of contrast in themes, characters and incidents besides adding to the textural density of the novel highlight the alienated life of the characters and their identity crisis. Bim's father leads an insensitive and callous life. Shanta Acharya observes :

> Quite contrary to expectations, Bim's parents are both portrayed as remote and far removed from the world of their children. They are both noted by their absence, they do not influence the lives of their children in any significant why. The father seeks refuge in the club playing bridge, unable to cope with the twin horrors of a diabetic wife and a retarded child [Acharya, *Explorations,* (ed.) Dhawan, 1982 : 250].

The action of the novel is divided between the house and the garden. The characters are found either moving into the house from the garden or are going out from the house into the garden. This to and for shuttling of the characters between the house and the garden suggests their human and natural identity. Their inability to harmonise thes two aspects generates identity crisis. The alliance of the human characters with the natural world is seen in the snail, the koel, the cat and the dog — all partaking in the drama of human experience. The bizarre translations of Raja and the profound lines of Eliot keep reverberating in Bim's mind. These 'poetic presences', skin to the calls of the koel outside, bring in the infinite dramas of self-identity into the action of the novel and refer to the affinity between art and life, between the human identity of the characters and their fictional identity. Bim becomes symbolic of mother India that accommodates all and accepts all, disowns and shuns none. The Mishra sisters represent a clash of values. They cannot wholly get rid of the past nor can they completely accept the present. The past and the present accentuates their isolation and self-estrangement.

The renewal of self-identity in another mould and pattern is the theme of the novel. The attempt of Bim to transcend her past identity is suggested when she mockingly enquires of Tara : "Do you know anyone who would ... secretly, sincerely, in his innermost self ... really prefer to return to childhood?" (4). Both sisters are afraid to face their past identity. The book divides itself into two parts — first, Tara's visit to the filthy and unkempt mansion on the banks of Jamuna in Old Delhi and the two sisters' memories of the past. This reminiscence unveils a past quite alien to the present, to the cheerful, chaotic childhood that one finds in a joint-family. Bim and Tara are the artistic equivalents and projections of all other Desai protagonists. Tara is a foil to Bim. The identity of the one is a passport to the identity of the other. Tara's weakness reveals Bim's strength but Tara's sensitivity to weakness also throws Bim's character in perspective. The novel reveals itself through the consciousness of Bim who is disgusted with her cloistered presence in the family. She feels she is unwanted, since she fails to get any response from anyone around. Bitterly lonely, she develops signs of nausea. Illness, both mental and physical, seems to infect the novels of Anita Desai. Caught in the contradictions within herself, Bim is unable to relate with her brothers and sisters. She feels split within and torn apart in "loving them and not loving them, accepting them and not accepting them. Understanding them and not understanding them" (166). Her emotional estrangement and turbulence is symbolised by the violent dust-storm raging outside. She longs to come out of the cocoon of her self to discover her true being and form viable relationship with others, and to make her fragmented existence "a whole, a perfect pattern" (*Ibid.*).

Bim's separation from her brothers and sisters accelerates in her the feeling of fragmentation and incompleteness, of the distintegration of her self. She feels isolated from her domestic milieu and is unable to co-ordinate and relate herself with others. Bim, who and felt herself to be the centre and had "stayed and become part of the pattern, inseparable" (56), now has the feeling of isolation and forlornness. Even when her own self is concerned, Bim is unable to relate it with its past life which symbolically suggests the estrangement of the modern individual in a transitional society.

The cruel, intolerant, puritanic and power-hungry life of Aurangzeb becomes a mirror in which Bim reckons the growth of her own self. She rejects Aurangzeb as an apathetic, ego-centric power-maniac. This symbolises her transition from hatred to love, from alienation to accommodation and from egotism to altruism. The life of Aurangzeb holds an epiphany to Bima's life. In moments of awakening, she becomes aware of the forces that hindered her quest for a truly emancipated self, and moves towards a new, genuine and authentic identity which she discovers in the embraces and kisses of her nieces. There is sunshine. The twitter of pigeons brings a note of joy. The air is reverberating with the excitement of the anticipated marriage, of release from staticity. The novel closes like *Where Shall We Go This Summer*? with hope. Anita Desai seems to dwell upon the theme of hope-despair-hope. The novel moves zig-zag. This optimistic atmosphere relieves the pervading gloom in the earlier parts. The identity of the resurrected and rejuvenated Bim, becomes the symbol of a resurrected and rejuvenated India — a nation having shunned her violent, bitter and eventful past is on the verge of a new beginning, a nation in search of a new identity. The last words of Aurangzeb bring to Bim a searing realization of the fundamental alienation of man : "Many were around me when I was born but now I am going alone" (167).

Alienation of the self in *Clear Light of Day* unlike Desai's other novels is not related to psychic illness but to emotional callousness operating within the domestic ambience of silence and staticity.

Alienation here finds expression in the to and fro shuttling of the characters between the past and the present, tradition and modernity. In this novel alienation leads to identification which is symbolised by the "clear light of day". The novel, nevertheless, ends in a positive note. Like the other novels of Desai, here, alienation does not lead to the annihilation and immolation of the self but to its rejuvenation and reidentification with the milieu. Ultimately all "opposing needs" and discords "seemed to mingle and meet at the very roots" (110) and Bim could see the clear light of day.

REFERENCES

Acharya, Shanta. "The Problems of the Self in The Novels of Anita Desai" in R.K. Dhawan (ed.) *Explorations in Modern Indo-English Fiction,* (New Delhi : Bahri, 1982).

Desai, Anita. *Clear Light of Day,* (New Delhi : Allied, 1980). (All citations from the text followed by page numbers in parentheses are from this edition of the novel.)

Gupta, Santosh. "Polarities of Imagination", in R.K. Dhawan (ed.) *The Fiction of Anita Desai,* (New Delhi : Bahri, 1989).

Interview, Anita Desai, *India Today,* December 1-15, 1980.

Pathak, R.S. "The Alienated Self in the Novels of Anita Desai" in R.K. Dhawan (ed.) *The Fiction of Anita Desai,* (New Delhi : Bahri, 1989).

Sharma, R.S. *Anita Desai,* (New Delhi : Arnold-Heinemann, 1981).

8

Character and Setting in Anita Desai's *In Custody*

DR. K. RATNA SHIELA MANI*

Compared with plot, theme, language, or character, as an aspect of fiction is sometimes relegated to a secondary position. But it is precisely place, "the named, identified, concrete, exact and exacting ...gathering spot of all that has been felt,"[1] argues Eudora Welty, that constitutes the real essence of a novel, "A novel", she observes "is essentially bound up in the local, the real, the present, and the day-to-day experience of life."[2] Place is an all-inclusive framework; it conditions a novelist's mode of characterization, his sense of direction — in brief, his entire point of view. In his study, *The Rise of the Novel*, Professor Ian Watt has shown that one of the distinguishing characteristics of the novel is that it gives its personages "a local habitation and a name". Localisation is a practical matter of placing the characters in an environment within which they can act out their stories. The descriptive passages take their place in the texture of the novel, and cannot be detached and enjoyed for their own sake, nor wished away from the novel without damaging its fabric.[3]

There is an organic relationship between the setting, the character and the point of view in a novel. The technique of background description, particularly description of landscape, in most novels, aside from localizing a scene or situation, projects through a skilful selection of colour and detail the mood of a character.[4] In the novel, participation of the reader in the moods of the characters is

* Lecturer, Department of English, Nagarjuna University, Guntur.

through the evocative power of descriptive passages. A novelist depicts the physical features, geographical boundaries, mountains and rivers, hills and forests and all that constitutes the region and important for its delineation. He describes the social, political, economic and religious conditions of the locale of his fiction. Time-induced changes and evolving consciousness also are portrayed. It is the place in fiction which makes the characters real. In this paper, an attempt is made to study how background is related to character in one of Anita Desai's recent novels *In Custody.*[5]

In Custody marks a departure from Anita Desai's earlier novels where the concentration was on the internal consciousness of the individual. *In Custody* depicts a world beyond the individual. This novel has a male protagonist who comes from a lower middle-class family and who seeks to reach out into a wider world in the hope of self-fulfilment. Deven Sharma is a lecturer in Hindi in a college in Mirpore, a small town near Delhi. He is portrayed as an average man completely lacking in initiative because of his timidity. However, he has literary aspirations and longs for distinction. The conflict between fantasy and reality is one of the themes in the novel. The story revolves round his weaknesses, and his trials and travails to become a success. He thinks that life so far has been "empty" and that "marriage, a family and a job had placed him in (a) cage" (p. 131). He resents the fact that he is chained to the necessity of "earning a livelihood" in order to "support his family". He longs to transcend the "entirely static and stagnant backwaters of his existence" (p. 104) and the liberating event is to be his interviewing the famous Urdu poet Nur Shahjehanabadi. The interview and recording of his memoirs end in a fiasco leaving his literary aspirations crushed. However, these humiliating experiences bring about a sudden change in Deven and he begins to look within to find his own strength and to know his real self.

In this novel, Deven is portrayed as "a diffident and awkward hero" and who feels himself a victim of circumstances. These dominant traits of Deven's character are doubly emphasized by the delineation of his background. Almost the first impression the reader gets on reading the descriptions of the background is its dreariness. Primarily, the protagonist is portrayed against two backgrounds — Mirpore and Old Delhi — both of which have been portrayed by the novelist in the most uninspiring and dreary terms. 'Carignano' in *Fire on the Mountain* symbolizes the psyche of Nanda and Raka with its bleak landscape. So also Mirpore with its dullness and barrenness reflects Deven's own personality. A series of negative images characterize the description of the town and the landscape to evoke the very sense of desolation and aridity of the place. Lacking a river the town had an artificial tank in which water is concealed by a covering layer of bright green scum. Water the source of life is beyond the reach of the town-dwellers indicating their state of lifelessness.

Almost the first thing which strikes the reader in the description of the place Mirpore is the numerous references to 'dust'; so much so 'dust' becomes a metaphor, an image characterizing Mirpore, which is symbolic of the dull arid life of Deven. As Viney Kirpal says 'Dust' with its connotations of unproductivity, sterility and death is more real to the people of Mirpore than soil, associated with vitality, creativity and growth.[6]

> The citizen of Mirpore...could not be blamed for failing to understand those patriotic songs and slogans about the soil, the earth. To them it was so palpably dust (p. 19).

Even the violence of religious riots causing diversion in the otherwise uneventful life can be buried easily by this ubiquitous presence of dust (p. 12). The neem tree outside Deven's house has covered the entire courtyard with its branches like "a dusty canopy" (p. 13), shutting out the sun and the air.

While travelling by bus to Delhi to seek an interview with Nur, Deven is beset with doubts as to whether this "rare opportunity would not also turn to dust" (p. 26). Apart his terrifying experience in the "perilous world of night-time bacchanalia" (p. 60) of Nur, Deven feels relieved to come back to the "safe dustbin" (p. 60) of his world in Mirpore. He wearily sinks back "onto the dust heap like a crust thrown away and moulder" (p. 67). Deven considers his family and his job as "heaps of rubbish" that obstruct his way towards literary fame and glory. But it is his own obsessive sense of insecurity and inadequacy and habitual timidity that become the stumbling block. He likes to project the view that he is the victim of other people and situations; but in fact he is the victim of his own doubts, a fact which he is aware of. Thus, Mirpore becomes an objective correlative projecting the dullness, boredom and apathy of Deven's life.[7]

If Mirpore stifles Deven with its dust and aridity, Delhi, the land of promise and glory is no better. The great city was "certainly larger, noisier, more crowded and chaotic" (p. 33). It too has its share of dust. The surroundings of his adored poet, Nur in the crowded Chandni Chowk show obvious signs of decadence which comes as a jolt to Deven. He refuses to connect this decadence to the life of the old poet, so greatly did he romanticize the poet and his world. But after observing Nur's life from closer angles, Deven comes to understand that even the poet, once a fiery symbol of Urdu literary world, has degenerated into a drunken, complaining, ill-tempered and whining old man. The sense of futility is accentuated by the house of Nur which is a picture of waste, neglect and lethargy. The predominant impression conveyed by the descriptions of Nur's house is that of gloom and darkness, even as dust symbolizes Mirpore.

> The room in which the poet lay resting...was in semi-darkness...the walls were lined with dark green tiles that added to the shadowy gloom...solid cushions...like objects carved out of this murkiness, heavy and palpable with gloom (p. 40).

This pictorial image is replete with words evoking an atmosphere of gloom-like 'semi-darkness', 'shadowy gloom', 'murkiness' etc. As in the other novels of Desai, the places and houses assume symbolic significance. They foreshadow certain crucial events that are central to the theme of the novel and important to the growth of the central character. Nur's house offers Deven, not the glories of poetry or the divine life of the poet but darkness, emptiness, secretiveness and death. The darkness of Nur's house signifies that his creative vision is gone into eclipse and that his entire life is darkened now with depravity and mediocrity. Deven has romantic visions of poets and their lives in sharp contrast of his own dismal existence. But Nur's place mocks at his fantasy with its unspeakable filth and noise.

Another impression evoked by Desai's descriptions of the locale of Mirpore is that of imprisonment, and the descriptions abound in words like 'prison', 'cage', 'trap'. Deven regards Mirpore as a prison where he is doomed forever to live a dull and empty life. He feels trapped in a net of mediocrity and inadequacy. But once he gets bogged down in the mire of Nur's life, he shockingly realizes that he is trapped equally in Delhi. Deven begins to feel that help offered by others to complete the project of interview with the poet is also an attempt to trap him further.

> Were those people really helping him to succeed in a unique and wonderful enterprise or simply locking him up more and more firmly in a barred trap?... All he knew was that he who had set out to hunt Nur down was being hunted down himself, the prey (p. 143).

Deven's fantasy about the poet is shattered when he realizes that Nur was as trapped as Deven was, that in fact Nur's cage was more prominent. Deven is now forced to accept Nur's life as another facet of reality.

The drunken revelry, the noisy melodrama enacted every evening in Nur's house seem to serve the purpose of driving away his loneliness. But it was too much for Deven who "hoped his former life of non-events, non-happenings, would be resumed, empty and hopeless, safe and endurable" (p. 183).

Another aspect of the character and setting of Deven is the colour symbolism. He regards his life as "grey clay" and a "field, bare of grain". 'Grey' is the only prominent colour in this novel in keeping with the drab world of the protagonist. It is colourless and meaningless. When he takes his son for a walk, in one of the rarely experienced happy moments "One brilliant feather of spring green fluttered down through the air" (p. 73) which is symbolic of the moment of laughter that enlivened the lives of father and son only for a brief moment. The colour 'green' which normally represents prosperity seems to Deven to signify death and destruction, as 'yellow' signifies dryness and lifelessness.

Thus, in this novel, the city and the town, Nur's crowded house with its noise and Deven's shabby house evoke the same sense of despair, besides a stifling feeling of imprisonment. Here, the city is not an antagonist as it too is smothered in dust and squalor objectifying the central character's plight. As in Mrs. Desai's other novels, here too, the landscape and the house reflect the psychic state of the protagonist.

Deven could never see any beauty or comfort even in the landscape. The stretch of land between Mirpore and the capital was so short that there was no really rural scenery — withered fields and tin smokestacks emitting black smoke, cement factories, brick kilns, motor repair workshops were all the landscape one sees along the highway "overtaking what might once have been a pleasant agricultural aspect and obliterating it with all the litter and paraphernalia and effluent of industry; concrete, zinc, smoke, pollutants, decay and destruction..." (p. 24). The landscape reflects the transition of the society. Even the prospect of meeting Nur, his idol, while travelling to Delhi does not make Deven happy owing to his own anxieties.

> Deven stared out at the white dust and yellow weeds, the leafless thorn trees, the broken fences, isolated tin and brick shacks and the scattered carcasses of cattle that littered the landscape and yet rendered it more bleak and more bare under the empty sky (p. 27).

The misery and wretchedness of his physical existence is paralleled by the bleak, melancholic surroundings. As Inamdar remarks, the wasteland outside correlates with the wasteland of Deven's mind.[8]

But these two settings Mirpore and Delhi and his shuttle between them teaches Deven to come out of his illusions and to face reality unflinchingly, gathering up the inner reserves of strength. Thus, though the portrayal of places and houses denote dereliction and death, they bring about a positive effect on the protagonist seen towards the end. As a critic remarks, the background of the city is used in the novel to concretize the process of Deven's defeat and his awareness of reality.[9]

Towards the end of the novel, when everyone deserts him, Deven suddenly finds his own strength and learns to accept his responsibilities with fortitude. He realises that having accepted the gift of Nur's poetry, he becomes the custodian of Nur's very soul and spirit, and this great distinction certainly has elevated him.

Viney Kirpal states, "this realisation is indicative of his growth as a human being."[10] Deven welcomes the 'greyness' of his life as it is better than darkness.

> The sky was filling with a grey light that was dissolving the dense darkness of night. It glistened upon a field of white pampas grass which waved in a sudden breeze that had sprung up, laughing, waving and rustling through the grass with a live, rippling sound (p. 204).

Consequent upon the resolution of the protagonist's inner drama, nature is seen to cover itself with beauty and splendour. The sunlight dissolving the darkness of the night before is symbolic of the emergence of the new courageous 'self' of Deven dispersing his previous timid, vulnerable self. His vague yearnings and illusory dreams are dissolved in the clear pool of reality. In this beautiful visual image of the landscape, the positive aspect of 'white' is brought out corresponding with the new mood of the protagonist. There is a delightful fusion of colour, light and sound reflecting the regenerated spirit of Deven. It also indicates the joyous affirmation of life that Deven arrives at after a long and arduous journey of the self.

REFERENCES

1. Eudora Welty, "Place in Fiction", *Critical Approaches to Fiction,* ed. Shiv K. Kumar and McKean (New York : McGraw-Hill, 1968), p. 254.
2. *Ibid.*
3. D.S. Bland, "Endangering the Reader's Neck," *Critical Approaches to Fiction,* p. 247.
4. *Ibid.,* p. 244.
5. Anita Desai, *In Custody* (London : Heinemann, 1984). All textual quotations are from this edition.
6. Viney Kirpal, "An Image of India : A Study of Anita Desai's 'In Custody'," *Ariel,* Vol. 17, No. 4, October 1986, pp. 127-38.
7. S. Indira, *Anita Desai as an Artist* (New Delhi : Creative Books, 1994), p. 159.
8. F.A. Inamdar, "Fetters of Illusion : In Custody", *Language Forum,* 14 : 1, 1988, p. 143.
9. *Ibid.,* p. 146.
10. Viney Kirpal, "An Image of India : A Study of Anita Desai's 'In Custody'," pp. 127-38.

9

Anita Desai's *Fire on the Mountain* and the Iconography of the Crone

CARMEN CONCILIO*

The virgin Maiden, the great Mother and the old Crone are the three faces of the pre-Christian Goddess of matriarchal times, of the Great Mother, or the Earth Mother; more simply, we could say that they represent the three stages of womanhood. Traditional Hinduism takes a somewhat different account of the Western female triad, seen as a global and dialectic embodiment of the Great Goddess or Mother.

Although an identification between the archaic Mediterranean Mother with the Hindu Mahadevi (or Mahamaya) is lexically possible, the evolutionary process modifying the primary theological identity of the archetypal Mother takes paths which are different in the East and in the West. However, if in Western mythology, the original Great Mother has evolved into three goddesses, representing the Virgin, the Mother and the Crone, in Hinduism the original all-comprehensive Goddess, the Mahadevi, has also generated a cluster of specialised female deities, who are emanations of her basic form, known as the Devi. As the Shakti (spouse) of Shiva the Devi splits her nature into a triad : Parvati-Durga-Kali.

While in literature both mother figures and young female characters are widely represented, the figure of the old Crone entails a far more disturbing iconography which nevertheless allows for a fair amount of different representations. It is particulary on

* Department of Foreign Languages, University of Turin, C.so.S. Maurizio, 10124 Turin, Italy.

the icon of the old Crone, as it appears in Anita Desai's novel *Fire on the Mountain* (1977) that my contribution will rest on.

The old Crone is a female who stands close to the Mahadevi, who is endowed with all sorts of positive and negative aspects, including creation, preservation and destruction. It is particularly on this potential for rejection, abandonment, death and destruction that this paper will focus on. In ancient religions, this powerful and darker figure is symbolically opposed — though equally valued — to the beautiful, sensual, divine giver of birth, light, love and nurture. To describe this dichotomy there is no better image than that of the goddess Kali, in classical Indian mythology, as an emanation of more reassuring female goddesses, such as Parvati, Sita and Sati.

First of all, Kali entails both the terrific beauty of a sensual seducer, and the terrible strength of an executioner of men. Iconographically, she is represented with a dark face and two pairs of hands — as remnants of the archaic female trinity. Maid (Kumari), Mother (Mahamaya Devi), Crone (Kali), or Creator, Preserver, Destroyer. Besides, the naked Kali is usually adorned with cut heads or human skulls as a necklace, with severed arms as a girdle and often her lips are smeared with blood. All her victims (both the enemies she kills in battle or the devotees who self-sacrifice themselves) are males. For these reasons, she has more affinities with her successors, the Greek Amazons and German Valkyries of the Western tradition, than to a proper *Karuna*, the "mother-love" figure of Eastern culture. Finally, Kali's iconographic representation also entails that conjunction of the powers of love and death, the drives of Eros and Thanatos, that Freud claims as the main attributes of the Goddess of Beauty as well as of the Goddess of Death.

I would not say that Nanda Kaul, the old female protagonist of Desai's novel, is a reincarnation of the goddess Kali, but rather, I would claim that she shares with the old Crone a certain pride, strong-mindedness, and authoritarian temperament as well as a potential for violence, of which Kali is an extreme representation. "She was grey (4)," says the extradiegetic narrating voice, thus hinting at her old age. Similarly the Crone, the most powerful of the Goddess's three personae, is described as an old woman. According to the ancient trinitarian scheme, the Crone has taken on the character of the "Grandmother". This equivalence between the Crone and the Grandmother can also be extended to Nanda Kaul, who in the first section of the novel is portrayed as reluctantly waiting for her great-granddaughter who is coming to visit her as an "unwelcome intrusion and distraction." She likes to be left alone in her villa at Carignano in the mountainous Kasauli region, she loves solitude and independence, thus showing a proud temperament. Nanda Kaul's seclusion in the mountains also establishes a further link with the goddess Parvati and her other intermediate emanation as Durga, for Parvati is called "the daughter of the Himalayas", while "nearly all of Durga myths associate her with mountains, usually the Himalayas or the Vindhyas [...]. These mountainous regions are areas considered geographically peripheral to civilized society and inaccessible except through heroic efforts."

Whereas in modern societies, and to some extent also in the traditional Indian extended family, elderly women tend to be marginalised, Anita Desai centres her novel on the character of an old woman, Nanda Kaul, who deliberately chooses a marginal place to live in. Immediately, the old protagonist identifies herself with the "barrenness and starkness (4)" of the surrounding landscape (as Parvati-Durga, the daughter of the Himalayas), and by showing disgust for some nestlings she confines her long past motherhood to a different time and topography :

> The old house, the full house, of that period of her life when she was the Vice-Chancellor's wife and at the hub of a small but intense busy world, had not pleased her. Its crowding had stifled her (29).
>
> She had been so glad when it was over. She had been glad to leave it all behind, in the plains, like a great, heavy, difficult book that she had read through and was not required to read again (30).

This radical refusal of her previcus but exhausted role as mother and wife (as Parvati, the loving spouse of Shiva) and her solitary retreat into an inhospitable landscape (as Durga, the vengeful warrior) are elements which exemplify what Kamini Dinesh calls "the negation of the role model", thus describing Nanda Kaul as neither a conventional stereotyped character, nor a role model either for readers or for writers.

Furthermore, Carignano was first inhabited by a married couple with children and then by a "long line of maiden ladies (8)", all English, before a native, Nanda Kaul, came there after the declaration of independence. Thus the house itself might be seen as the temple of the trinitarian Goddess, as it was inhabited by the Maiden, the Mother and, eventually, by the Crone. Yet, if the house is a temple, then it is the residence of the two terrible goddesses who respectively represent the intermediate and final emanation of Parvati, namely Durga and Kali, since in the past all the male inhabitants of the house risked or underwent violent deaths.

The married couple lost their seven children there, and when the roof of the house was hurled down by a storm it caused the death of a coolie. Apparently, many of the women living there manifested violent attitudes. One almost killed her husband with a knife, and it is said that his ghost still haunts the house; another was famous for her temper and she reported to have "climbed onto his [her gardener's] back and whipped him around the garden, yelling 'No marigolds, understand?'... (8)"; another used to grow strange herbs which were supposed to cure scorpion bites, and once she killed her cook with a fork, in the attempt to save him from choking. This line of women also seem to share some of the characteristics often attributed to Kali, the terrible Crone : a violent attitude, magic and obscure powers as administrators of death on their consorts (Kali is portrayed as usually standing or dancing on Shiva's prone or dead body). Therefore, if the house is a temple at all, it is a temple devoted to rituals of domestic and uncouth violence.

Undoubtedly, a strong propensity to be quickly angered is Nanda Kaul's most typical feature, a trait she obviously shares with Kali. Her straight posture, "for she made a point of keeping her back as straight as a rod (11)", reveals her uncompromising character, her uprightness being the distinctive mark of her double nature, imbued with a numinous fierceness. A letter brought by the postman is the diegetic medium which introduces the new characters : Nanda Kaul's daughter and grand-daughters. Nanda Kaul's daughter, Asha is writing about her daughter, Tara, who is perpetually ill-treated by her often drunk, unfaithful and violent husband, who has now been appointed as a Diplomat in Geneva. The problem is they cannot bring the little daughter with them, since she is still recovering from typhoid. Nanda Kaul not only disapproves of Tara's passivity and miseries, but she is also not inclined to accept her great-grandchild, Raka, in her house.

Thus, while Asha personifies the domineering and interfering mother, ready to rush from one of her daughter's household to the other's, apparently Nanda Kaul is the personification of the wise Crone, who lives in seclusion and in isolation. Yet, here the trinitarian scheme is further developed, for if Nanda Kaul is the old, barren and dry woman, her daughter and grand-daughter represent two different kinds of mother-figures, while her great grand-daughter, Raka, is the image of the unconscious maiden. Four generations of women are thus represented in this novel, though the narration mainly focusses on Nanda Kaul and Raka, the old Crone and the (only apparently) inexperienced Maiden.

Little Raka is immediately identified as an intrusion and a distraction, because all Nanda Kaul "wanted was to be alone (17)." Yet, she has to accept the role of "universal educator of the young" which is proper of elderly women. Besides, in her being mother of mothers and fathers, in her intellectual, though silent defence of Tara's rights against her violent husband, and in her acceptance of Raka as if in her lap, Nanda Kaul might also be assimilated to the Goddess Durga of the Hindu Vedic pantheon, as she who is Inaccessible, the Leader of the Mothers, who contains within herself her counterpart : Kali the dark-faced.

While comparing herself to the regal detachment of the eagle, "gliding on currents of air without once moving its great muscular wings which remained in repose, in control (19)", Nanda Kaul is called back to her domestic duties by a cuckoo. In that way, her thoughts are diverted from a timeless dimension of self-abandonment and proud loneliness to the real time of her domestic and repetitive and unenjoyable chores.

By the way, the old Crone is often associated with wisdom, her totem being the wise owl, a bird symbolising enlightment. Nanda Kaul preferably identifies herself with the eagle, less in its rapacious attitudes than in its elegance, regal superiority and self-sufficient independence. Furthermore, "in all cultures, flying was the archetypal model of the soul's journey to heaven'', such an ability is also attributed to the Crone. Nanda Kaul poses her attention on the hovering flight of the eagle, thus hinting to her own eternal and final flight : ''She had wished, it occurred to her, to imitate that eagle-gliding, with eyes closed (19)''. However, while the eagle symbolises the eternal dimension of time, and therefore of life after death, the cuckoo seems to be an expression of the real time, specifically Nanda Kaul's present death-in-life. It cannot be a chance that Nanda Kaul reads Gogol's *Dead Souls*.

Apart from the letters, Nanda Kaul's other contact with the real world is through the telephone, an object of hate rather than pleasure. The announcement of Ila Das's visit is met with the same non-enthusiastic spirit which Nanda Kaul previously showed on hearing of her great-granddaughter's arrival. By now, her familiarity with loneliness has slowly changed into a familiarity with death : ''She would imitate death, like a lizard. [...] She had practised this stillness, this composure, for years, for an hour every afternoon : it was an art, not easily acquired (23).'' This familiarity with sleep and death, this ''sense of negation of life'', once again makes of Nanda Kaul an affiliate to the figure of the Durga for she is called ''she whose form is sleep''. This is further proved by the image of Nanda Kaul as the ''still fixed eye in the centre (24)'' of a whirlpool of children, guests and servants spinning around her. This characteristic also reminds us of the iconography attached to the goddess Kali, with her central ''third eye of mystical insight'', which is also an evil eye, a piercing gaze from which nothing can be hidden.

Nanda Kaul speaks with relief about her loneliness, as if it were a conquest, afraid that her great-grandchild's arrival could spoil her tranquillity. For Kasauli is described as a place of light and space, where ''hills melted into sky, sky into snows, snows into air (28)'', a place that her husband, a scholarly man who read many languages, had liked to call the *Abendleuchtung* (28)''. The German world *Abendleuchtung*, meaning ''dusk'', hints at the sunset. The hour of ''cowdust'', also engenders an allusion to the time of the day when the Gods can descend on the earth and mingle with human beings, thus attributing to Kasauli an eerie atmosphere. Kasauli is the place where sky and earth meet, where the soul's final flight is easier for the sky is closer. Similarly, Nanda Kaul's solitary presence in such a landscape and her dreams of flight once again allow for her iconographic stigmatization as Durga.

The second section of the novel opens with Raka's unwelcome arrival. In the very first lines Nanda Kaul expresses her perplexity in relation to the child's name : "Raka - what an utter misnomer, thought Nanda Kaul [...] Raka meant the moon, but this child was not round faced, calm or radiant (39)". Raka is the goddess of the full moon, and in the *Rigveda* she is associated with abundance, bounty and riches, she is a would-be mother figure. However, Raka is not compared to the round, calm, radiant face of the moon here, but rather, implicitly to the darker side of the moon, and therefore to the darker aspects of the goddess, that is to Kali "the black one". Besides, she is described as having "a pair of extravagantly large and somewhat bulging eyes (39)", and this is another iconographic characteristic of Kali the Crone. In this way her affiliation to the genealogy of wicked women in Kasauli is made explicit.

Besides, Raka shares some common features also with her great-grandmother. They are both skinny, to the point that while embracing each other, "Each felt how bony, angular and unaccommodating the other was and they quickly separated (40)". Similarly, Kali "especially in her early history, is often depicted or described as emaciated, lean, and gaunt". Moreover, to Raka's eyes the interior of Carignano seems like "a blackened, fire-blasted cave in which one fiery, inflamed eye glowed and smouldered by itself (42)". Here the house is described as the obscure forge of the goddess Kali, she who has a third glowing eye, for the great-grandmother is a potential fury, who consumes her passion within herself.

Because of their proud and independent attitude, the two female characters hardly interact. It is Ram Lal, the cook, who establishes a friendly relationship with the child and it is surprising that the first warning he gives her is not to roam at night near the ravine where the burnt out rubbish from the Pasteur Institute is collected (as if it was natural for a child to go out at night). There, he says, there are "bones and ashes of dead animals (44)", the remains of the guinea pigs, ghosts of people who died of rabies, and jackals. Raka accepts this admonishment by pressing her "pale lips" and immediately Nanda Kaul observes : "How pale you are, child. Didn't you rest at all? (44-5)".

Here Raka is represented as bearing vampire-like features, since, rather than becoming pale after hearing the spectral stories about the Pasteur Institute, she seems to partake both physically and naturally with such a place, as Kali the queen of the "cremation ground : where she sits on a corpse surrounded by jackals and goblins. [...] She sits on a corpse in the crematorium ground, and is surrounded by skulls, bones, and female jackals." Raka is fully at ease in the ravine, where there were "splotches of blood, there were yellow stains oozing through paper, there were bones and the mealy ashes of bones (48)" and jackals. Finally, the "*Kalevala* even gave the name of Kalma (Kali Ma) to the Goddess who reigned over graves," and the Black Kali is also the Mother of Diseases (a hint at the Pasteur Institute, as well as at Raka's typhoid), as the black-featured mother of such spirits as Pleurisy, Colic, Gout, Phthisis, Ulcers, Scabies, Canker, and Plague.

Raka is further described as a "perceptive child (46)", always set in motion by an exploratory drive. Insight and lively intuition are also the main characteristics of Kali as shakti, that is of Kali the powerful one. Raka usually goes out, roaming on her own in the Kasauli landscape of stones and thornbushes till dusk, and she comes back "with her brown legs scratched, her knees bruised, sucking a finger stung by nettles, her hair brown under a layer of dust, her eyes very still and thoughtful as though she had visited strange lands (46)". Iconographically Raka's appearance is not reassuring, in exactly the same way as Kali's icons fail to reassure. Where Kali is black, Raka is sun-tanned; like Kali, Raka has disheveled hair; where Kali is depicted with a lolling tongue and a mouth stained with blood, Raka is always described with her finger in her mouth and her pocket stained with the red juice of the berries she devours, because like Kali, who "is described as ever hungry", Raka "always rose hungry from the tea-table and her evening rambles about the hills were also forages for food, she searched for berries and pine nuts along the paths to allay the hunger that grew and growled inside her small flat belly (55)".

Apart from her ugly appearance, what also strikes Nanda Kaul is her loneliness and total indifference : "But Raka ignored her. She ignored her so calmly, so totally that it made Nanda Kaul breathless. She eyed the child with apprehension now, wondering at this total rejection, so natural, instinctive and effortless when compared with her own planned and wilful rejection (47)".

Here Nanda Kaul reveals her inner nature. Her own loneliness and isolation is a pose. It is a mask used in self-defense against a world which has caused her pain and sorrow. In contrast, Raka's solitude is not imposed by external events, it is a natural attitude. And after the physical and behavioural similarities between the two female characters, here Nanda Kaul declares explicitly their affiliation : "Nanda Kaul saw that she was the finished, perfected model of what Nanda Kaul herself was merely a brave, flawed experiment. [...] like her own great-grandmother, Raka wanted only one thing — to be left alone. (47-8)". Thus the assimilation of the young Raka to the old Crone is here stated explicitly. Raka is the perfected model of her great-grandmother. She has inherited her features and temperament; she is her natural continuation.

During one of her exploration trips, Raka comes across a serpent. In the past she had seen bits and pieces of the skin of a serpent, or had heard the movements of a serpent in the grass, but "she had never seen the whole creature before (49)". This episode is commented on by critics as the epiphany by which Raka enters adulthood, and they compare it to the scene of the club, where Raka is horrified by the sight of men and women with severed heads, wearing symbols of death at a fancy dress party, shouting and shaking like animals. A scene which reminds Raka of her father's bursting fits of madness after such parties, when he came back home and reduced her mother to a "wet jelly", "squelching and quivering (72)" on the floor. Thus, another aspect of domestic violence against women is introduced almost silently in the narrative.

Fire is the other element which attracts Raka, and Kali also burns the corpses of her enemies. The first, to mention forest fires is Ram Lal during a wind storm, and Raka seems excited at the thought of the garden and forest on fire, while the cook explains that in Kasauli there is not enough water to put out the_repeated fires in the summer draughts. The second, to mention forest fires is Nanda Kaul, when she explains that what Raka has taken for the rising full moon is, in fact, a big fire, while the moon is not nearly full. Raka observes the fire as a distant, silent, threatening dream of destruction, while the reference to the incomplete phase of the moon might be taken as a hint at the immaturity of the maiden.

Raka's lonely roaming is seen as a manifestation of her "genius" or her "daemon (64)" but also as a similarity with her great-grandmother who is ready to admit : "Raka, you really *are* a great-grandchild of mine, aren't you? You are more like me than *any* of my children or grandchildren. You are *exactly* like me, Raka (64)". Moreover, Nanda Kaul also thinks of leaving the Carignano villa to her great-grandchild after her death. In this way, it seems that Raka, too, is assimilated to the mythical figure of Parvati the daughter of the Himalayas, in her quiescent phase, before she reveals her other powers as Kali.

It cannot be pure chance that after receiving the news of her mother's new breakdown, Raka heads for the burnt house on top of the hill, to inspect that vision of destruction. While Carignano is the house that "inscapes the life of Nanda Kaul" and mirrors her self and existence, the burnt house, instead, mirrors Raka's wild nature. This sinister interest of Raka's ("a morbid, psychopathic love for the dark, destructive, mysterious aspects of life") is once more underlined by her assimilation to the crazy goddess Kali : "No one ever came here but Raka and the cuckoos that sang and sang invisibly. These were not the dutiful domestic birds that called Nanda Kaul to attention at Carignano. They were the demented birds that raved and beckoned Raka on to a land where there was no sound, only silence, no light, only shade, and skeletons kept in beds of ash on which the footprints of jackals flowered in grey (90)".

Further, Raka is described as "appealed, driven and inspired" by such scenes of death and destruction, and also at ease in Carignano, but ready to "burst from its shell like an impatient kernel, small and explosive (91)". Here is the first reference to Raka's affinity with fire, for "she felt the yellow light strike a spark down her fingertips and along her arms till she was alight, ablaze (91)", as if Raka-Parvati could metamorphosis into Raka-Kali, the queen of burnt corpses and jackals. Then she runs away as a human torch amidst the "mad" call of the cuckoos and on seeing her the old caretaker of the house exclaims : "The crazy one from Carignano (91)". Raka begins to show something of the spirit of Kali the mad and frenzied destroyer. However both Nanda Kaul and Raka could be classified as crazy, because of their seclusion and strange behaviour.

After some unsuccessful attempts on the part of Nanda Kaul to gain her great-grandchild's attention and trust by telling her stories about her own child-hood and of her loving father, the second section of the novel closes as a replica of the first one, with a phone-call by Ila Das, announcing her visit. Again, the name of the visitor is that of a minor goddess, "associated primarily with the sacrificial cult of the *Rg-veda* : Ila (Ida in the Brahmanas) seems to be associated with the sacrificial offering itself, specifically the cow from which many sacrificial objects were taken".

Ila Das is described in the third section of the novel as the victim of the assault of some school-boys, who in the end take her umbrella and crash and kick it till it is stuck among the railings of the fence which runs along the road. If the doomed umbrella taken from Ila Das is on one level a mock-sacrificial object, it also anticipates issues of more violence to come. By the way, significantly, the first section of the novel is entitled "Nanda Kaul at Carignano", the preposition "at" giving a sense of permanence; the second section is entitled "Raka to Carignano", the preposition "to" stressing the arrival without anticipating permanence or departure; while the third is entitled "Ila Das leaves Carignano", as if her arrival was the prelude to her ultimate departure.

Ila Das's visit is welcomed exactly as Raka was before her, as an inevitable intruder : "Nanda Kaul looked down from her height, having invited her to tea, having failed to put her away out of sight and mind (112)". Nanda Kaul's tall figure in spite of Ila Das's short stature is compared to Ila Das's fall to a lower social status, which she underlines by mentioning her friend's "manorial hall" compared to her own "village hut down below (113)". As if from the plains of their common past, Ila Das brings past memories to the unwilling ears of Nanda Kaul who had escaped from her past to the top of the Kasauli mountains. But if Nanda Kaul does not want to see her past life resumed under her eyes, Raka prefers "the ravine with its snakes, bones and smoking kilns — all silent, and a forest fire to wipe it all away, leaving ashes and silence (120)''. Silence, the need for silence also is a common feature for both Raka and Nanda Kaul. The latter admits : "I never cared for music myself. It makes me *fidget.* I greatly prefer silence (119)''. Above all, silence over her past shame caused by her husband's unfaithfulness.

Ila Das had a hard life, though in a different way, made as it is of privations and poverty, nevertheless she still cares for the social problems which continue to plague India. On the contrary, Nanda Kaul has never experienced such an engagement, she smoulders her rage within herself and her retirement. Ila Das still fights against local superstitious priests, who deny the children the possibility to be treated in hospitals, and let them die. Furthermore, Ila Das is conscious of the role of women in the process of modernisation that India is undergoing after Independence : "the women are willing, poor dears, to try and change their dreadful lives by an effort, but do you think their men will let them? Nooo, not one bit (129)''. Therefore, Ila Das is aware of the subordinate condition of women, especially evident in the practice of child-marriage, that Indian legislation has abolished and Ila Das is still trying to stop.

Ila Das's final comment on the dry weather and on the risk of forest fires is just an echo of Nanda Kaul's brooding over the lack of water in Kasauli if compared with the richness in lakes and rivers of the Kashmir of her childhood. But that dryness has permeated Nanda Kaul, who is dumb to her friend's request of help, and indifferent to her friend's social involvement to improve life for women. Both Nanda Kaul's recollections of her childhood, spent in lakes and rivers, and Ila Das's umbrella in a dry season and in the evening hours are emblems of a lost womanhood, of a maternal female world, which has been destroyed by males. Nanda Kaul's husband is the cause of her present aridity and selfishness, while Ila Das's good-for-nothing brothers are the cause of her negated womanhood or even motherhood, since she could never marry.

Nanda Kaul's recommendation to her friend not to preach against the priest, and the grainseller's reproach not to go out at night alone are just anticipations of what is going to happen. Ila Das falls victim of the ambush and rage of Preet Singh, who wants to marry his seven-years-old daughter to a widowed man, and does not accept Ila Das's intrusion in that matter. Ila's sacrificial death and rape catches the reader by surprise, as a signal of that blind violence that uncoils in the darker corners of India.

The death of Ila Das is announced as was her arrival : by a phone-call, from the police station. In this sudden and incredible revelation, Nanda Kaul breaks down and becomes conscious of all the lies she has told herself and Raka of a happy life with her father and her husband, who had married her only to cover his life-long relation with a Christian, Miss David : "She did not live here alone by choice — she lived here alone because that was what she was forced to do, reduced to doing (145)". And while the reader is doubtful about Nanda Kaul's surviving the bad news, Raka excitedly calls her : "I have set the forest on fire. Look, Nani — look — the forest is on fire (145)".

Because of its shortness, *Fire on the Mountain* is structured like a short story, or rather like a novella, with the climax at its very end. Thus, in the space of four pages, as many critics have noticed, the climax of this novella is consumed in a fire, and Raka has shown her true face as Kali the destroyer.

The fire is an act of will : Raka had gone to the kitchen and had taken a box of matches to set the forest on fire, to stop the two ladies lying about their happy past, to "wipe it all away", to reduce all its stories and violence to silence. Whatever is latent in Nanda Kaul, her resentment, her rage and vengeance is patent in Raka. Parvati the spouse, has become Durga the inaccessible, before Raka made her appearance and fully displayed her powers as Kali, the fury emanated by Parvati-Durga. Metaphorically, the full moon has ripened and Raka has consciously set a whole world on fire. In spite of her youth and white complexion, which are the reassuring aspects taken by Gauri, the goddess emerging from Parvati's will to get rid of her black colour, she has inherited the dark and fierce spirit of her great-grandmother, thus appearing in her many facets as the goddess Kali.

Her fire has been interpreted in many ways and Premila Paul and R. Padmanabhan Nair in their essay, "Varieties of loneliness in

Fire on the Mountain'', provide a whole set of hypotheses. Raka's incendiarism is read as vengeance against the adult world; or fire is seen as a passion for purification through apparent destruction. According to R.S. Shama, ''the fire consumes the fictive world of Nanda Kaul and leaves the reader smouldering under the impact of a tragic awareness that he had never anticipated. The only reality he has finally left with is the reality of fire that symbolizes the funeral pyre — the ultimate consummation. Apparently, Raka is the only survivor of this three-woman-story and she is identified with the triumphant knowledge.''

All these interpretations are satisfactory enough, for fire is a symbol of purification, of death and rebirth from its own ashes; it is a sign of Raka's rebellion against a violent world, but it is also Raka's handy execution of her great-grandmother's spiritual hate of the world. However, the final fire as well as the often mentioned forest fires are the objective correlate of those domestic and silent acts of violence that plague Indian family — and social-life. After all, literally, Nanda Kaul is a widow who dies in a fire (though we are not sure if she had already died when she heard the news of Ila Das's murder), and this is a reminiscence of the practice of sati (suttee), that is of women who burned themselves on their husband's funeral pyre, outlawed in 1928. Furthermore, fire is one of the major causes of domestic incidents in India, as shown in the much discussed recent film *Fire*.

The whole novel, or novella, is built on the attempt to give central focus to what is marginal. First of all, an old woman, representing the marginalised of society, becomes the main protagonist of the story. Secondary characters like Raka and Ila Das introduce other stories of violence within the main narrative. But Raka is a child herself, and paraphrasing the words of Kinsley, both the old (or dead) woman and the infant have a liminal nature. Neither has a complete social identity. Neither fits neatly or at all into the niches and structures of normal society. Both Nanda Kaul and Raka have been excluded from human relationships. ''One who approaches Kali in these roles is awakened to a perception of reality that is difficult to grasp within the confines of the order of dharma and a socialized ego.'' Thus the fire also represents this final knowledge and reciprocal recognition. The fact that Raka calls her great-grandmother "Nani" in the last episode and had done so only twice before, is a farther proof of a deeper recognition, like the infant who on the battleground cried so desperatley in order to attract Kali's attention, and conquered her as a mother. Actually, the novel concludes with a double confession. On the one hand Nanda Kaul confesses she has made up all sorts of fantasies and stories, while Raka confesses she has set those same stories on fire.

Besides, Nanda Kaul's apparently tranquil story of retirement in the mountains allows for a whole set of secondary plots to be hinted at. Subplots concerning ill-treated wives, children who die without medical assistance, for Western medicine is not accepted all over the country, child-marriages as a tradition which goes against the laws of modern India, but still persists in rural areas, as well as Nanda Kaul's own unhappy marriage, Tara's unhappy marriage, Ila Das's hard life spent for the benefit of her male brothers who dilapidated her family's riches, these are all examples of the condition of women and children in modern India, but these themes are introduced almost silently, delicately, as if from the sidestage of the main narrative stream. Child-marriage, the practice of sati, widow-remarriage, reforms over property, dowry, inheritance, are all issues which have been raised by the All India Women Conference, since its first steps as the Women's Indian Association, in 1917.

However, Anita Desai masters the art of the novel so as not to turn it into a social pamphlet. Thus, all the explosions of violence in the novel are put to an end by a huge fire, as if the goddess Kali had come back to destroy the world in order to re-create it, according to her iconography of life-giver and life-destroyer or according to the inner rhythms of the divine mother (Mahadevi) which are also the rhythms of Hindu cosmology.

Dr. Carmen Concilio is Full Time Researcher in English Literature and Literatures of the English Speaking Countries at the University of Turin. She has published essays on Canadian, Caribbean, South African, Australian and Sri Lankan Literature. She has co-edited the Volume "Coterminous Worlds, Magic Realism and Contemporary English Literature" (Amsterdam : Rodopi, 1999) forthcoming.

REFERENCES

1. "An old woman, a great grandmother, may be irrelevant and hence not very useful and even burdensome in a domestic set up. But she can have great artistic relevance and potential in this author's fictional world. Anita Desai has touched upon such a subject in an earlier short story, 'Great Mother'." Premila Paul & R. Padmanabham Nair, "Varieties of Loneliness in *Fire on the Mountain*", in *Indian Women Writers,* R.K. Dhawan ed. (New Delhi : Prestige, 1991), set I, Vol. III, pp. 216-235 : 217.

2. "This many-named Goddess was the first Holy Trinity. Her three major aspects have been designated Virgin, Mother, and Crone; or alternatively, Creator, Preserver, and Destroyer. The same trinitarian pattern can be traced in all the Goddess figures of Indian, Arabian, Egyptian, the Middle Eastern, Aegean and Mediterranean cultures, and among Celtic and Teutonic peoples of Northern Europe. In India, one of the earliest homes of fully developed Goddess worship, within historical times, a Brahman priest-hood tried to replace the original female trinity with three male gods, Brahma the Creator, Vishnu the Preserver, and Shiva the Destroyer. [...] They wrote in the Tantrasara that the Triple Goddess alone was the One Primordial Being, the Creatress of the three gods themselves." Barbara G. Walker, *The Crone, Woman of Age, Wisdom and Power* (New York : Harper, 1985), pp. 21-22.

3. "In some areas, the Goddess was represented as three-faced or three-headed, like the Hebe-Hera-Hecate trinity of archaic Greece. In other areas, she was three individuals who were still somehow one, embodying the same spirit like the grandmother, mother, and daughter of the matrilineal clan." Walker, p. 22.

4. Anita Desai, *Fire on the Mountain* (Bombay : Allied Publishers, 1977), p. 3. Further references will appear parenthetically in the text.

5. "Carignano" is the name, Peliti, an Italian caterer gave to a villa in the mountains, not too far from the city of Simla where he ran a very successful Grand Hotel, a famous Simla rendezvous for cakes, gossip and flirtation. The landscape in Kasauli might have reminded him of the Piedmont region in Northern Italy, where he came from, thus he named the villa after a small village at the foot of the Piedmontese mountains.

6. Kinsley, *Hindu Goddesses* (New Delhi : Motilal Banarsidass, 1986), p. 99.

7. See Kamini Dinesh, "*Fire on the Mountain.* Negation of the role model", in *Between Spaces of Silence : Women Creative Writers* (New Delhi : Sterling Publishers, 1994), pp. 107-112 : 107.

8. "Throughout the novel, Carignano is associated with death, and is a place where memories reside." Premila Paul & R. Padmanabhan Nair, p. 223.

9. Walker, p. 31.

10. Walker, p. 45.

11. Walker, p. 74.

12. Some critics have compared the treatment of time in Anita Desai's and Virginia Woolf's works. Here, too, Nanda Kaul's consciousness of the shift between the eternal time, symbolized by the flight of the eagle, and real time, symbolized by the cuckoo's calling, is similar to Mrs. Dalloway's shifting experience of interior time and the real time measured by the Big Ben. See

Asha Kanwar's "Anita Desai and Virginia Woolf : A Comparative Study", in *Indian Women Writers,* 1991, set I, Vol. III, pp. 7-21, and "Anita Desai's *Clear Light of Day* And Virginia Woolf's *The Waves*", 1991, set I, Vol. IV, pp. 26-42.

13. Dinesh, p. 108.
14. Kinsley, p. 100.
15. "The Gorgon's evil eye was attributed to many other manifestations of the Crone. [...] As a postmortem judge, she was usually credited with a piercing gaze from which nothing could be hidden. Her Egyptian name as Mother of Truth and Justice, Maat, derived from the universal mother-syllable Maa (Ma). In Egypt this also meant "to see", and it was shown in hieroglyphics as an eye. In the Middle East, the Crone had several manifestations as an all-seeing eye, notably the huge-eyed Syrian Goddess Mari who could search men's souls." Walker, p. 58. "Scottish legends said of the Caillech that she sometimes had one eye in the middle of her forehead, like statues of Kali with her central 'third eye' of mystical insight; and that she gave birth to monstrous giants with several heads and arms apiece : obvious recollections of typically Hindu deities." Walker, p. 77.
16. Alessandro Monti, "Da Gauri a Gausra in The Time after Cowdust, (Alessandria : Edizioni dell'Orso) forthcoming.
17. Kinsley, p. 15.
18. "Like other forms of the Great Mother, the Ephesian Goddess had her Virgin, Mother and Crone facets, often signified by the new moon, full moon, and waining moon." Walker, p. 23.
19. "There are many statues and paintings of the entity that Erich Neumann called the most grandiose form of the Terrible Mother : India's Kali Ma, the archetypal Crone. [...] In her typical pose, Kali Ma squats on top of her consort Shiva, who lies dead under her feet. She rips open his belly, and drags his entrails into her mouth. [...] She scrowls fiercely. She sticks out her tongue. Her eyeballs bulge." Walker, p. 71.
20. Kinsley, p. 126.
21. Kinsley, pp. 116-117; 124.
22. Walker, p. 76.
23. Walker, p. 76.
24. "In India this feminine wisdom figure was usually called Shakti, an almost untranslatable amalgam of wife, mistress, queen, power, genius, strength, authority, mind, vulva, woman, and cosmic energy. Each god needed his own Shakti." Walker, p. 59.
25. "In the Mahanirvana-tantra, too, Kali is one of the most common epiteths for the primordial sakti. [...] the uniting of opposites (male-female, microcosm-macrocosm, sacred-profane, Siva-sakti). Kinsley, p. 123.
26. Kinsley, p. 126.
27. S.P. Swain, "The Incarcerated Self and the Derelict House : A Study of the house image in Anita Desai's Novels", in *Indian Women Writers,* 1995, set III, Vol. 2, pp. 31-36 : 33.
28. P. Paul and R.P. Nair, p. 228.
29. It is surprising that among the studies on the the figure of "the crazy

woman'' which compare Anita Desai's *Cry, the Peacock* to Margaret Atwood's *The Edible Woman*, and Desai's *Baumgartner's Bombay* to Margaret Laurence's *The Diviners*, none takes into account a comparison between Desai's *Fire on the Mountain* and Laurence's *The Stone Angel*, for the characters of Nanda Kaul and Hagar share many characterisitics. See Sunaina Singh's ''The 'crazy' Ones in Anita Desai and Margaret Atwood''; and D.K. Pabby's ''Widening the Human Perspective through Multiculturalism : The Fiction of Margaret Laurence and Anita Desai'' and ''Multicultural Ethos in the Fiction of Margaret Laurence and Anita Desai : A Comparative Note'', in *Indian Women Novelists*, 1995, set III, Vol. 2, pp. 36-65.

30. Kinsley, p. 15. Moreover, Ila may be another name for Durga. In Sanskrit it may mean both ''earth'' and ''mother''. She is the goddess of earth who, with Sarasvati and Mahi, forms the trinity which bestows delight.

    P.P. Piciucco. ''Destructiveness, self-destruction and violence seem to be among your privileged settings. Do you think this is due to your sensibility and/or personal experiences or as a sort of 'cultural inclination' the Bengalis have towards the Kali myth?''

31. A. Desai : ''You see, I don't think the Indians are an extremely peaceful people. In India one is always running up against tremendous violence or threats of violence. It is a certain element in the atmosphere which has many causes, really. It comes from a huge population which crowds the country, it comes from extreme poverty, it comes from a sense of powerlessness and frustration.... I have always felt that there was a state of tension that could erupt any time to violence, and not to acknowledge that in my writing would have not been true to it. And the Kali myth explains a great deal of the Indian psyche, how the destructive is very much a part of everyday life. The destructive and the creative lives are very close together in India and they prevail so much of life. And out of this has born so much : poetry, music, art, laughter, pleasure in living. The two seem to lie very close together. This belongs to the way Indians experience life. I have seen the same thing in Mexico where, at the same time, there are extremely deep, dark and destructive forces and life, colour, pleasure, crowds, beautiful objects. The two seem to need to exist together.'' See Pier Paolo Piciucco's ''Interview to Anita Desai'' in this Volume.

32. Kinsley, pp. 225-234.

33. Kinsley, p. 131.

34. Kinsley, pp. 126-137.

35. See also the two Volumes almost entirely dedicated to Anita Desai of the already mentioned series : *Indian Women Novelists*, 1991, set I, Vol. 2, and 1995, set III, Vol. 2, pp. 9-128.

36. ''So much for my commitment to the English Language. Now for the problems this is supposed to have created for me. I think I have simply side-stepped them — by not writing the kind of social document that demands the creation of realistic and typical characters and the use of realistic typical dialogue. By writing novels that have been catalogued by critics as psychological [...] I have been left free to employ, simply the language of the interior.'' Anita Desai, ''The Indian Writer's Problems'', in *Indian Women Writers*, 1991, set I, Vol. 2, pp. 7-10 : 9.

37. Kinsley, (Durga) p. 101; (Kali) p. 130.

10

Raka As a Metaphor for Ruined Childhood in Anita Desai's *Fire on the Mountain*

DR. B. BRAHMANANDA CHARY*

Anita Desai does not attribute any ideology to her characters. She aims at exploring their psychological crises and struggles. In some of her novels she portrays the usual psyche of children too. *Fire on the Mountain* is one such novel and Deasi seems to assert in it that if a child is denied love and affection owing to negligence and irresponsibility on the part of the parents, he or she may turn out to be a problematic, maladjusted child.

Raka of *Fire on the Mountain* is perhaps the most complicated and mysterious child character in the entire gamut of Indian fiction in English. She presents an intriguing picture to the readers by her unusual behaviour. Raka means the moon. But Raka, the character, is not round faced, calm or raidant. In fact, animal imagery is profusely used to describe her in the novel. To her great-grandmother Nanda Kaul, she appears like "one of those dark crickets that leap up in fright but do not sing, or a mosquito, minute and fine, on thin, precarious legs". Raka's "Extravagantly large and somewhat bulging eyes" (39)[1] make Nanda Kaul feel more than ever her resemblance to an insect. Besides, she has "large and protruding ears" (40).

Raka does everything so silently and secretly that Nanda cannot discover what she does with herself all day long. She finds out that 'The child had a gift for disappearing — suddently, silently. She

* Lecturer, Department of English, Vijayanagar College of Commerce, Vijayanagar Colony, Hyderabad.

would be gone, totally, not to return for hours'' (45). She returns with her brown legs scratched, her knees bruised, sucking a finger stung by nettles. Her eyes look very still and thoughtful as if ''She had visited strange lands and seen fantastic improbable things the lingered in the mind'' (46). Sometimes she emerges from the dark ''like a soundless moth'' (46).

Raka is like ''a rabbit conjured up by magician — drawn unwillingly out of the magic hat, flashing past Nanda Kaul, then vanishing in the dark of a bagful of tricks'' (47). As long as Raka is out of view, Nanda would wait for her arrival. But when she comes, Nanda turns a look on her ''that was reproachful rather than welcoming'' (47). But Raka never stops to take notice of it.

> She ignored her so calmly, so totally that it made Nanda Kaul breathless. She eyed the child with apprehension now, wondering at this total rejection, so natural, instinctive and effortless when compared with her own planned and wilful rejection of the child (47).

Raka has the gift of avoiding what she regards as dispensable. Gradually, Nanda finds Raka to be ''the finished, perfected model of what Nanda Kaul herself was merely a brave, flawed experiment'' (47). Like her, Raka does not love company: ''She had not a dog's slavishness to companionship'' (56). She outrightly rejects ''the very thought of school, of hostels, of discipline, order and obedience'' (59). She has a non-conformist and detached self.

With her undemanding nature and independent existence, Raka leaves Nanda wondering what an extraordinary child she is. No normal child will be like Raka. She ''was not like any other child she (Nanda) had known, not like any of her own children or grandchildren. Amongst them, she appeared a freak by virtue of never making a demand. She appeared to have no needs'' (47). She seems to have given up all the childhood pleasures and desires. Children of her age often have stock interests: fairy tales, adventure stories, flowers, bufferflies and the like. Raka, on the contrary, regales in ugliness, danger and destruction. Her imagination is weird and she is irresistibly drawn to strange things.

If a child finds the world hostile, the easiest course for her is to withdraw from it. But, Raka instinctively learns to expect nothing from it. There is no move on her part to participate in life, to strive for achievement and to socialize. That is perhaps why the rocks, symbolising lifelessness, attract her. She has lost what Rollo May calls "inten-tionality"[2], meaning the faculty of entertaining intentions with the help of which one can relate oneself to the world.

To Raka's unusual behaviour is added to craving for setting something on fire. When Ram Lal expresses his fears about the human being knocked over and the fire being spread, Raka asks him in excitement: "Will it set fire to the garden?....Will it set the hill on fire?" (53). She has a mysterious urge to see fire on the mountain. Her desire for destruction is symbolic of the burning rage within herself. It is a secret yearning for a companion who is akin to her, not with an interest to share or bear the wilderness of her life but as a consolation. The deprivation of loving care has created disturbance in her subconscious mind making her emotionally blank and inclined to set the world on fire. Raka is a victim of 'Emotional deprivation,"[3] to use a phrase of Leland H. Scott. Usha Pathania also rightly says that Raka's "embarrassing, loveless childhood fills her heart with distrust and suspicion. She, therefore, turns her back upon human beings and their so-called safe, cosy and civilized world and develops a strong fascination for the ugly, lonely, rugged and desolate aspects of nature."[4]

Any normal child would want the company of an elder while visiting tourist spots or other places. But Raka never likes such company. She wants to do everything on her own. For example, while going to Monkey Point, Raka does not want her great-grandmother to accompany her.

> She had planned to come to Monkey Point alone, on a solitary afternoon expedition, without anyone's knowing, secrecy was to have been the essence of it, she relished it so — Raka had all the jealous, guarded instincts of an explorer, a discoverer, she hated her great-grandmother intently watching her ascent, clenching her hands with tension when the goats nearly knocked her off her feet or when she slipped on the loose pebbles (60-61).

By this it becomes evident that Raka has a strange fascination for being left alone. She even takes delight in being not cared for at all. When she is at the top of Monkey Point she feels "light and exhilarated, airborne as a seed or a blade of grass" (61). Quite extraordinarily, Raka takes delight in imagining that she does not have anyone and she is all alone : "I'm shipwrecked, Raka exulted, I'm shipwrecked and alone. She cluing to a rock — my boat, alone in my boat on the sea, she sang" (61-62). This quality in Raka disturbs Nanda Kaul and makes her think: "Raka's genius. Raka's daemon" (64).

The way Raka moves about in the dark makes her appear queer and strange. It is impossible for any normal child — for that matter even adult — to wander about in the dark like Raka does. She finds darkness, rather than light, friendlier to her. She is at home with the things of the darkness and is afraid of the "hairy young men" of the club because there is something "some alarming about them, to her, than in the wails of jackals or the sudden rattles of the night jars in the darkness" (68). It is abnormal that laughter and happiness do not appeal to Raka. They instead appear to be repulsive to her.

On being encouraged by Ram Lal, Raka goes to the club to have the vision of "ladies dressed as queens and men as princes" (68). But when she peeps into the ballroom, she is shocked. She thinks that the scene is lunacy rampant. The drumming of the band and blowing of paper horns frightens her :

> She wished she could close her eyes. She wished she were a million miles away from the band. She tried to think she was asleep and this was a nightmare (69).

Raka flees this scene like an animal being pursued, sobbing the while, "*Hate* them — *hate* them...." (71). The perverted acts of the people dressed in a bizarre fashion unlock the hidden memories of her own father and his wild behaviour at home:

> Somewhere behind them, behind it all, was her father, home from a party, stumbling and crashing through the curtains of night, his mouth opening to let out a flood of rotten stench, beating at her mother with hammers and fists of abuse — harsh, filthy abuse that made Raka cower under the

> bedclothes and wet the mattress in fright....and her mother lay down on the floor and shut her eyes and wept. Under her feet, in the dark, Raka felt that flat, wet jelly of her mother's being squelching and quivering, so that she didn't know where to put her feet and wept as she tried to get free of it. Ahead of her, no longer on the ground but at some distance now, her mother was crying (71-72).

Raka comes back to the world of reality only when a jackal howls. After the club incident, a peculiar change comes over her thin, pale face :

> Her eyes darkened, as if with a secret she would not divulge. She was no longer the insect, the grasshopper child. She grew as still as a twig (72).

However, Raka does not stop going to the ravine to wander. She moves about chanting defiantly under her breath : I don't care — I don't care — I don't care for *anything*!" (73).

Raka is drawn to the fire, when she sees it for the first time : "Shivers ran through her, zigzag, leaving streams of sweat in their wake" (74). During that night she keeps "getting out of bed and coming barefoot into the drawing-room to look out of the window and see the fire spread" (75).

One may think that Raka is cold towards Nanda Kaul and does not want to develop intimacy with her because of her (Nanda's) reserved nature. But the textual evidence shows that Raka does not have intimacy even with her mother. She does not miss her in the least. She does not feel home-sick. She moves about in Carignano as if as lived there eversince her birth.

This strange attachment on Raka's part to the place may be interpreted as her way of forgetting all the suffering associated with her home and parents. "Her traumatic childhood" says Shanta Krishna Swamy, "has hardened her into a hard little core of solitary self-sufficiency and now recovering from a bout of typhoid, her spirit is defiant enough to go chanting."[5] Intimidated since birth, anything destructive, lawless, uncompromising and ruthless excites her. Krishna Swamy continues : "The conventional sweet smells and sounds of childhood are ignored, she feels drawn by scenes of devastation and failure. The forest fires tingle her and she bursts from the shell of Carignano like a sharp keen-edged explosive to set fire to the mountains."[6]

She goes to such places where no ordinary persons dares go. She is attracted to a land "where there was no sound, only silence, no light, only shade, and skeletons kept in beds of ash on which the footprints of jackals flowered in grey" (90). The nurseries and bed rooms of her infancy do not attract her because of their sickly sweet smells of illness, sadness, drink, medication, milk and tension. Similarly, the clubs and parks of the cities in which she has lived do not interest her as "no one had given her the necessary pass, the key" (91). What attracts Raka will be frightening enough to any normal child :

> It was the ravaged, destroyed and barren spaces in Kasauli that drew her : the ravine where yellow snakes slept under grey rocks and agaves growing out of the dust and rubble, the skeletal pines that rattled in the wind, the wind-levelled hill-tops and the seared remains of the safe, cosy, civilized world in which Raka had no part and to which she owed no attachment (91).

At no point of time has Raka experienced anything that is affectionate and kind. She has grown up with repulsive and abhorrent feelings. The burnt house on a hill allures Raka and the forest fire that can burn everything to ashes haunts her and ultimately leads her to set the forest on fire. As Raka's world consists only of broken, devastated and appalling objects, withdrawal comes to her naturally. But "it is a morbid state of rejection of the unbearable reality which always hovers in Raka's mind,"[7] says Kunj Bala Goel.

Childhood is a formative period when a person has intrinsic desires for spiritual health. The child discovers the beauty and sweetness of human relationships through love. Raka's parents have no time or inclination to fulfil her emotional needs. Her mother Tara is in such an unhappy predicament that she cannot do anything to help Raka. Her shattered mental equilibrium and deteriorating physical strength render her helpless. Her father has not time to look after her well-being. Consequently, Raka's "Traumatic experiences deprive her of child's innocent trust and feeling of joy in the company of others."[8] With the result, unlike other normal children, she is not interested in stories about people, about relations. Her curiosity about people and what they do has been blunted.

Raka does not like even the presence of Ila Das and Nanda Kaul. She feels disgusted with the company of the two old ladies. The longer Raka is in the company of her great-grandmother, the more she wants to run away from her. She is bored with Nanda's unreal account of her childhood. Nanda's boring narration makes her "ache for the empty house on the charred hill, the empty summer-stricken view of the plains below, the ravine with its snakes, bones and smoking kilns — all silent, and a forest fire to wipe it all away leaving ashes and silence" (120). Games too do not have any appeal for Raka. An Adult resignation and philosophical reserve are found in Raka as for games and play.

Raka is a victim of an unwholesome, empty and hopeless childhood environment. She spends her childhood and develops her consciousness in a home which reeks of disease and moral decay. Her mother is sick forever and father is found drinking at all hours. They are just not worried about the emotional growth and adjustments of Raka.

Such an unhappy home environment creates fear, insecurity, distrust and anxiety in growing children. For healthy growth, a child needs an orderly and secure world. For creating order, parents-child exchange of ideas is essential. Discussing the positive influence of a harmonious familial interaction upon the psyche of a growing child, Sudhir Kakar comments : "An individual's identity and merits are both enhanced if he or she has the good fortune to belong to a large, harmonious and close knit family."[9] For Raka, childhood means a nightmare, violence and terror, because she has seen them taking place in her house and they have left an indelible impression of her tender consciousness. It is because of this, when Nanda Kaul tells about her childhood as being happy and her father being affectionate, Raka concludes that they are perfect lies. Raka's final act of setting fire to the mountain is then not merely an act of violence, but also an act of purification as it might burn away the lies and the make-believe world of Nanda Kaul and the mental agony of her own.

Raka alleviates her suffering by resorting to violence. It is a means of escape for her. By the act of setting fire to the forest, she saves her ideal self from being totally destroyed. Like a rubber ball hit hard against the wall, Raka bounces back on the cruel and false world with a vengeance.

REFERENCES

1. Anita Desai, *Fire on the Mountain* (New Delhi : Allied Publishers, 1977) 39. All the parenthetical page references are to this edition.
2. Rollo May, *Love and Will* (New York : Northern, 1969). Quoted by Usha Bande in *The Novels of Anita Desai* (New Delhi : Prestige, 1988) 223.
3. Leland H. Scott, *Child Development* (New York : Rinehart and Winston, 1967) 317.
4. Usha Pathania, "The Filial Ties — A Bane : *Fire on the Mountain*," Indian Women Novelists, III, ed. R.K. Dhawan (New Delhi : Prestige, 1991) 210.
5. Shanta Krishna Swamy, "Anita Desai — The Sexist Nature of Sanity," *The Women in Indian Fiction in English* (New Delhi : Asia Publishing House, 1982) 273.
6. Swamy 262.
7. Kunj Bala Goel, *Language and Theme in Anita Desai's Fiction* (Jaipur : Classic Publishing House, 1989) 43.
8. Pathania 209.
9. Sudhir Kakar, *The Inner World : A Psycho-Analytic Study of Childhood and Society in India* (Delhi : OUP, 1981) 121.

11

A Focus on Anita Desai's 'Games at Twilight'

B. VYAGHRESWARUDU*

Anita Desai has a collection of short stories: 'Games at Twilight' (1978) to her credit. The author of the highly acclaimed novel, 'Fire on the Mountain' and six other novels, has shown her craftsmanship even in the shorter fiction *i.e.*, short story. Her short stories which are witty, evocative, tender and perceptive reveal her skill and dexterity in handling this genre. She uses all her creative techniques and talents even in her short stories. She works with the same material as in the novels but on a small scale. As against her early novels which are about withdrawal, some of her stories make contact with the outer world. She takes up themes like the tension between convention and exploration, family solidarity and individualism, social requirements and the impersonal factors (like death and art) which transcend them. Her characters are individual persons with keen sensibility and zest for life and they view the world with astonishment, with humour and sometimes with pain. Many of her characters are children, women, employees, artists and introverts. In these stories, one finds the colours, smells and sounds of India. Her delicate strength of observation, 'hypotically beautiful style', quietly precise characterization and gentle irony with a tinge of humour add a new dimension to her short stories.

The title story 'Games at Twilight' — is an indepth study of psychology of children at play. When the children decide to play, hide-n'seek' Ravi, in an attempt to come victorious in the game

* Head, Department of English, S.K.B.R. College, Amalapuram.

hides in a dark lumber room for hours together suppressing his fear. As he anticipates his victory over others, his fear dissipates. When he comes out to declare himself victorious, nobody recognises his victory as the children have left the old game and now playing a new game — "funeral game". His victory becomes a pathetic realization of his own insignificance. 'The ignominy of being forgotten' pricks and makes his heart heavy. In this story Desai has successfully developed and depicted the struggle between Ravi's 'self-assertion and desire for recognition'. In Ruth Prawer Jhabvala's work the social background is more important than the characters, in Kamala Markandaya's, the stress is as much on the main characters as on the diverse background, but in Anita Desai's, the inner climate, the climate of sensibility, is more compelling than the visible action. As Iyengar puts it "Her forte.... is the exploration of sensibility — the particular kind of modern Indian sensibility that is ill at ease among the barbarians and the philistines, the anarchists and amoralists."[1]

As Desai's forte is the exploration of sensibility — the sensibility of her characters, she focuses her searching lens on the visible bit of reality which is like the tip of a submerged iceburg. The purpose of her writing is to explore this submerged truth and she does it through the exploration of the psyche of her characters. In the story 'Games at Twilight, she creates an intense moment of psychological struggle in the mind of Ravi to explore deep into it. She is interested in "delving deeper and deeper and into a character, a situation, of a scene rather than going round about it."[2]

As the usual narrative mode is inadequate for her purpose, she chooses the subjective mode and adopts the strategy of sustained use of imagery. "This mode gives ample scope for introspection, analysis, reflection and reverie." In this story, 'Games at Twilight', Desai makes use of many apt images and symbols 'to crystalize the various levels of consciousness and illumine the states of mind'. "All the characteristics of symbolic style musicality, pictorialness and synaesthetic experience are found in her short stories."[3]

The metaphorical prose comes to her rescue in delineating her characters who suffer from the stress of the soul and overburdened emotions. Desai takes up her images from a large variety of sources depending on the aptness of the situation. "Her most important source is nature and she has a whole range of images drawn from vegetable and plant life, birds, animals and other natural phenomena."

In the story "Studies in the Park", we find another kind of withdrawal, withdrawal from material pursuits, from participation in the rat race. Suno, in a bid to get first in his examination, finds a suitable place in a park and sticks to his books. But books are 'like parasites and like parasites they suck him dry'. Under the overwhelming pressure of study, he gradually loses his ability to function suitably, both physically and psychologically. Desai describes Suno's state of hopelessness.

"I lay sluggishly on a heap of waste paper under my tree and read without seeing and slept without sleeping... I felt as if we were all dying in the park, that when we entered the examination hall it would be to be declared officially dead... I don't work myself any more — I mean physically, my body no longer functioned" (p. 29).

At his point in the story, Suno sees a young beautiful woman on a bench, in the park, her head lying on the lap of a man, who is caressing her face. One finds this same image in her novel 'Where Shall We Go This Summer' where Sita recollects this scene in the park as the only happy memory she has. This vision of tender relationship between the couple creates an emotionally moving moment. Suno's extreme reaction to tension is both distressing and horrifying. He develops an apathy towards studies. 'Life becomes for him search and is no longer a race'. This story depicts a universal theme — parent's ambition and society's competitiveness which sandwitch students like Suno. Some of the well written lines in this story run like poetry. They are 'very crisp like the delicate strokes of a sculptor or finishing touches of a great painter'.

In the story 'Sale', as in the 'Studies in the Park', proving one's worth is the central struggle. A poor artist, who is compelled to sell his paintings to support his family finds it difficult to survive in a competitive and sensitive environment. A party of prospective buyers encourages him with a hyprocritical show of friendship and praise his paintings. They bargain many pieces of art but when the poor artist, who is badly in need of money, asks for some advance, they show their teeth and empty pockets. Customers' callous reaction produces that intense moment in which the story is tied together. The reader is drawn into sympathy with the artist's hopeless position. In this story Desai gives no names to her characters as if to present the universal predicament of the artists and snobbery of the artless and heartless customers. These three stories are practically powerful in their overall impact.

The stories like 'A Devoted Son', 'Surface Textures', 'The Accompanist', 'Pigeons at Day Break', 'The Farewell Party', 'Private Tuition by Mr. Bose' and 'The Pineapple Cake' though skilfully written, containing excellent imagery and unusual characterization, some of the stories fell short in their emotional power. Some lack unified structure of a well developed conflict.

In 'A Devoted Son' the devoted son, Dr. Rakesh, fulfils the dreams of his parents. He gives his ageing father the full benefits of filial duty and medical science. But his father finds life a chore and desires to die. This story is both touching and comic in the insight it reveals of human psychology of the old man and dutiful doctor son. Though the story has 'no unity of time', the singleness of effect is achieved by Desai by concentrating on certain traits in her principal characters. Some critics find fault with Desai for shifting of focus from Rakesh to Varma. 'Had the dentire story been narrated with Varma in the spot-light, it might have had greater effect'.

In 'Surface Textures' Desai starts the story from Shiela's point of view and then switches over to Harish point of view and this lack of unity in its structure weakens the potential power of the story. In this story Harish, a Government servant, who becomes intensely preoccupied with textures of objects, finally becomes a Swamiji. As a character study, the story lacks depth.

In 'The Accompanist', Desai delineates the emotional state of a Tampura Player. The company of Ustad Rahim Khan makes a street urchin an accompanist. The alchemic touch of the master turned the crude and base boy into a noble and gentle accompanist. But once, he recollects and confesses, how his calm has been destroyed, his devotion shaken when his childhood friends had mocked at him. But he is convinced after some soul-searching that he can never become 'Ustad' in his own right and feels 'Does a mortal refuse God'.

In 'Pigeons at Day-break', Desai takes up the same theme as in 'Devoted Son'— 'The theme of old age and the unreasonable claims of a patient'. Asthmatic Basu always feels uneasy about something while his generous and devoted but too talkative wife, though irritates Basu with her talk, does all her best to provide some comfort to her husband. The news about supposed power cut seems to cut the very chords of life of Basu. In 'The Farewell Party', Desai presents both the hollowness and want of social life. The 'Cinderella-like friendliness' that pervades in the society is well revealed in the party. Through this story, Desai mocks at the snobbery of highbrows. In the story 'The Private Tuition by Mr. Bose', Desai presents the hardships of a middle class private teacher. It is a punishment to a teacher to be asked to teach an unwilling learner. Mr. Bose in the midst of domestic chorus, tries his best to teach Sanskrit to Pritam, who coughs limitating his favourite screen actors and shows little interest in studies. He is rather forced to read and teach Bengali Poetry to Upaneet, a girl of fashion, who comes more for mischief and mockery than to learn anything. Her presence irritates the house-wife as Upaneet's cunning glances are more on the teacher than on the book. Her presence seems to spoil the harmony of the home. Nagging, Mr. Bose lets her complaining child cry all the while. When Bose asks her to keep the child quiet, she finds a tough time to control the child. There is an exchange of heated dialogues but at the end of the day they have to come to terms with each other as their's is a 'lovers' quarrel'. In the story 'Pineapple Cake' Desai presents a glimpse of Westernized parties and pomp and show associated with them.

'Scholar and Gypsy' is a story about the clash of cultures, about redefinitions of meanings in life. It presents an American Couple's reacting to their experiences in India. David, in his scholastic pursuits, dislikes gypsy way of Pat. Pat dislikes the urban social life of Bombay as she considers it to be primitive. As they move from the city to hills David feels estranged from her. Pat prefers to join Hippies in their Search for Nirvana. But David returns to Delhi and his thesis. The Psychological revelation and analysis in which Anita Desai shows a keen interest gives a new dimension and direction to the themes of her stories as well as novels. In the story, each event acquires importance and it directly or indirectly debunks the protagonists of their old selves or outerposes and moves them towards some kind of self-revelation and assessment. "It is this position *vis-a-vis* their former selves which changes."[4] In this story many of the details used by Anita Desai to create the characters of David and Pat are well selected. She paints an exceptionally vivid backdrop for their actions. But Desai fails here because of her unconvincing dialogue — as she uses British-English overtones and Victorian attitudes in the portrayal of an American couple.

Anita Desai in her novels takes up many complex themes, ranging from the relationships between men and women between children and parents, between men and society, sexual repression to psychological struggle of the characters. As a fiction writer she turns her searching lens on the problems of women especially on their sexual and emotional responses which are crystalized into feminist statements taking up questions of education, jobs, reality, marriage and motherhood, discussing areas of freedom in both psychological and philosophical terms. But in her short fiction, she deals with ordinary themes but many of the stories contain the seeds which later germinate into great novels. Some of her stories are precursors of her great novels. In her short stories her style shows to even more advantage than in the novels. The best ingredients of her style in short stories are childhood memories and the haunting feelings surging out of a romantic heart. In Iyengar's words : "As we remain mesmorised by Anita Desai's verbal artistry and her uncanny evocation of atmosphere, her tale unfalteringly glides by and we force a rendition of the veil of happening or a memory to gain entry into the realm of personal experience and attain the desired finale of acceptance."[5]

REFERENCES

1. K.R. Srinivas Iyengar, *Indian Writing in English,* New Delhi, Sterling Publishers Pvt. Ltd., 1985, p. 464.
2. Jasbir Jain, *Stairs of the Attic, the Novels of Anita Desai,* Jaipur; Printwell Publishers, 1987, p. 14.
3. S. Indira, *Anita Desai as an Artist,* New Delhi, Creative, 1994, p. 4.
4. Jasbir Jain, p. 155.
5. Iyengar, p. 745.

12

Tradition and Deviation — A Study of Anita Desai's Novels

DR. S.P. SWAIN*

In dealing with the interior landscape and the psychic odyssey of the characters, Desai has extended and enlarged the thematic horizon of the Indo-Anglian novel. Her major novels tend to disappoint the reader due to their one-dimensionality, turning the characters wooden and insensitive. They are not kaleidoscopic in their thematic projection. In most of them there is a repeated and droll harping on the isolation of the self. However, they are deeply moving in their existential and socio-psychic import. Microcosm of man's endless struggle for survival, they voice the anguished ennui of the caged bird that symbolises the modern man. Emblems of remonstrance and psychic protest, they strive for the protection and preservation of their dignity and self-esteem in a patriarchal society. Indignantly promiscuous and inordinately self-conscious, they long for mutual understanding and reciprocation of love and respect.

Anita Desai speaks to us not only of the tumult of the human soul but also of its depth, its poetry and pathos, its beauty and compassions. It is through "the quality of mind and soul alone" (Iyengar 1962 : 343), that Anita Desai's novels would be a major contribution to literature. That is why the existential predicament in her novels has the unique touch of the universal. Her tender, flexible, malleable and moribund sensibility whipping inanities into awe and wonder becomes at times, as in Fire on the Mountain, too

* Department of English, Rourkela Municipal College, Rourkela.

melodramatic to make the story artistically coherent and aesthetically satisfying. The "fire" in *Fire on the Mountain* and the "light" in *Clear Light of Day*, have an insignificant and trivial link with the central plot and as such have a dim symbolical and metaphorical relevance, which, instead of ennobling and satisfying the artistic sensibility of the readers often bewilders them. Her hold on the reader's mind loosens. The readers instead of identifying themselves with her artistic sensibility, get alienated from it. Desai endeavours to offer the reader a slice of life but fails to impart the required voltage. The action at times detonates to poetic and philosophical speculations on existence and essence which the readers find too arduous to grapple with. The readers are so much repelled by the peculiar psychic set-up of her novels that they fail to take stock of the gravity of the alienated self's existential plight.

Dealing with the thoughts, emotions, and sensations at various levels of consciousness, Anita Desai found the technique used by D.H. Lawrence, Virginia Woolf, William Faulkner and Henry James quite suitable for her purpose of character delineation. Hence we have the use of flashbacks and the stream of consciousness technique in some of her novels, mainly in her first novel, *Cry, the Peacock* which to R.S. Sharma, is "the first step in the direction of psychological fiction in English" (Anita Desai 127). Very few Indo-Anglian novelists have paid so much attention to form and technique. Prof. Srinivasa Iyengar rightly observes :

> Since her pre-occupation is with the inner world of sensibility rather than the outer world of action, she has tried to forge a style supple and suggestive enough to convey the fever and fretfulness of the stream-of-consciousness of her principal characters (*Indian Writing in English* 1973 : 16).

This inner world of sensibility rendered through splendid poetic prose gives a "peculiar poetic quality" (Sharma 1981 : 14) to Desai novels.

Alienation is basically a western concept and in imitating this idea in her novels, Anita Desai remained at heart no less traditional than western. To her, alienation is more related to the emotional and mental moods and attitudes of her characters than to their spiritual, moral or ethical temperaments. The alienated self in Desai experiences the pangs of emotional isolation, not the spiritual and intellectual angst of a Raskolnikov or a Roquentin. The struggle of the alienated self in Desai is more similar to the Kafka protagonist than to the Camus hero. The Camus hero is nauseated and stifled. He seldom delights in his alienated existence but a Kafka hero does. Anita Desai's pro-tagonists never dodge the harsh reality of existence. They encounter it single-handedly. They delight in despair. Nirode in *Voices in the City* longs to move from failure to failure. The Desai protagonist is not an instance of bureaucratic alienation of Kafka's "K".

Alienation in Nathaniel Hawthorne suggests not only physical isolation but also psychic imperviousness. To him alienation is insulation. But in Desai, alienation seldom manifests in imperviousness. Desai protagonists are not like the Hawthorne hero who basks in the sunshine but is as cold as death. Hawthorne's treatment of alienation unlike that of Desai's, has moral and religious concerns. There is some similarity between the solitary self in Hawthorne and the sequestered self in Desai. Both undergo a gradual disintegration of their personality and both are the pictures of suffering arising from a sense of deep gloom sometimes thrown over their mind (monodic self) by morbid reflections on death and despair. Both are the manifestations of thanatophobia and both frantically long to break out of their cocooned self in quest of something more real and more palpable than their shadowy and hollow existence. But Desai protagonists in no way contribute to the tradition of the romantic hero as a sad clown as does the Hawthorne hero.

Like the Kafka protagonist, Desai heroes too, encounter the distressing conflict between external and internal obligations. Maya's conflict in *Cry, the Peacock* is between her obligations to the dead Toto and her biological obligations to her husband; Nanda's in *Fire On the Mountain* is between her filial obligations to Raka, her grand-daughter and to her unrequited psycho-emotional urges for self-isolation; Sita's in *Where Shall We Go This Summer*? is between her external life on the island and her emotional life as a housewife.

The Alienated self as portrayed in the novels of Anita Desai is not an instance of total alienation. The lone self in Desai novels does not undergo the pangs of alienation as does Hemingway's

Santiago, who stands isolated from every entity and group. Even from God.

Anita Desai portrays women as not totally cut off from familial and social ties but women who remain within these orbits and protest against monotony, injustice and humiliation. Woman in her novels is not a mere goddess or a robot but a self-actualising and self-realising individual. The names of Desai women like Maya, Sita and Raka are suggestive of their epic and mythic parallels to them (*i.e.* their names). They are ideals rather than facts. Maya says : "As a child, I enjoyed, princes like, a sumptuous fare of the fantasies of the Arabian Nights .... Indian mythology ... lovely English and Irish fairy tales ..." (Cry, the Peacock 89). Even Nirode's attitudes are also partly governed by the Greek Myths and contemporary Western philosophy. Thus Anita Desai imparts a fancifully mythopoeic colouring to the alienation of her characters. Save R.K. Narayan and Raja Rao, no other Indo-Anglian novelist has resorted to this strategy. To Raja Rao, myth is a legend, to Narayan it is a social reality, but to Anita Desai, it is a psycho-emotional reality. Unlike Raja Rao and R.K. Narayan but like Arun Joshi, Anita Desai resorts to the stream-of-consciousness technique which serves as an experience of the private inner world. Desai adopts the special narrative technique of setting apart from the main fictional narrative, the fragmentary passages which imply the theme of alienation.

In Bharati Mukherjee and V.S. Naipaul, it is the sense of "exile" that leads to the alienation of the characters. But in Desai, it is not so. Anita Desai's novels do not deal with the theme of exile : "... exile has never been my theme" (Desai Interviewed, Rajasthan University Studies in English 69) says Anita Desai. Her main thematic concern is how people cope with society, alien or not alien, without losing their sense of self-identity and individuality. In Mukherjee, it is people and cultures in collision but in Desai, it is people and people in collision, in Mukherjee, it is cultural confrontation but in Desai, it is psychic confrontation. Desai protagonists are emotional orphans. Emotionally maimed, they hail from fractured families. Their parents are either dead physically or psycho-emotionally (*i.e.* absent and uninvolved in their life). Jasbir Jain observes :

> ... they (the protagonists) either disown or are disowned by their families. Maya's only memory of her mother in Cry the Peacock is the photograph on her father's desk (134); the Ray children in *Voices in the City*, all four of them, are alienated in different degrees from their mother, their only surviving parent, as well as from their father, who is now dead, Sita's mother in *Where Shall We Go This Summer*? had run away from home leaving her children to the care of a father whose concerns lie outside the family, Sita had imagined she came into world motherless. A similar withdrawal, from her parents, is there on part of Sarah in *Bye-Bye, Blackbird*, who by marrying an Indian, has at one stroke, placed herself outside the family and the cultural situation. The children in *Clear Light of Day* resent the long absences of their parents and are aware only of their exists and entrances ... (*Stairs to the Attic* 113-114).

Like the novelist herself making a bold deviation from tradition in her approach to the fictionalisation of artistic ideas and ideals, Desai characters "carry very little of their parents in them; it is as if they were consciously rejecting whatever little they may have inherited. They prefer to go in the opposite direction" (*Ibid.*, p. 116). But heredity figures only marginally in her novels. In tracing the positive and negative effects of heredity on her characters, Anita Desai fails to supply the required voltage. Hence it is not as strong as in the novels of Emile Bronte, George Eliot or Thomas Hardy.

Delineating in novel after novel the pitiable and awful plight of the alienated self, especially of housewives, facing single-handed the torments and tortures of their insensitive and temperamentally callous husbands, Anita Desai has rendered a new dimension to Indo-Anglian fiction. This is further enlivened by her unconventional concern with the inner reality of the characters and their psychic topography. Desai denies the importance of theories in the shaping of artistic imagination. A work of art should grow from within, from the writer's inner beckonings and compulsions :

> I think theories of the novel are held by those of an academic or critical turn of mind, not the creative. A writer does not create a novel by observing a given set of theories ... he follows flashes of individual vision, and relies on a kind of instinct that tells him what to follow and what to avoid, how to veer away from what would be destructive to his vision. It is these flashes of vision, and a kind of trained instinct that leads him ... not any theories (Atma Ram, "An Interview with Anita Desai", *World Literature Written in English* 100).

Thus Anita Desai eschews traditional practices and gives free reins to her individual vision. Edgar Allan Poe, Henry James, E.M. Forster are at once critics and creative writers. Not Desai. She propounds no systematic theory of the novel against which to gauge the merit of her literary creations. Most of the Indo-Anglian novels are the result of a deliberate planning and plotting. In the case of Desai, they are an instinctive outcome of her inner motivations and compulsions — her desire to show as well as to see. It is a natural and vegetative growth. The object that triggers her imagination could be very trivial and insignificant — "a leaf dipping under a rain drop, a face seen on the bus, or a scrap of news read in the papers" (Ram, *op. cit.*, p. 99). Her fictional world witnesses the chaotic strife between the self and the society. Society here is a conscious entity, perpetually administering its gravitating influence and grip over the despairing self, which is enmeshed in the bewildering texture of the social gossamer and struggles unsuccessfully for an escape. The self struggles and falters, falters and struggles again. In almost all her works, save a few meant for the gratification of the puerile adolescent taste, this bold and chaotic tussle of the self for a release from the stranglehold of a pandemonic and hollow society is conspicuous. In her interview with Yasodhara Dalmia, Desai speaks of "the terror of facing single-handed, the ferocious assaults of existence" (Desai interviewed, The Times of India 13). These assaults of existence are the outcome of a society in which norms and values have degenerated. Her protagonists are socio-psychic rebels, recalcitrant selves, who find it difficult to compromise with the milieu. The self frantically endeavours to escape but in the process enters another world equally disturbing and disheartening. Thus it lies cloistered in a world, where there is a perpetual and persistent struggle between the physical and the psychic, leading to the triumph of the latter over the former. The temporal existence of the self in contrast to the eternity of the soul is the crux on which the fictional tapestry of Desai rests. The flux of recollections and ruminations that perpetually keep haunting the psyche of the characters is an aspect of the individual self which is at loggerheads with the socio-psychic reality. Desai mirrors the mythic reality of our life through the complex interaction of the self and the society. The reader is lost among some dark forgotten city streets where the sunlight seldom falls, streets pull of shadows, phantoms and skeletal beings, anaemic and cadaverous : streets smelling of generations of anticipated death and regretted birth, dread and desolation, worn-out clothes, cold and damp wood. And as one walks through, the street usually ends in cul de sac. Desai seldom offers any acceptable solution or clear-cut conclusion. There are hardly any abrupt revelations or surprises. Not even much overt anguish or vivid emotions. There is a kind of aerial drowsiness and an awful equanimity. There seems no noticeable effort at carrying the narrative forward. The novelist prefers to meander from episode to episode in a dubious wilfulness. The impression, thus generated, is very deceptive. Desai creates a hazy and blurred landscape, slotting in a story here and a suggestion there. The jigsaw puzzle she presents is incomplete and fragmentary, and the final picture that emerges is anything but impoverished and dull. Unlike R.K. Narayan, Mulk Raj Anand and Bhabani Bhattacharya, Anita Desai is chiefly concerned with the portrayal of inward or psychic reality of the characters. To use her own words, not "the one-tenth visible section of the ice-berg that one sees above the surface of the ocean..." but "the remaining nine-tenths of it that lie below the surface" (Desai, "Replies to the Questionnaire", Kakatiya Journal of English Studies 01). She "probes deep into the inner recesses of the psyche of the character and delves deeper and deeper in a character or a scene rather than going round about it" (Jain, "Desai Interviewed", Rajasthan University Studies in English 68). She prefers the private to the public world. For her, literature is neither a means of escaping reality nor a vehicle for parading political, social, religious and moral ideas. It is an exploration and an enquiry. Desai imparts no messages, preaches no morals. Like Jane Austen, she works on a narrow canvas, her "two inches of ivory". Narayan, Anand and Bhattacharya have opulence of subject matter, richness of experience. But a woman novelist, has her limits. Yet her novels have intensity, though not variety. Unlike Raja Rao's, they are occasionally abstruse and abstract. Since Desai believes that literature should deal with most enduring matters, less temporary and less temporal than politics, she is opposed to the art of delineating contemporaneity or documenting socio-economic reality. There are occasional allusions to contemporaneity but they are not deliberately or elaborately dealt with. Only in *Clear Light of Day*, we find a reference to the partition riots and the assassination of Mahatma Gandhi.

In dealing with the problem of the alienated self, Anita Desai has adopted a realistic/metonymic mode of writing. Dr. Madhusudan Prasad attributes alienation in Desai's novels to temperamental incompatibility of the characters. But the feeling of alienation in most of her characters is psychotic and psycho-neurotic. It is neither the alienation of Savithri in R.K. Narayan's *The Dark Room* nor that of Madeleine in Raja Rao's *The Serpent and the Rope*. It is the alienation of a psychically malformed character in quest of an authentic selfhood.

Unlike Narayan and Malgonkar, Anita Desai does not believe in a pre-conceived plot. She does not believe in its linear movement in terms of exposition, conflict and resolution. For her, the plot is just an idea occupying one's subconscious mind, a fragment of her imagination and a flash of her vision. Desai prefers pattern and rhythm, which is natural, to plot, which is artificial and mechanical, something superimposed upon the aesthetic vision of the artist. In such an organic whole, fragments are so integrated and interrelated that together they lend artistic unity and picturesque intelligibility to the work of art : "the perfect novel achieves the perfect balance, with just as much story or as much fantasy as its structure can bear, no more" (Ram, "Desai Interviewed", WLWE 100).

In *Cry, the Peacock*, it is the character of Maya and in *Voices in the City*, the voice of the metropolis Calcutta that smothers other voices and lends organic unity to the novel and sensitivity to the caged isolation of the characters. Anand, Narayan and Bhattacharya wrote for social documentation, and hence they selected characters from amongst socio-economic preys and predators. Anita Desai, on the other hand, is concerned with the delineation of psychological reality, and hence prefers such characters who are peculiar and eccentric rather than general and commonplace. Most of her major characters do not have fixed personalities. They are either entirely imaginary or an amalgam of several different characters. Desai conceives each character as a riddle and a mystery and believes that it is the duty of the novelist to solve this riddle and unravel this mystery. Her characters are almost sick of life and listless playthings of their morbid psychic longings. Most of her female protagonists are abnormally sensitive and unusually solitary to the point of being neurotic : Maya in *Cry, the Peacock*, Monisha in *Voices in the City*, Sita in *Where Shall We Go This Summer* and Nanda in *Fire on the Mountain*. This is conveyed through her stream of consciousness technique, her use of flashbacks and lyrical language. To Dr. Brijraj Singh, her novels are "an extended piece of music, subtle, sensitive, sensuous ... complex and richly integrated in its total effect" ("The Fiction of Anita Desai", The Humanities Review 43). English in the hands of Anita Desai becomes so flexible and tractable that it not only yields to the steerings and churnings of her intellect and the movement of her pen but also rises to such poetic heights so as to mirror and manifest her visions and views. In dealing with the psyche of the characters, their motivations and compulsions, she moves along the labyrinthine and dimly-lit corridors of inner reality.

The English novelists before Anita Desai studies man and his world in relation to the objective social reality. They used their art as a powerful "public instrument" (Daiches 1965 : 01) to present social problems but Desai walks out on such a traditional approach to fiction. She writes neither for providing entertainment nor for the dissemination and propagation of social ideas. Her main pre-occupation is to study human existence and human predicament, her exploration being a quest for self. She is the novelist of psycho-emotional situations and her theme is the individual against himself and against the milieu. Like Joseph Conrad, she has a double function — to pull away the individual from the social milieu, so that "he can be put in extremis, and to act as an agent of self-confrontation" (Allen 1954 : 303).

The Indo-Anglian novel till 1970s treated themes of political and social import. It exhibited a splendid array of limited, contrarious items : princes and paupers, saints and sinners, whitemen and babus, farmers and labourers, untouchables and coolies, prosperity and adversity, cities and villages. Mulk Raj Anand, Bhabani Bhattacharya were pioneers in this field. Writers like Raja Rao, Kamala Markandaya and Khushwant Singh dealt with more impressive and sophisticated themes like the country's independence movement, East-West encounter, tradition and modernity, materialism and spiritualism. The very notion of gauging the unexplored recesses or an individual's mind, of transcending the narrow and shallow conscriptions of the physical self was alien to them. It is only with the arrival of Anita Desai that such long-neglected themes were given an emotionally poetic treatment. She paraded them in sophisticated poetic cut-outs. Thus by shifting the realm of her novels from outer to inner reality and fathoming the nocturnal recesses of the human psyche, she brought the Indo-Anglian novel into the mainstream of European and American fiction. An important phase in the growth of fiction in India, as elsewhere, is the gradual shifting of focus from the external world to the inner world of the individual, capturing the atmosphere of the mind, and directly involving the reader "in the flow of a particular consciousness" [Lawrence, "Morality and Novel", Lodge (ed.) 20th Century Lit. Criticism 130]. A housewife with selected family ties, Anita Desai, George Eliot and Virginia Woolf resemble one another. Solely concerned with the inner weather of the characters, Desai is a painter of their kaleidoscopic and prismatic moods, their wills and conflicting choices. Her predecessors dealt with political turmoils and social evils. She discusses problems of temperamental incompatibility, conjugal chaos and inharmonious man-woman relationship. "The great relationship for humanity", says D.H. Lawrence, "will always be the relation between man and woman. The relation between man and man, woman and woman, parent and child will always be subsidiary" (Dalmia, "Desai Interviewed", The Times of India 13). Due to rapid industrialisation, growing awareness among women of their rights and the westernisation of our attitudes, man-woman relationship has become a popular concern for R.K. Narayan in *The Dark Room* and *The Guide*, Raja Rao in *The Serpent and the Rope*, Mulk Raj Anand in *Gouri*, Bhabani Bhattacharya in *Music for Mohini*, Manohar Malgonkar in *A Bend in the Ganges*, Arun Joshi in *The Foreigner* and *The Strange Case of Billy Biswas* and Kamala Markandaya in *The Nowhere Man*. Anita Desai, on the other hand, has given this theme a unique treatment. In her novels, most protagonists are alienated from the world, from society, from families, from parents and even from their own selves, because they are not average people but individuals who are unable to communicate with the people around. Unable to relate themselves with the milieu, they drift into their own sequestered world where they spin their dreams which never materialise. Mrs. Desai elaborates upon this aspect of her protagonists in her interview with Yasodhara Dalmia :

> I am interested in characters who are not average but have retreated, or been driven into some extremity of despair and so turned against, or made a stand against, the general current, it makes no demands, it costs no effort. But those who cannot follow it, whose heart cries out 'the great No', who fight the current and struggle against it, know what the demands are and what it costs to meet them (''Desai Interviewed'', The Times of India 13).

Unlike the other Indo-Anglian novelists, Anita Desai's predominant concern is not with society or social forces but the individual psyche and its interaction with social values. While the other Indian Novelists in English ''have been content to record and document'' (Desai, Quest 43), she is solely interested in the psychological aspect of the characters. In her review of Amitav Ghosh's The Circle of Reason, she shows her discontent for the novelists who prefer the ''outer'' aspect of an individual to the ''inner'' aspect and prefer the social to the psychological novels (India Today 149).

Anita Desai dealt though on a subjective plane, with the theme of East-West encounter, ''the conflicts and reconciliations or two cultures'' (Mukherjee 1947 : 64), Indian and Eurasian in matters of love, sex and marriage. Look at Raja Rao in *The Serpent and the Rope*, Kamala Markandaya in *Nectar in a Sieve, Some Inner Fury and Possession*, Bhattacharya in *A Dream in Hawaii*, Manohar Malgonkar in *Distant Drum and Combat of Shadows*, Nayantara Sahgal in *A Time To be Happy*, Arun Joshi in *The Foreigner* and Anita Desai in *Bye-Bye Blackbird.*

In Indo-Anglian writings, the theme of violence and death has been dealt both emotionally and spiritually. Leslie Fiedler refers to two stages in the treatment of violence in fiction : the urbanisation of violence and the ennobling of violence. In the first stage, "violence is transferred from nature to society, from the given world that man must endure to the artificial world he has made, presumably to protect himself from ravages of the first" (Love and Death in the American Novel 489). Thus we find the association of large metropolitan cities like Paris and London with the elements of crime, violence and poverty. In Desai, we hardly find any such association. Only in *The Voices in the City*, is Calcutta associated with sinister and demoniac elements. In Indian writing in English, there are virtually no war novels and the only acts of violence and death that recur are either around the freedom movement and partition of the country or around famine, flood and poverty. Hence, violence in Markandaya's novels is due to poverty, in Anand and Bhattacharya to economic disparities and exploitation, in Raja Rao, Manohar Malgonkar and Chaman Nahal to independence movement and the country's partition, in Nayantara Sahgal, to the bickerings of politicians and in Arun Joshi, to the conflict between tradition and modernity, primitivism and civilisation, or to incommunication and insubordination. Anita Desai says Darshan Singh Maini "is a disturbing and demanding presence in Indo-Anglian Fiction" [K.K. Sharma (ed.) *Indo-English Literature* 216].

The treatment of violence and death in Anita Desai's novels is quite different. Now it is psycho-emotional, now hysterical projections and symbols of her own contrite and sensitive psyche. Desai's protagonists are moved by the muffled whisper of individuals, leaking of taps, creaking of shoes, chattering of birds, ticking of clocks, rattle of vehicles and the thumping of pedestrians. They stand apart. They are highly poetic and nervy. "Anita Desai", says R.S. Sharma, "seems to be struggling towards the mastery of a violence which seems to threaten not only her protagonists but also her own introvert self. Right from *Cry, the Peacock*, this violence has persisted and permeated in her works as a kind of inevitability, forcing one to conclude that it has some kind of inevitability, ... metaphysical or psychological significance, not yet explored or analysed'' (Anita Desai 167). This violence is psychical end clinical. *Cry, the Peacock* begins with the death of Toto, the pet dog and ends with the death of Gautama. Maya, the protagonist, is deeply moved by the astrologer's prediction of the death of one of them. She associates herself with the peacocks and their knowledge of life and death. She is obsessed by death and her death-wish issues out of her frustrations and dejections in life. In *Voices in the City*, violence and death are largely due to the 'demoniac' and 'death city' of Calcutta. Violence has been poetically and symbolically represented through the images of birds and animals who act as preys and predators. In *Bye-Bye, Black Bird*, violence has been sarcastically portrayed through jeers, taunts, sarcasms and aspersions of the white towards the blackbirds. Sarah, for instance, is the victim of individual and social violence, the victim of derisions of her countrymen for having married an Indian. In *Where Shall We Go This Summer*?, Sita is so much horrified by the violence rampant in our society that she is reluctant to deliver her fifth child. She undergoes fits or depression in her lone struggle to assert her identity. She is a split self and it is her desire to 'stay whole' (107-108) that evokes in her the urge to escape to the island of Manori. She looks at the raucous and greedy crows attacking a young eagle and reflects : ``There was much black drama in this crow theatre ... murder, infanticide, incest, theft and robbery'' (*Where Shall We Go This Summer* ? 38).

Nanda Kaul in *Fire On The Mountain* withdraws into the secluded world of Carignano for peace and tranquility but is upset by the rape and murder of Ila Das — a scene too horrific and ghastly to bear. In keeping with her theme and technique, Anita Desai makes a liberal use of symbols, though instinctively and subconsciously. What matters to her is the movement of the object, not the object itself, the quintessence and not the essence. The reiterative use of symbols not only enriches her work of art, it elevates it to aesthetic and transcendental heights. Even the title of some of her novels, like *Cry, the Peacock*, are highly symbolic. Her symbols lend docility, flexibility, richness and pliability to her works. They add to their mythopoeic beauty.

Concerned mainly with the nocturnal and nebulous atmosphere of the psyche, Anita Desai is a psychological novelist whose characters are different from those of Raja Rao, Sahgal, Narayan, Bhattacharya, Markandaya and Malgonkar, who deal with the socio-economic or political or philosophical aspects of a character. What matters for Desai is the motivation, the conscience, the psychic tension of these characters. Unlike the other Indo-Anglian novelists, Anita Desai creates an opulent gallery of characters, though dominated by the female. Most of her protagonists are hypersensitive females. They are hypo-chondriacs. Each is presented, as an inscrutable individual, enigmatic and eccentric. Neither are they chosen from the common rung of the society nor are their problems related to food, clothing and shelter. They are rebels and their rebellion is not so much directed against society as against individuals. Their problems are neither physical nor social. They are psychical and emotional.

In dealing with psychic maladies, Anita Desai strikes a new note. Her characters suffer from various complexes and mental diseases, which impede the healthy growth of their personality. A particular trait in a character, a tragic flaw develops into a psychic malady making the character neurotic and hysterical which in turn breeds a morbid and contrite temperament. Maya suffers from father-fixation, Nirode from claustrophobia and Dev, from Caliban complex.

A unique feature of Desai's characterisation is her dexterous handling of objective correlatives. These objective correlatives project the alienation and identity of the characters. It is, in fact, their state of alienation that motivates them in their quest for identity. For the first time in Indo-Anglian literature, Anita Desai makes an associative use of landscapes and myths, symbols and images (esp. of birds and animals) for characterisation. This animal imagery shows that we still retain in our nature a portion of that primitive animal identity. In the words of Dr. B. Ramachandra Rao, "Anita Desai evokes the necessary mood and elicits the right emotion from the reader through a series of objective descriptions" (The Novels of

Anita Desai 10). Since she belongs to the upper middle class and has a limited or no access to the infernal and filthy lanes of power-hankering politicians and diehard criminals, her characters are polished and sophisticated and are verily an imitation of life. Yet her feminine and domestic sensibility seldom strays beyond the narrow confines of family life. Working on such a limited canvas, she has been able to create masterpieces in Indo-Anglian literature that have won her the coveted Sahitya Akademic Award.

Desai records the psychic oscillations and tensions of her near-neurotic characters and articulates them through hints and suggestions, symbols and images. Albeit, there have been many women writers before Desai, such as Kamala Markandaya, Nayantara Sahgal and Ruth Prawer Jhabvala, yet none has her exotic feminine sensibility of depicting love as an ennobling ideal in man-woman relationship.

As has been pointed out, Desai's fiction tends to conform to both American and English tradition. It takes its form and tone from polarities and irreconcilables. Oddities and eccentricities of character, disintegration of personality and morbidity or temperament, the prose of order and the poetry of disorder, alienation and depersonalisation of identity constitute the tradition she draws upon. One remembers Virginia Woolf for whom ... "Life is not a series of gig-lamps symmetrically arranged; life is a luminous halo, a semi-transparent envelope surrounding us from the beginning of consciousness to the end" (*The Common Reader* 177).

Desai prefers 'pattern' to plot, Hopkinsian 'inscape' to external incident, cubist composition to cumulative accumulation of facts. Unlike R.K. Narayan and Mulk Raj Anand, she employs 'the language of the interior' to portray the compulsions and tensions of her characters, most of whom suffer from 'emotional and intellectual consumption'.

The theme of immigration and consequent alienation of the self has been the thematic pre-occupation of Indo-Anglian novelists like Naipaul, Kamala Markandaya and Bharati Mukherjee, but they are chiefly concerned with cross-cultural and racist encounters between the characters on socio-cultural plane. Seldom do they deeply and punctiliously probe into the psyche of the characters like Anita

Desai. What differentiates Anita Desai from them is her capacity to transform such alienational experiences into the monument of living art. It is neither the concern of an absurdist nor the enigma faced by an existentialist but the simple, homely rendering of emotions of individuals who face abnormal situations in living and partly living every moment of life on an alien soil in a strangely fascinating way.

S. Sujatha maintains that Anita Desai's protagonist faces the predicament of the tragic isolation of the individual and consequent sense of the absurdity of human life ("The Theme of Disintegration", *The Commonwealth Review* 49) but to me the Desai protagonist is confronted with the very reality of existence. It is never absurd, for, Maya, Monisha, Sarah, Sita, Nanda and Tara, all battle with a reality hard to bear, a workaday reality. Their problem is our problem, their plight is everyone's plight. What is absurd is real and it is the reality of absurdity that the Desai protagonists are confronted with. Hugo Baumgartner's alliance with the cats might sound absurd but it is real. Hugo the kitten is isolated from the mother cat (*i.e.* his mother). Hence his transference of love to the cats in whom he possibly sees the 'maternal image'. Kai Nicholson rightly opines that the life and death of this German Jew, a refugee from Nazi terror, is close to reality ("Are We Expatriates", *The Commonwealth Review* 14).

Historical themes like partition dealing with alienation have found an important place in the novels of Mulk Raj Anand, Manohar Malgonkar, Khushwant Singh, Attia Hosain, Chaman Nahal and Nayantara Sahgal. In Desai too, there are allusions to historical incidents in *Clear Light of Day* but it is patchy and sketchy. Such references only serve as a foil to the alienation of the protagonist. Like R.K. Narayan, (with reference to Waiting for the Mahatma) he remains silent about the horrors of the partition. She builds her novels round the struggle within the self, the dismal and morbid moods of men and women. Like Arun Joshi, she explores the depths of human psyche against the muddling social backdrop.

To Desai, writing is a means of discovering one's identity, of unravelling the hidden truth of life. Narayan's use of irony, Raja Rao's acceptance of Indian metaphysics is irrelevant to Mrs. Desai's fictional needs. Even the doctrinaire humanism of Mulk Raj Anand and the sanguine exploits of Kushwant Singh and Malgonkar are alien to her art of fiction. On a small canvas, she weaves the web of the protagonist's anguished odyssey.

Anita Desai's works clearly indicate the direction Indian fiction was taking in the hands of the third generation of urban writers. It is the turning inward of Indian fiction from the romantic tryst in gardens or on river-banks to a more meaningful exploration of the world of reality. What matters to her is the character and not the tale, the situation and not the environment, the depth and not the dimension. Esoteric and secret passions and tensions occupy her interest.

Desai's novels are autobiographical, in the sense they mirror her 'quiet' temperament. Her novels exude the feeling of gentle isolation. In the words of Dr. Atma Ram, "Whereas a man is concerned with action, experience and achievement, a woman writer is more concerned with thought, emotion and sensation" ('Desai Interviewed', WLWE 102).

Prof. Jasbir Jain rightly points out :

> The world of Anita Desai's novels is an ambivalent one; it is a world where the central harmony is aspired to but not arrived at, and the desire to love and live clashes — at times violently — with the desire to withdraw and achieve harmony. Involvement and stillness are incompatible by their nature, yet they strive to exist together (*Stairs to The Attic* 16).

Desai's novels plumb man's perennial dilemmas : love versus hate; action versus inaction; possessiveness versus renunciation. They are mainly concerned about things that every individual longs for — the courage to live and the capacity to love as well as be loved. Most of the characters in her novels are characters without roots. It is their alienated state that propels them from crisis to crisis, sucking in its wake several other characters. They are presented mostly as seekers — questers through love — questers for identity. Emotionally and psychically perturbed, they are relentlessly and maniacally driven by undefined hunger and feverish lust which bring about their own fall. Incapable of silent submission and ungrudging suffering, they somehow pull the load of life. The Desai heroines are 'Pativratas', and yet are unhappy and gloomy, for they do not have the mental strength to be Nora (Heroine of Ibsen's play, *A Doll's House*). Desai's Monisha, Sita, Maya and Nanda Kaul — all aspire for a socio-psychic emancipation. They crave for the liberation of their feminine self from the shackles of a socio-psychically maladjusted environ. They desire to stay whole but when offered the choice, they retrace and retract.

Desai's concern for violence and conflict, for isolation and guilt link her with Camus, Hemingway and Sartre, rather than with her Indo-Anglian contemporaries. Despite these continental affiliations, she is unique in her own way in dealing with the past and its haunting obsession; death and its grim horror; love with its anguish and alienation, now savage, now still.

Anita Desai has made the landscape not just a backdrop but an environment reflecting the isolation and nostalgia of the alienated self. She uses memory, in a series of internal monologues to give us an access to the characters' minds. Through the psychology of association, the reader is made to participate triumphantly in the characters' movements back and forth in time. The world outside reason appears to be the major dimension of her work, where she probes the manifestations of the irrational in human relationships.

In *Cry, the Peacock*, Maya's abortive marriage to Gautama with its lack of emotional attachment stands in sharp contrast to her jolly and love-laden infancy. Maya's childhood remembrances overshadow her present with gloom and foreboding and bring about her alienation from her time-bound present. Time, that had preserved and ensconced her past, destroys her present. Desai admits that her novel is about 'time as a destroyer, as a preserver and about what the bondage of time does to people' ('Desai Interviewed', *India Today* 142). The mind's time occupies a more prominent place in Desai's novels than clock-time, and sometimes the passage of clock-time is transcended by the characters in moments of vision. Desai's intention is to portray the moment 'whole', so that the very texture of life is revealed. In her novels mind's time is not shown in conflict with linear time, but is depicted as one unified whole that is central to human experience. Like Virginia Woolf, Desai is obsessively involved with the characters' past as a key to their consciousness, their psycho-emotional life. Her pre-occupation with reminiscential thoughts takes the form of nostalgia. Like Virginia Woolf, she makes use of the stream of consciousness as an integral part of her fictional craft. But while Virginia Woolf uses parentheses to ensure the continuity of thought, Anita Desai uses dashes to the same effect :

> He notices a dead branch on one of the silver oaks and, with a small muscle at the corner of his mouth twitching — for he is particular about garden — he complains of the laziness of the gardener (*Cry, the Peacock* 39).

Reality, for Desai, is neither metaphysical nor socio-political. She has given an existential dimension to the three most vital human predicaments — anguish, alienation and despair. Plot development in her novels is not a spatio-temporal progression. It leads to the protagonist's self-discovery. A letter, a telephone call, and a forest fire, triggers off a chain of situations and incidents that intricate and complicate the plot. "My novels are no reflection of Indian society, politics or character. They are a part of my private effort to seize upon the raw material of life — its shapelessness, its meaninglessness" ("Desai's Comments", *Contemporary Novelists* 348).

D.F. Karaka is one of the first novelists to depict the plight of the alienated self in *There Lay the City* (1942). The narrator-protagonist here lives an insulated life with an expatriate sensibility. Karaka portrays the impact of the urban milieu on the psyche of the stranged self, a theme which Desai chooses for her novel, *Bye-Bye, Blackbird*. While alienation of the protagonist in Karaka is self-imposed, in Desai, the alienation of Sarah, Adit and Dev is due to their inability to adopt an alien culture. Karaka gives physico-spiritual dimension to the alienation of the protagonist, whereas Desai treats the problem psychologically. The alienation of Karaka's protagonist is physical, spiritual and social, whereas Desai's is temperamental.

In R.K. Narayan, the serio-comic and hapless plight of the 'lone self' assumes an ironic and sarcastic dimension. In *Swami and Friends*, alienation of Swaminathan's father from his son and his mother is the outcome of the generation gap between the son and the father. This alienation may be called socio-historical or socio-biological. Chandran, in *The Bachelor of Arts*, finds his friends 'scattered like spray', but unlike him, they were 'at grips with life, like a buffalo' caught in the coils of a python (154). Desai's protagonists, too, are at grips with life, but their encounter is psycho-emotional and psycho-physical, not socio-economic and socio-political. In Narayan, the characters remain alienated, without losing their intrinsic hold on the comic perception of life. Raja Rao's alienated individuals like Govindan Nair and Ramakrishna Pai in *The Cat and Shakespeare and Ramaswamy* and Madeleine in *The Serpent and the Rope* face the pull of the transition in society from the old to the new, they face the emerging realities of Indian life. They set out on a quest for self-awareness and self-fulfilment in a world replete with social anomalies and incertitudes. Rao's protagonists experience alienation mainly on the metaphysical and mythical plane, occasionally on the mystical. Sarah and Maya in *Bye-Bye, Blackbird and Cry, the Peacock*, share an alienation, purely emotional and psychic, while Rosie and Marco in Narayan's *The Guide* pass through an intellectual alienation. Narayan's protagonists face alienation with compromise and conciliation, Desai's with defiance and combat. Narayan's heroes remain humorously alienated from the milieu. This alienation is ironic and comic, while Desai's is hysteric and oneiric. Alienation in Narayan chiefly operates on the domestic and social plane. His protagonists, like Jagan, flee from the milieu. Their alienation is socio-religious and socio-cultural. In Naipaul, alienation leads to the forging of a new identity and a new life. It leads to the transformation of the native into an expatriate sensibility. Such transformation of identity hardly occurs in Anita Desai. Her characters alienate in order to involve themselves in a frantic quest for their identity. Alienation leads them into a blind alley, where they decay and decompose. In Desai, the alienated self is a 'mind forged manacle'. The earlier Indo-English novelists like R.K. Narayan, Mulk Raj Anand and Raja Rao were concerned with the dilemma emanating from alienation, whereas their successors, Arun Joshi and Kamala Markandaya dealt with the impulse behind alienation and its harrowing effect upon the individual. In Mulk Raj Anand, alienation is solely limited to the socio-political milieu. The 'lone self' in his novels is an underdog and a downtrodden.

Manohar Malgonkar, unlike Anita Desai, seems aware of the problems and predicaments of the alienated self in all their magnitude. The alienation of the Eurasian young woman in his novel, *Combat of Shadows*, represents the feeling of the rootless and the spineless, who oscillate and waver between their choices and wills, like O'Neill's *Yank*. In *Ruby Miranda*, the novelist portrays "the awareness of rootlessness, of not belonging, of not being wanted, even being despised..." (Malgonkar, Combat or Shadows 103).

Ruby is a lonely lady leading a de trop existence. The feel of alienation in Ruby and her English lover, Henry Winton, has been polarised. Winton does not feel it so deeply as Ruby, who deems it a problem of life and death, of bitter survival in the threatening milieu. Gian Talwar in *A Bend in The Ganges*, peevishly shies away from reality, but in Anita Desai, the protagonist encounters it single-handed. Malgonkar depicts his protagonist, a bewildered wanderer between two worlds ... the Indian and the English in the midst of cross-cultural contacts. In Desai, we have it in *Bye, Bye, Blackbird* and, to some extent in her latest novel, *Baumgartner's Bombay*. But she does not deal with the problem so overtly, so revealingly.

In Kamala Markandaya, the alienated individual is portrayed against Indian socio-ethnic scene with 'a particular contemporary relevance' (Kumar, "Tradition and Change" Books Abroad 508) which we do not find in Desai's 'lone outsider'. Helen of *The Coffer Dams* and Saroja of the *Two Virgins* feel cut off from their heritage, forgetting what they knew. It is a case of alienation from nature as well as from the self. However, alienation in Markandaya, is only superficial and skin-deep, since it neglects the psychic aspect. Kit, in *Some Inner Fury* clings to the British Raj and apes Western Culture only superficially. In *Possession*, it is the possessive and mundane love which alienates Val from the milieu and unites him with Lady Caroline. The alienation of Srinivas in *The Nowhere Man* is no doubt, instinctive but it lacks penetration and finesse. Srinivas is rooted in his cultural ethos. The psychic and the temperamental factor hardly counts. Uma Parameswaran believes that Markandaya's portrayal of the alienated self in her novels is without any authorial commentary. She has artistic instinct to know where the roots of the protagonists are, but she does not possess sufficient artistic care to do full justice to her subject ("India for the Western Reader", Texas Quarterly 123). In Raja Rao and Markandaya the alienated self's quest for identity takes a social-phisophical direction but in Anita Desai it is socio-psychic.

Balachandra Rajan, too, deals with the dilemma of the rootless individual. Though Rajan's approach is searching, he fails to capture the essence of Indianness. He misses the Indian topography and ethos on account of his mixed sensibility. Alienation of Krishnan in *The Dark Dancer* is social and of Nalini in *Too Long in the West*, cultural and environmental. Krishnan's callousness and apathy towards his family and his cynical view of the society drives him to a state of rootlessness. Alienation in Rajan does not end up in gloom and despair, while in Desai's major novels it does. It brings about self-recognition and self-restoration in the protagonist. In Rajan, the phenomenon of alienation is all-pervasive. It is diffused in the entire atmosphere, but in Desai, it is confined to the psyche only.

Nayantara Sahgal handles alienation more persistently and resolutely. The solitude of Sanad Shivpal in *A Time to be Happy* is the outcome of a clash of values. It is the outcome of his upbringing in an anglicized atmosphere. Moral disorder and cultural chaos breed alienation in Sanad which is not the case with Desai's protagonists. In Sahgal's *This Time of Morning*, Rashmi's estrangement from her husband is due to her unfulfilled 'freedom of sex'. Her desire to be ultra-modern alienates her from the emerging socio-cultural scenario. Her approach to life alienates her from the society. In Desai, the protagonist does not look at life from the surface. He is committed and involved. Communication gap between man and man and the disintegration of social values in a culture-ridden society bring about the alienation of her protagonists. Sahgal uses political background to focus marital alienation of three young couples — Inder and Saroj, Jit and Mara and Dubey and Leela, in her novel *Storm in Chandigarh*. Dubey's longing for companionship with his wife Leela reminds one of Gautama's alienation from Maya in Desai, *Cry, the Peacock*. But while in Desai, alienation is set against a socio-psychic background, in Sahgal we see it against a socio-political backdrop. In Desai, it is the disintegration of human values and the emotional and psychic void in characters that alienates them from the milieu.

Arun Joshi's treatment of alienation is unvarnished and ingenuous. It takes on an eternal dimension. Sindi Oberoi in *The Foreigner* is 'a perennial outsider' (Quest 101). Forever forlorn in the world, he shirks even ordinary responsibilities. His alienation is a projection of his self, it is within himself, it is spiritual : "My foreignness lay within me ..." (Joshi 1974 : 61). Sindi is alienated from everything save himself. His alienation is not geographical. It is spiritual. Joshi's Billy in *The Strange Case of Billy Biswas* escapes into the saal forests of Maikal Ḥills to be suckled in a creed outworn. There is a heathen and a pagan element in Billy's alienation from society. But the alienation of Naipaul's *Billy in A House* for Mr. Biswas is unreal and superficial. In Joshi, the lonely self encounters the void both within and without. In Desai, it sees the void within. Joshi's execution of the outsiders' point of view is verily engaging and impressive. In Desai, it is diffusive and distracting. In Joshi the protagonists are always alone. In Desai of the later novels like *Clear Light of Day, The Village by the Sea* and *In Custody*, they move from a state of alienation to that of 'mythic acceptance' [Sivaramakrishna, KJES 3 (1),1978] and stoic resignation. In her treatment of alienation, Anita Desai is different from Arun Joshi. In Desai, alienation is psycho-emotional and intellectual but in Joshi, it is spiritual. It is the alienation of the soul.

The protagonists of many Indo-Anglian novelists are 'alienated from nature and society' (Glicksberg 1963 : 128). Desai's protagonists are torn from their socio-psychic self, and psycho-emotional milieu. In Joshi and Raja Rao, alienation leads to cultural schizophrenia, in Desai, it results in a psycho-emotionally oriented identity crisis. Desai paves the way for a new kind of novel — the novel of psychic sensibility. Desai protagonist is a lone individual, and not a social man. In most other novelists the hero is country-bred, but in Desai, he is an urbanite. "No other writer, it is said, is so much concerned with the life of young men and women in Indian cities as Anita Desai is" (Kohli, Times Weekly 3). Alienation in Desai, at times, assumes schizophrenic dimensions, where the character loses all contact with reality. Maya, in *Cry, the Peacock* says, "I strolled with him slowly across the lawn, feeling that an unreal ghost stalked beside me — a body without a heart, a heart without a body — what was he" (196)? Anita Desai and Raja Rao deal with the philosophic detachment of the hero, what Raja Rao renders in prose, Desai does in poetry. Raja Rao is concerned with dry facts, Desai with the mellifluous outpourings of the lone individual. Rao renders his philosophical speculations through dull, monotonous prose whereas Desai ventilates her lyrical thoughts through soothing and poetic prose. Desai uses depth-psychology in her study of women. She expertly explores the psychic reverberations of her female characters : Maya's masochism, Monisha's neurosis, Sarah's expatriation and Sita's regression. In Desai, the conflict is not so much between society and the lone outsider, as between 'Yes' and 'No', between two polarised and ambivalent choices and wills of the human psyche in the crisis of a transitional society.

Like Karen Horney, Anita Desai believes that childhood experiences determine conditions for neurosis but they are not the sole cause of trouble in adult life. In her interview with Jasbir Jain, she agrees that experiences of childhood are no doubt vivid, yet adult life has its traumatic experiences. Desai does not fully expose the childhood of her protagonists, but whatever flashbacks she provides are enough. Her characters tend to lose their 'vital self' in the course of their growth from infancy to adulthood. Sita struggles to 'connect'. Nirode 'spurns' everything. Bim, Nanda and Raka wish to 'forget'. Each wants to guard his/her identity but fails. Most of them are estranged women in quest of a new self, a new identity.

In Carson McCullers, grotesquerie serves to symbolise the disordered and the fragmented society, in Anita Desai it projects the demented, derailed and disintegrated self in the face of antagonistic and apathetic socio-psychic forces. If McCullers anatomises the malady of the emotionally disturbed society, Desai probes the psyche of the emotionally disturbed self. Man's search for a God, his desire for a harmonious world is the basis of McCullers' work, while in Desai, it is man's search for his roots, his desire to belong. Grotesquerie in McCullers is organically integrated into the mosaic of her work, it serves as an objective correlative, which lays bare the wounded psyche of the alienated self. The search for identity in McCullers ends in integration whereas in Desai, it ends in frustration and misery heightening the individual's feel of alienation. The protagonist in McCullers fails to reciprocate or respond in love. He cannot communicate, since he is either physically or spiritually maimed. But in Desai, lack of response in love and failure in communication arise from some psychic malady or trauma.

McCullers' is grounded upon spiritual alienation, Desai's vision upon socio-psychic alienation.

Like Edward Albee's dramatic personages, Desai protagonists face the problem of incommunication. They want to articulate their human problems. Against the forces of isolation, they strive to assert themselves. Albee's heroes realise the presence of an in-built sense of alienation in the very fabric of the society, with everyone separated from everyone else. Desai protagonists too, arrive at such an awareness but only at the unconscious plane of their existence. Jerry in Albee's play *The Zoo Story* suffers the pangs of alienation and experiences the utter lack of communication. But there, the concern of the dramatist "is unavoidingly metaphysical while Anita Desai has noticeably confined herself to the mundane reality of life. Transcendental American concern is missing here" [Singh, in Prasad (ed.) *Response* 236].

In Conrad, the alienation of Lord Jim leads to his immoral 'jump' from the Patna. His alienation is spiritually stultifying and annihilating. It is deep-rooted and death-like. Such alienation is foreign to Anita Desai. It does not propel one into such nocturnal and ghastly corridors of life. Alienation in Desai is neither moral nor spiritual, it is intellectual and emotional. The death of Lord Jim reminds us of Monisha in Voices in the City, who asserts her identity by committing suicide. But in Monisha, the 'death-wish' springs from her psychic maladjustment and not from moral or spiritual vacillation as is the case with Lord Jim.

Unlike Conrad, Desai does not make the individual's alienated plight spiritually baffling and morally humiliating and ridiculous. Conrad projects the theme of estrangement and isolation of the self through marine and spiritual images, Desai through animal and stellar images, the images of prey and predator and at times through natural images like day and fire. The existential dilemma of the sequestered self is more profound and intense in Conrad than in Desai. In Conrad, it extends beyond psychology to philosophy and, in a sense, to the socio-political subjective milieu. In Desai, it touches the cloistered socio-psychic world. The despair of her protagonists is the despair of a Yank or an emperor Jones. It is the despair and derangement, of not belonging. Anita Desai's narrative like Shouri Daniels' fictional plot, moves from emotional outbursts to philosophical musings. In Daniels, the problem of alienation assumes a comic and extravagant dimension through the disjointed and loose extravaganza of its structure, but in Desai, it functions within the family save in *In Custody* and *Baumgartner's Bombay*. It lacks the element of humour and comedy. Shouri Daniels' novels are a conglomeration of the elements of fantansy, absurdity, irony, sarcasm, philosophy, comedy, lofty wisdom and nostalgic reminiscences. They are an extravaganza of creative ingenuity. The alienation between Mira and her husband Nanjundan is religious. It is an alienation of two cultures — East and West — which result in a clash, the clash between tradition and modernity, generating identity crisis. The novels of Desai, like those of Daniels, explore the bedimmed and beguiled psyche of the protagonist who has gone through intense and fiery moments of conflict. The protagonist is a 'lone explorer' of his identity.

Anita Desai's novels are a blending and binding of both exterior landscape and interior vision. In *Clear Light of Day* and *Baumgartner's Bombay*, there are allusions to communal disharmony and political turmoil and in *Bye-Bye, Blackbird*, there are notes of East-West encounter. But here these allusions are peripheral and incidental, in Raja Rao, Arun Joshi, Kamala Markandaya, and B. Rajan, they are central and functional.

In dealing with the problem of alienation, Anita Desai makes abrupt change in the narrative focus. The scene rolls on from character to character and we have "the rhetoric of characters in opposition which causes them to reveal each other's values as well as the values in the situations" (Springer 1978 : 32).

Anita Desai simply skims over the surface of a character's life without making deep psychological probing without graphically portraying the inner turmoil of the alienated self. Artistic devices of monologue and soliloquy have not been fully exploited to analyze the alienation of the self. Hence the reader fails to get a comprehensive picture of the psychic malady of the solitary self and simply left to wander from one speculation to another. Kalpana Wandrekar has very aptly pointed out this defect in relation to the character of Sarah in *Bye-Bye, Blackbird* :

> When Sarah refuses to play with her childhood toys, we are kept ignorant about the emotions felt

> by her at that time.... At the tea party we are told that she is relieved but we are not told what exactly she feels, the turmoil in her mind.... None of the vehicles of monologue and soliloquy is fully exploited to analyze Sarah's character.... The outer reactions we see, but what goes on within is often known only to the character and its creator ("The Ailing Aliens", *Image of India in the Indian Novel in English* 48).

In *In Custody* and *Baumgartner's Bombay*, Desai explores the psyche of a male protagonist outside the circumscriptions of familial ties and obligations. She makes a departure from her earlier obsessive pre-occupation with the interior landscape of hypersensitive and neurotic women. In *In Custody*, the artist protagonist, Deven, is endowed with a different kind of sensibility. He is not an alienated self, in the sense the female protagonists of Desai's earlier novels are. For Desai was "conscious of the need to write outside oneself, to be able to feel oneself into completely different personalities from one's own" (Sheth, "Desai Interviewed", Imprint 84). Suresh Saxena maintains that *Baumgartner's Bombay* is "a complete departure from her earlier writings" (*Commonwealth Literature* 237). But it is not. The alien plight of Hugo has an apparent similarity with that of the blackbirds in *Bye-Bye, Blackbird.* From the nostalgia of the blackbirds, Desai shifts her focus to the estrangement of the exiles. Each of her novels is a step forward in the growth of her fictional self, where the immured spirit passes through spontaneous self-realisation and self-discovery.

In the novels of Anita Desai, the theme of disharmony and discord is confined to the family and at times to the maladjusted or ill-adjusted self. Loneliness and unrequited love drives Desai heroines to the jaws of death, often manifesting in madness or suicide. Desai deals with the alienation of upper-middle class people of society. Her protagonists, like the characters in Charlotte Bronte's novels, suffer from lack of parental love, disturbed infancy, broken homes and Oedipus or Electra Complex. Disgruntled with their existence, they often opt out of the mainstream of life. Alienation in Desai characters often manifests in immoral ties and activities which we hardly find in any other Indian Women Novelist save Shobha De.

Alienated from their selves, Desai protagonists search for their identity in the milieu through self-discovery and self-identification.

REFERENCES

Allen, Walter, 1954. The English Novel, London : Penguin.

Daiches, David, 1965. The Novel and the Modern World, Chicago : Phoenix Books, University of Chicago Press.

Dalmia, Yasodhara, "An Interview with Anita Desai", The Times of India, April 29, 1979.

Desai, Anita, "Reply to the Questionnaire", Kakatiya Journal of English Studies, 3 (1978).

— "Comments", Contemporary Novelists, ed. James Vinson, New York : St. Martin's Press, 1972.

—, 1980. *Cry, the Peacock*, New Delhi : Orient Paperbacks.

—, 1982. *Voices in the City*, New Delhi : Orient Paperbacks.

—, 1982. *Where Shall We Go This Summer*, New Delhi : Orient Paperbacks.

—, 1985. *Bye-Bye, Blackbird*, New Delhi : Orient Paperbacks.

—, 1977. *Fire On the Mountain*, New Delhi : Allied Publishers.

—, 1980. *Clear Light of Day*, New Delhi : Allied Publishers.

—, 1983. *The Village by the Sea*, New Delhi : Allied Publishers.

—, 1984. *In Custody*, London : Heinemann.

—, 1988. *Baumgartner's Bombay*, Harmondsworth : Penguin.

(Textual Citations, if any, are from these editions of Anita Desai's Novels.)

Fiedler, Leslie, 1966. Love and Death in the American Novel, New York : Dell Publishing Co.

Glicksberg, Charles, 1963. Tragic Vision in Twentieth Century Literature, South Illinois University Press.

Iyengar, K.R. Srinivasa, 1962. *Indian Writing in English*, Bombay : Asia Publishing House.

—, 1973. — (Second Revised Edition) —.

Jain, Jasbir, "Interview with Anita Desai", Rajasthan University Studies in English, Vol. XII (1979).

—, 1987. *Stairs to the Attic : The Novels of Anita Desai*, Jaipur : Printwell.

Joshi, Arun. 1974. *The Foreigner, Bombay*, Asia Publishing House.

Kohli, Suresh. "Indian Women Novelists in English", Times Weekly (8 November 1970).

Kumar, Shiv. K. "Tradition and Change in the Novels of Kamala Markandaya", Books Abroad, 43/4 (Autumn 1969).

Lawrence, D.H. "Morality and Novel", in David Lodge, ed. *Twentieth Century Literary Criticism*, London : Longman, 1971.

Maini, D.S. "The Achievement of Anita Desai" in K.K. Sharma (ed.) *Indo-English Literature*, Ghaziabad : Vimal, 1977.

Malgonkar, Manohar, 1964. *Combat of Shadows*, London : Hamish Hamilton.

Mukherjee, Meenakshi. ''A Review of The Foreigner'', Quest, 60 (Jan.-March '69)

Nicholson, Kai. ''Are We Expatriates'', The Commonwealth Review, Vol. IV, 1992-93, No. 2.

Parameswaran, Uma. ''India for the Western Reader : A Study of Kamala Markandaya's Novels'', Texas Quarterly, Summer 1968.

Rao, B. Ramachandra, 1977. "The Novels of Anita Desai : A Study", Ludhiana : Kalyani.

Saxena, Suresh. ''Anita Desai's Search for Roots in Baumgartner's Bombay'', Recent Commonwealth Literature, ed. Dhawan *et al.*, New Delhi : Prestige, 1989.

Seth, Ketaki. ''It is fatal to write with an Audience in Mind : An Interview with Anita Desai'', Imprint (June, 1984).

Seth, Sunil. ''Interview with Anita Desai'', India Today, December 1-15, 1980.

Sharma, R.S., 1981. *Anita Desai*, New Delhi : Arnold-Heinemann.

Singh, Brijraj. ''The Fiction of Anita Desai'', The Humanities Review, III, 2 July-December, 1981.

Singh, C.P. ''The Visitor and the Exile : A Study in Anita Desai's Bye-Bye, Blackbird'', in Prasad (ed.) *Response : Recent Revelations of Indian Fiction in English*, Bareilly: Prakash, 1983.

Sivaramakrishna, M. ''From Alienation to Mythic Acceptance : The Ordeal of Consciousness in Anita Desai's Fiction'', Kakatiya Journal of English Studies, 3/1, (1978).

Springer, Mary Doyle, 1978. "A Rhetoric of Literary Character : Some Women of Henry James", Chicago : The Univ. of Chicago Press.

Sujatha, S. ''The Theme of Disintegration : A Comparative Study of Anita Desai's Cry, the Peacock and Bharati Mukherjee's Wife'', The Commonwealth Review, Vol. IV, 1992-93, No. 2.

Wandrekar, Kalpana. ''The Ailing Aliens : Anita Desai's Bye-Bye, Blackbird as a Symptomatic Study in Schizophrenia'', in Pandey and Rao (ed.), *Image of India in the Indian Novel in English 1960-1985*, Bombay : Orient Longman, 1993.

Woolf, Virginia, 1953. *The Common Reader* (First Series), London : Hogarth Press.

13

Images of Alienation – A Study of Anita Desai's Novels

DR. S.P. SWAIN*

In Anita Desai's novels, imagery lends a poetic, lyrical colouring to the problems of the estranged self and project reality through "artistic parallels more powerful and eloquent than common collocation of words" (Prasad 1984 : 54). Besides enriching the artistic and aesthetic value of the novels, images in Desai, enlarge the critical and interpretative horizon of her art. They suggest the protagonist's totality of experience and build up the overall tonality of the novels. Images in Desai are not confined to the world of art only. There are scientific images too. Both these images produce esthetic effects and impart a tangible shape to stirred up emotional states of the alienated self. To Anita Desai, "it is the image that matters, the symbol, the myth" (Srivastava 1984 : 04). There is in her a persistent search for the most appropriate symbols and images in the expression of the subterranean and the subconscious.

Image may be an epithet, a metaphor, a symbol or a simile in the form of a mental picture. It derives its origins from 'imago'. It is an 'artificial imitation' of the external form of any object, while 'symbol' deriving its origin from symbolism, is something which stands for, represents or denotes something else (not by exact resemblance, but by vague suggestion, or by some accidental or conventional relation).

Anita Desai's mastery over words is manifested in her felicitous

* Department of English, Rourkela Municipal College, Rourkela.

and deft use of images. Her imagery is always in character which suits the lone plight of her characters. In Desai's novels, the struggle of the alienated self takes place through a dialectic of images, through an intricate pattern of imagery. Her novels are based on the texture of a rich and splendid medley of images which is functional rather than decorative. The core images of alienation are found enmeshed with other images arising out of it. Each image holds within it the seeds of the self's own destruction and Desai's dialectical method is a constant building up and splitting down of the images that come out of the character's alienational experience. The images do not conflict with or contradict each other but are in perfect harmony and accord with the nature of the character's alienation. Sometimes these images become congested and dense. Desai does not make use of scientific and Biblical imagery in her novels. Most of the Desai novels deal with images suggesting the identification of human beings with the forces of isolation. Through imagery, Desai achieves the polarisation of the opposites. In her novels there are a number of symbols which have a contextual signification. In Anita Desai's novel characters are found to be 'thinking in images', *i.e.* images which strike the mind as the projection of other minds in immediate contact with social realities. Thus Maya's character is projected through Monisha, Monisha's through Sita's and so on.

Anita Desai uses symbolic and functional imagery as the sole ingredient of her art. Her images are literal, metaphorical and frequently symbolical. Imagery in Anita Desai may be considered to constitute the poles of an axis on which her fictional world revolves. The symbolic world of her fiction, the themes of despair, death, desolation and socio-psychic fragmentation have been picturesquely presented through telling and tantalising images. Imagery in her novels, besides articulating the estranged sensibility and the changing moods of her introverted characters, reflect their mental isolation. Botanical, zoological, meteorological and colour images add to the aesthetic beauty and textural density of her novels. Besides these primary images, she employs certain stray images which move along the periphery of her works but are nonetheless important to the theme of alienation. Of all the contemporary Indian English novelists, Anita Desai is avowedly the most powerful imagist novelist in whom images give a poetic and lyrical colouring to the problem of the alienated self.

Cry, the Peacock, Desai's maiden novel, teems with numerous striking images illuminating the dark and shadowy realms of Maya's consciousness and her deteriorating psychic states. The botanical image of the "sapless and sere neem tree" which figures in Part-II, Ch. 2, of the novel and the image of "the silk-cotton trees" whose "huge, scarlet blooms" were "squashed into soft yellowish miasma" (34), symbolically project the inner void and isolation of a childless housewife. The images of petunias and lemon blossoms suggest the temperamental isolation between Gautama and Maya, unlike Gautama, is able to distinguish the smell of the petunias from that of lemon blossoms. To Maya, Gautama's hand appears as cool and dry as the bark of an old and shady tree. "The blossoms of the lemon tree were different, quite different : of much stronger, crisper character, they seemed cut out of hard moon shells, but a sharp knife of mother-of-pearls, into curving scimitar petals that guarded the heart of fragrance...." (19).

But who guarded the heart of Maya? For her, Gautama is a repelling, not a refreshing presence. The limes reveal the flagging love-life of Maya and Gautama, an ill-assorted couple languishing in silence and incommunication.

In *Fire on the Mountain*, Nanda Kaul wants to withdraw from the milieu and merge with the pine trees. Free from all "unwelcome intrusion and distraction" (3), she longs for the privacy, seclusion, tranquility and solidity of trees : "She stepped, backwards into the garden and the wind suddenly billowed up and threw the pine branches about as though to curtain her" (3). The news of Raka's visit to Carignano shatters Nanda's hope for privacy and isolation. Raka's arrival would pose a threat to her "privacy achieved only at the very end of her life" (36). The image of the "yellow rose-creeper" that "had blossomed so youthfully last month but was now reduced to an exhausted mass of grey creaks and groans again" (17), symbolises the wilting and withering of her hope for a cloistered life.

In *Baumgartner's Bombay*, Hugo's isolation during his infancy is portrayed through the image of the 'fir-tree' : "... he did not belong to the picture-book world of the fir-tree...." (36).

Botanical and zoological images occur in clusters to denote the isolation of Nanda. Residing in the mute, and desolate milieu of Carignano, she seeks an identity, different from all bewildering passions, the identity of "a charred tree trunk in the forest, a broken pillar of marble in the desert, a lizard on a stone wall. A tree trunk could not harbour irritation nor a pillar annoyance. She would imitate death, like a lizard. No one would dare rouse her. Who would dare?" (Fire on the Mountain, 1977 : 23).

No one dare rouse her, since she would attract no one's concern for her tense and trying moments. She should prefer total isolation : "She asked to be left to the pines and cicadas alone ..." (3).

Alienated from her great-grand-mother, Raka begins to listen "to the wind in the pines and the cicadas all shrilling incessantly in the sun with her unfortunately large and protruding ears, and thought she had never before heard the voice of silence" (40). The sighing of the pines and the cicadas inspires in her the urge for isolation silence and serenity.

Raka's isolation is instinctive and unimposed. It is spontaneous and natural. It is the isolation of a roe, playful and fanciful. She could often be found : "... scrambling up a stony hillside ... or wandering down a lane in a slow straying manner, stopping to strip a thorny bush of its few berries or to examine an insect under a leaf..." (46). Wishing to be left to the pines and cicadas, Nanda withdraws herself totally from the world of "bags and letters, messages and demands, requests, promises and queries" (3). Raka and Nanda, components of "the bareness and stillness of the Carignano garden", of "the starkness of rocks, pines and mountains" (4), want no one and nothing else. Seeking an absolute isolation here, she fancies she could merge with the pine trees and be mistaken for one. "To be a tree, no more and no less" (4) is all she desires. She wants to be alone and to have Carignano to herself in this period of her life, "when stillness and calm were all that she wished to entertain" (17). The imagery used highlights Nanda Kaul's longing for a secluded and still life. Nanda despises almost everyone who comes her way : her haughty, complacent daughter, Asha, her pale and fragile granddaughter Tata, her elusive, volatile and cadaverous great-granddaughter Raka and her old, decrepit and emaciated companion Ila Das.

In *Voices in the City*, Anita Desai uses the image of the 'weed' to portray the dehumanisation of Nirode. He is "a dripping gargoyle, grotesque, offensive, comic" (54). Nirode is wearied by his own incertitude in which "he swept back and forth like a long weed undulating under water, a weed that could live only in aqueous gloom, would never rise and sprout into clear day light..." (63-64).

Look at Amla's reaction to Monisha's withdrawal and confinement : "This sister had wandered away into some unholy garden of her own, stood there now like one of those lifeless statues on the brink of the stone fountain, and seemed not to realise that the fountain was dry and what confronted her was no ripple and tickle of cool water but only dry, hard flag stones" (149).

There is also Aunt Lila's garden which with its oppressive spirit of melancholy preys upon Amla and her thoughts. Aunt Lila has allowed it to "run wild" with its "dark unbreathing atmosphere", its "unmown grass" and "its infertile trees, contrasting sharply with the garden in Kalimpong" (148). The garden is a veritable picture of abandonment and neglect with none to domesticate it with mown grass.

Dharma also has a garden. He finds himself "inexorably drawn away from his island, back to the mainland again" (223-24). One is reminded of the garden of Carignano in *Fire on the Mountain* which, too, presents a dreary, desolate, forlorn picture suggesting Nanda Kaul's isolation.

Of the different kinds of images, zoological imagery insistently impinges on the reader's consciousness in *Cry, the Peacock, Where Shall We Go this Summer?*, and *Fire On the Mountain*. The image of dead Toto, besides introducing the death motif in *Cry, the Peacock*, serves as the symbol of an abandoned self doomed to loneliness :

> All day the body lay rotting in the sun. It could not be moved onto the verandah for, in that April heat, the reek of dead flesh was overpowering and would soon have penetrated the rooms.... Crows sat in a circle around the corpse, and crows will

> eat anything, entrails, eyes, anything. Flies began to hum amidst the limes, driving away the gentle bees and the unthinking butterflies (5).

Gautama, the fly, is driving away gentle bees like Maya and the dead Toto, to utter desolation and isolation. The image of dead Toto is projected in different forms to describe Maya's psychic derangement and her ineluctable obsession with death. Several disturbing and horrifying images of slimy, creeping, crawling creatures such as rats, snakes, lizards and iguanas figure in close succession in a crescendo till Maya pushes Gautama over the parapet.

The image of rats suckling their young symbolises Maya's harrowing obsession with her childlessness : "Rats will suckle their young most tenderly. I know this, as now I lived quite near one, with seven young ones nestling between her legs..." (145-46).

The image of the domestic cat is metamorphosed into the horrifying iguanas. On seeing it, she wails out :

> 'Iguanas' My blood ran cold, and I heard the slither of its dragging tail even now, in white day light. Get off — I tell you, get off Go (147).

Maya stands for the domestic cat who under pressure goes wild and neurotic like the iguanas. The iguanas suggest her neurosis and melancholy. The animal images in Maya's mind indicate her submerged instinctive drives.

Maya is exasperated to hear the cooing of the doves. She must drives them away? yet dares not disturb their amour. The doves in a mood for mating, cooed to one another. But, could Maya coo to Gautama? Oh, no their mating was to Maya, an omen of ill-fortune, of alienation, for their coo was a tedious repetition of the fatal words, 'Go Away' (35). The alienation of the copulating doves is an ephemeral one, whereas hers is far more enduring. Theirs is natural and instinctive, hers, though natural, is self-imposed and compulsive. With the mounting tensions in her aberrant mind, Maya thinks of rats and lizards, projections of her abandoned self and her fast disintegrating sensibility.

The image of the caged monkeys on the railway platform stirs and excites her agony. She too is caged within her nostalgic remembrances. It signifies her loss of privacy, her isolated life, a life of domestic imprisonment. It is her self-image. The monkeys boisterously struggling inside the cage for liberation and release remind Maya of her own alienation and estrangement. She is sensitively prone to self-reflection which dismantles her emotional stability and self-identity. Her thought-current transforms itself into a swift flux of fragmentary images frothing to the surface under the impact of certain external stimulus.

The image of the peacock and its anguished shriek for mating call "Piya, Piya" reaches out to Maya. She responds woefully to it, but not Gautama :

> 'Can you hear them, Gautama?
> Do you....?'
> 'Hear what?' (175)

Gautama remains listless to the cry. He is isolated from the milieu. He has no sexual urge. Maya the 'pea-hen' fails to get a response from Gautama, the 'peacock'.

In *Voices in the City*, the prey-predator image forms an integral part of the zoological imagery. Amla's longing to flee is expressed through the image of the horses bursting forth to release themselves from the massed impatience and the lust of the mob. The horses symbolise the possibility of isolation and escape from the pressures of conformity. The prey-and-predator image occurs in the race-course scene in which a horse, while running fast, falls on the ground hurt, and then a flock of hungry birds swoops down. We remember the abandoned corpse of Toto, encircled by crows and rotting in the sun. The characters in the city live corpse-like, isolated from the general current of life, going their own way. Calcutta itself is imaged as an ugly, ghastly monster in whose lethal grip the three desperate preys — Nirode, Monisha and Amla — gape and gasp for breath. Monisha calls Calcutta "this devil city" (117), "unrelenting city" (236). Images of putrefaction, like filth, squalidness and adversity create in Monisha a distaste and dislike for the city. Amla keenly feels the demonic, ogre-like presence of the city, its throbbing pulse attracts as well as repels :

> ... this monster city that lived no normal, healthy and red-blooded life but one that was subterranean, underlit, stealthy and odorous of mortality, had

> captured and enchanted — or disenchanted — both her sister and brother... (150).

The city with its callousness presents a subtly tilting picture of aloofness to Amla :

> At every turn, on every road, the city thrusts its ugly apathy at her like a beggar thrusting his mutilated hand through the window and laughing because he knows she must pay him her conscience money... (193).

Amla calls Calcutta a 'harsh' and 'insidious' city. It is a city with a brooding, dull, weary and vacant face. "... this city, this city of yours, it conspires against all who wish to enjoy it, doesn't it?" (153) Vacant and brooding and at the same time rapacious, the city has a Janus-like existence. This ogre and monster city gobbles Monisha, while it leaves the remaining two — Nirode and Amla — awfully battered and shattered. Calcutta is an 'overpopulated burrow'. Its sewers and gutters are choked with 'grime, darkness, poverty and disease'.

Washed in the monsoon, Calcutta presents a moving picture of desolation end dissolution, decay and disintegration :

> ... watching the sodden walls of unlit houses peel away in the wet, film posters dissolve and fade, seeing motor-cars and trams stranded hub-high in water, noticing how the crowds had melted away, vanished and only a solitary rickshaw — heroically mobile amidst all the waterlogged vehicles — churned and splashed nobly through... (54).

The solitary rickshaw, 'heroically mobile amidst all the waterlogged vehicle is an apt image symbolising the 'singlehanded struggle' of Nirode in the suffocating and stifling environ of the city.

In *Where Shall We Go This Summer*?, the tumult and chaos in Sita's mind has also been symbolically projected through the image of the monsoon winds :

> I wanted the book to follow the pattern of the monsoon to gather darkly and threateningly, to pour down wildly and passionately, then withdraw

> quietly and calmly (Ram, "Desai Interviewed", WLWE 97-98).

Again in *Fire On the Mountain*, we have an image of the whirlpool pointing to Nanda Kaul's incarceration and staticity : "... life would swirl on again, in an eddy, a whirlpool of which she was the still, fixed eye in the centre" (24).

The imagery of urban squalor, soulless pursuit of the characters for material prosperity and mundane pleasures create a cumulative impression of alienation. Spiritually alienated, they are doomed to rave and roam for ever in the desert of desolation, disturbed infrequently by vague forebodings and apprehensions.

In *Bye-Bye, Blackbird*, the image of the city occurs in a different perspective. It points to the void of existence, which is mutely repulsive and incomprehensively cold. The silence and emptiness of the houses and streets of London make Dev uneasy. The hollowness of the city bewilders him : "... the houses and blocks of flats, streets and squares and crescents — the English habit of keeping all doors and windows tightly shut — of guarding their privacy — It remains incomprehensible to him. It never fails to make Dev uneasy to walk down a street he knows to be heavily populated and yet finds it utterly silent, deserted — a cold wasteland of brick and tile" (70). Acutely tormented by the agony of silence and solitude in the city, he develops a disgust for London. He becomes a rebel like Nirode, the artist-rebel in *Voices in the City*. The Waterloo station serves as an image to reveal the emotional estrangement of the black-birds. The lone and solitary image of the station — all smoggy and hazy — objectively projects the isolation of the blackbirds in England. In that hazy atmosphere, none could see the other. Each remain alienated from the other behind the thick screen of smog. None could even hear the other. Alienation — physical and emotional — persists throughout. The melancholic haze of departure and the anguish of separation seem to have seized every word and feeling of the couple :

> As in an old film, the dialogue was blurred, almost inaudible, merely an accompaniment to the scene — words snatched away and sank into the haze of departure, the fog of preconceived absence. (257)

Monisha sees Nirode as a "broken bird" in the aviary, alienated in his own way and subdued and silenced by the fever and fret of life : "Lying on a mat in his tin-shed room, so solitary on a roof-top splattered with pigeon-droppings and a million cigarette stubs that speak of nights of insomnia and despair ... (125-126).

In *Where Shall We Go This Summer*?, Anita Desai emblematically delineates the conflict in Sita's life through the image of a crowd of crows attacking an eagle, "wounded or else too young to fly" (38). This trivial incident serves as an apt objective correlative to Sita's alienation from her husband.

The image of the jelly fish has been used to highlight Sitat's entanglement and her consequent alienation :

> Perhaps I am only like the jelly fish washed up by the waves, stranded there on the sand bar. I was just stranded here by the sea, that is all. I had not much to do with it at all, she sadly admitted... (149).

Sita's identification with the jelly fish only suggests her castaway and shipwrecked self, an image which is repeated in *Baumgartner's Bombay, in the depiction of* the alien plight of Hugo Baumgartner.

In *Fire On the Mountain*, Raka is "a mosquito flown up from the plains to tease and worry" (40) . Raka (literally means the moon) is ironically likened to one of "those dark crickets that leap in fright but do not sing" (39). She is "lizard-like" (42), "a pet insect" (54), "higher than the eagles" (61), or "a mosquito, minute and fine" (39). Raka moves about in Kasauli like a 'soundless moth', solitary and isolated.

Nanda Kaul views Raka as "an uninvited mouse or cricket" (85), stealthily entering the barren and rugged world of Carignano. Pining for a secluded life, she would lie down motionless like "a lizard on a stone wall" (23).

Through zoological images, Anita Desai juxtaposes the animal world with the human to suggest the cannibalistic and predatory nature of man. Preet Singh's sexual assault on Ila Das, for instance. Ila's cold-blooded rape and murder is gruesome and horrifying. Carnal images indicate our low instincts and desires, our base and ignoble motives. Reference to animals serves as an interface imagery.

In *Cry, the Peacock*, the isolation between Maya and Gautama is brought out by the image of the horse, a symbol of animal blindness and apathy to the splendour of nature. The denizens of Calcutta in *Voices in the City*, are compared to "gutter rats" and "apparitions seen in delirium" (97).

In *Clear Light of Day*, the despair and isolation of Bim is projected through the image of the mosquito :

> They had come like mosquitoes — Tara and Bakul, and behind them the Misras, and somewhere in the distance Raja and Benazir — only to torment her and mosquito-like sip her blood. All of them fed on her blood — Now when they were full, they rose in swarms, humming away, turning their backs upon her (153).

The zoological image of a snail, slowly, resignedly making its way from under the flower up a clod of earth only to tumble off the top onto its side — "an eternal, miniature Sisyphus" (2), symbolically illuminates the character of Bim in *Clear Light of Day*, who withdraws herself from the El Dorado of life to shoulder all alone the responsibility of looking after her mentally retarded, dumb brother, Baba, and her widowed Aunt Mira. She is a "lone crusader" in the arena of life's "conflicts and confrontations".

In *Baumgartner's Bombay*, we see the loneliness and destitution of Hugo shivering on a hot summer night "as abjectly as a dog who senses he is about to be turned out into the street ..." (133). Baumgartner's rootlessness, his sense of not belonging, his terrifying loneliness have been articulated through the image of the dog. Feline and canine images, a part of the zoological imagery, play a crucial role in crystallising the predicament of the self living in closed and sequestered worlds. Desai stresses Hugo's homelessness through the image of cats. As time rolls, the cats flock round him, the cats that haunt the alleys of Colaba, homeless and nomadic like himself : "Baumgartner could contemplate homelessness for himself but not for his cats.... His room filled and overflowed with them, with their scrawny progeny..." (204).

Throughout, Hugo remains an outsider, a flotsam panting for self-identification and self-projection :

> An isolated youth in an increasingly unsafe and threatening land and then, a solitary foreigner in India — like a mournful turtle — Baumgartner carried everything with him; perhaps it was the only way he knew to remain himself (109).

'Captivity' and 'internment', an extension of the image of entrapment and encagement "had provided Baumgartner with an escape from the fate of those in Germany, and safety from the anarchy of the world outside" (131). Hugo's isolation is a kind of protection. But to Elaine Y.L. Ho, it is desperation and destruction :

> His squalid room is cut off from, but also hemmed in by, the poverty and degradation of the streets. It is a marginal refuge from the real world and from a past that lingers and that he cannot retrieve meaningfully ; nor will the past allow him to survive in his marginality (WLWE 104).

Nur in *In Custody* is a veritable prisoner of his own self. He "had not escaped from his cage for all that — he was trapped as Deven was, even if his cage was more prominent.... Still it was a cage in a row of cages. Cage, cage, Trap, trap" (131). This image of the trapped animal and menagerie brings to our mind the lone selves of Maya, Nirode and Dev. The stress on the words, 'Cage' and 'Trap' bears out the quagmired self of Deven both in his public and private life. Without any control over these forces, Deven remains alienated and ruffled. "An agonised dog" (126), he is left out in the cold, reeling under the throes of the agony of life.

The vehicles of steel, though devised to save time, are in reality "self-destructive". The self is imprisoned in its desire to save time : "A vehicle of steel is only a steel trap. Man is not set free by the aeroplane, he is trapped in it" (153). Getting trapped is also getting isolated from the self as well as the society.

Auditory image in Desai is a part of the synaesthetic imagery. The sounds produce anticipatory sensations. In *Fire On the Mountain*, Raka hears the call of the cuckoos, but instead of dutiful domestic birds, they emerge as symbols of demented birds that rave and beckon Raka on to faery lands forlorn where there is "no sound, only silence, no light, only shade" (90). The sound that carries with it the sensation of solitude is symbolically an echo of Raka's own voice crying for isolation.

The house is a recurring image that resonates in the novels of Anita Desai. In Attia Hossain's *Sunlight On a Broken Column*, the house stands for country, home and families divided against each other and in Arun Joshi's *The Last Labyrinth*, it is the symbol of dirt and squalor. It is a whore : "... money was dirt, a whore. So were houses..." (11). But in Desai, the house stands for the individual self divided from within. It is the symbol of despair and desolation. House imagery in Desai evokes a sense of desertion and incarceration. It throws light on the musings of the lacerated self's immured existence. In her novels, the house occurs as an inorganic imagery serving as the focus of her thematic vision. It is metaphorically pictured through the symbols of walls, boundaries and barriers.

In *Voices in the City*, there are allusions to large Victorian houses "screened by royal palms" (125) and "old Georgian houses lined still" (142) which indicate gloomy and dejected minds, languishing in self-isolation and solitary confinement. "The houses here have aged with grace, and faintly lit by low gas lamps glowing a pale blue in the foliage ... grown very old and deserted long ago to the vicissitudes of soot-black rain and plaster peeling sun" (125). Nirode fears his isolation from his own past, his childhood home. The image of the house is projected through the symbol of a "shell". Nirode is encaged in his "small shrunken shell" (110). But he steps out of it for self-expression. In Desai, there is a curious merging where the body becomes the house often referred to as a 'shell' or a 'cage'.

The house to Monisha is a prison. In the first few pages of the novel, the concept of her husband's house as a prison, cage comes across very strongly. She does not belong to it, does not relate to it. Her husband, on the other continues securely in his own cage. To him, the house is a symbol of safety and shelter. The house to Monisha is also an object of intimidation. The four tiered balances with metal railings were so intricately criss-crossed that one could not so much thrust one's head through them. "Enclosing shadows like stagnant well water" (109), it was enough to depress her. She longs to thrust her head out of the window but the bars are too closely set. After all what was there to see. Other houses, other walls and other bars. In the privacy of her room, she is oppressed by a terrifying sound that repeats like the motif of a nightmare, from which there seemed no escape. The atmosphere in and around the house seemed to stifle her self-expression. She is encaged in the house. Like Nirode, she cannot step out of it. It is impossible to avoid in any corner of this house, "the damp pressure of critical attention" (159).

Nirode, "stared across the road at the white, cell-like suburban houses with their barred windows" (72). To him these houses where "there are no ethics" (117) serve as the symbol of a lacerating and disintegrating sense of anguish and agony. He says to David, "And have you taken a room at that robbing house again" (67). To him they are "slaughter houses" (42) that ruin our sensibility but to Dharma his house was "as quiet as his face" (46). Desai uses the image of the house to portray men and women leading scattered and disunited lives in this city of commerce : "Lives spent in waiting ... always behind bars, those terrifying black bars that shut us in, in the old houses, in the old city" (120).

In *Where Shall We Go This Summer*? Desai makes an artistic and symbolic use of the house imagery. The house here is linked with the pale and melancholic psychic life of Sita. In Bombay, she lived in a flat on a height, but now isolating herself from the hubbub and commotion around, she retreats to the house built by her father in Manori Island. She has the desire to set the house right but she discovers, to her amazement, the house abandoned in a sorry and awful state :

> .... a waste of ashes she saw, the cold remains of the bonfire her father had lit here to a blaze. Ashes, white and waste. Dust lay as casually as sound on a beach, spider webs spanned the corners of the unfurnished room like skeletal palm leaves. The odour was bats and mildew, and silence boomed like the silence of undersea caves. It had no air of providing shelter from the sea or the beach ... it was as much a natural part of them as an abandoned shell or lump of twisted driftwood (28).

The house, besides exposing the battered and fractured self of Sita, projects her wish to withdraw into an isolated and illusory world of impregnable silence and muted movements. But later, realising the futility of her living in an imaginative world of illusions, she compromises with the harsh realities of existence and returns to Bombay.

The use in *Fire On The Mountain* is a static and iterative image appearing in clusters with the image of the garden and other botanical and inorganic images as portrayed in the picture of the Carignano : the house that consoles Nanda and satisfies her :

> She turned around and gazed at her house instead, simple and white and shining on the bleached ridge. On the north side, the wall was washed by the blue shadows of the low, dense apricot trees. On the east wall the sun glared, scoured and sharp. It seemed so exactly right as a house for her, it satisfied her heart completely (5).

Nanda Kaul's house becomes her refuge. Desai sharply contrasts this with "that house — his house, never hers", (18) the perfect house she dutifully ran for her husband and family but to which she never really belonged.

Carignano, the desolate and haunted house in Kasauli inscapes the life of Nanda. But unlike Sita, she does not live in Carignano by choice. She lives there under compulsion deserted by her sons and daughters after the death of her husband. Yet she is content with its stark, secluded end sunny splendour. Symbolically, the seclusion and serenity of Carignano defines the stillness and freedom, Nanda has been able to achieve in her old age. Carignano is Nanda and Nanda Carignano. The humming and hectic part of Carignano is made out of Nanda's own past — the past that goes back to her days as a house-wife. It is juxtaposed with her awfully busy life in the past — ordering "too many servants" (29) entertaining "too many guests" (29) and tending "so many children" (29) and grand children. But Carignano, like Nanda, is burried in the silent spaces of inner vastness.

The image of the burnt house "at the top of the hill" (90) used in Chapter 18, Part-II, of the novel, mirrors the wild and unbridled nature of Raka with her irrepressible desire to set the forest on fire and her irresistible attraction towards "the ravaged, destroyed and barren spaces in Kasauli" (91) :

> At the top of the hill was the burnt house she had come to visit. It was only the charred shell of a small stone cottage. The verandah roof was already torn off and flung onto the hillside, the paving stones on the floor were cracked and gaping. The doors swung rotten, the window-frames hung askew, shattered glass lay amongst the cinders. The stairs were a tumable of rocks and weeds... (90).

The house imagery used in this novel is chiefly functional in nature. The house in this novel has its own history, that relentlessly links Nanda to other tormented and exiled women. Even this tranquil mountain resort, Carignano, that résonates in Nanda's experience, explodes and culminates in the rape and murder of her childhood friend, and alter ego, Ila Das.

In *Clear Light of Day*, the house throws light on the variegated moods of Tara and the behavioural eccentricities of Bim. The image of empty rooms suggest abandoned husbands. The old unchanged decrepit house in Old Delhi to which Tara returns evokes the feeling of stagnation and the resultant sense of boredom and nausea. Raja and Bim feel alienated in their own shabby house. In contrast to the house of Hyder Ali where there is company, colour and charm, his (Raja's) own house is "dismal, dusty, grimy and uncharming" (49).

In Part-II of the novel, we have the subtle image of a house abandoned by Hyder Ali. Bim too, is abandoned by Raja and Aunt Mira. Look at the neighbours derelict houses in Chapter 1 : "On the either side of their garden were more gardens, neighbours' houses, as still and faded and shabby as theirs, the gardens as overgrown and neglected and teeming with wild uncontrolled life..." (23-24).

Throughout, the house image figures as an ominous and threatening presence characterised by a detonating and a palpitating silence. This static image of the house symbolically projects Bim's stifled anger and acerbity, her longing for silence and staticity. The house lingers long in the reader's mind. It becomes a symbol of the past to which both Tara and Bim try to feel indifferent since they abhor returning to their childhood, "all that dullness, boredom, waiting" (122) where life seemed to have bypassed them. Bim's "dark and smouldering" (140) house horrifies her. Looking at the past she gets terrified and grows despondent to such an extent that she "seemed to stampede through the house like a dishevelled storm ..." (148). Tara eventually becomes reconciled to her life in the house which at the outset only seemed to appease her expectations from life. She frees herself "of this shabby old house that looked like a tomb in the moonlight" (159).

In *Village By The Sea*, Hari's house in the village, Thul, serves as a symbol of neglect and abandonment :

> The hut should have been rethatched years ago ... the old palm leaves were dry and tattered and slipping off the beams. The earthen walls were crumbling. The windows gaped, without any shutters. There was no smoke to be seen curling up from under a cooking-pot on a fire as in other huts... (9).

The house image brings out the forlorn self of Hari as well as the rural folk of Thul who crushed under poverty and despair, live split lives on the verge of decay and death.

The derelict house in *In Custody*, reflects on Deven's failure to form congenial and harmonious conjugal ties. It also reveals the couple's marital isolation and conjugal chaos leading to insanity.

Siddiqui's dilapidated, derelict and blackened house, which has neither lights nor curtains to colour the gloom, symbolises his incarcerated and immured self-seeking an escape into the open and lucid atmosphere of Delhi. The kitchen in the house which is "unspeakably filthy" (134) serves as an image of waste and putrefaction projecting the isolation and neglect into which the house has fallen. Deven is vaguely pleased, rather nauseated to look at this house "blackened by neglect" (134) which symbolises the "state in which everyone else lived in Mirpore" (134).

In *Baumgartner's Bombay*, the house serves as a contrast

between the protagonist's past and the present. Hugo Baumgartner's "old, crowded, slum-like house off Free School Street, in the lane too narrow for traffic but wide enough for people, pigs, stray dogs, even a few intrepid rickshaws" (171) serves as a contrast to the European quarter he had known before the war — its great houses with deep verandahs and green shutters, high walls and tall palms ... (171). But the house hardly provides any refuge to the disconsolate and expatriate self of Hugo from the conundrum of city-life :

> Not that the house provided any kind of shelter from the city. Down at the bottom of the lane there was a gap in the wall where the gate had once been and one entered through that into the walled compound that was really only partially walled since the wall had crumbled and in many places disappeared, allowing beggars, cattle, stray dogs and vendors of the whole locality to wander in and set up wherever they found space (174).

Even then Hugo "entered the house, mounted the stairs, careful not to step on the beggars and lepers and prostitutes who inhabited every landing, and at last achieved the small cell that was his room. He had no sense of being walled away from the outer world as he had had in the camp" (175).

The house is concerned with the quest for self-identification. Be it Nanda, Sita or Deven, the house serves as a symbol of consummation. Having relinguished her present self, Nanda Kaul totally merges with the house. The organic alien identifies with the inorganic alien — the derelict house. This identification of Nanda with the house is an assertion of self. For most of the protagonists in Desai the house is the symbol of their decaying and moribund self. Disgruntled with their self-existence, the characters have a frantic desire to assert their identity with the forlorn and forsaken house. Besides portraying the sickening self of the alienated protagonists, the house image brings to the surface their straying into the world of death and desolation, of illusions and longings, in quest of meaning and value. It lays bare the inner rumblings of their psychic life. The house brings about a spatio-temporal continuity to the alienated self in its quest for identity in a world as menacing and lonely as the house in which the lone self strives and thrives. The house in Desai novels is not only a symbol of shelter and protection but also of incarceration and laceration. It is the house that fails to house the abandoned self.

In Clear Light of Day, Bim's emotional estrangement is projected through the image of a flock of mynahs and the dog who serve as a foil to her isolation :

> Bim said nothing. In the small silence, a flock of mynahs suddenly burst out of the green domes of the trees and, in a loud commotion of yellow beaks and brown wings disappeared into the sun. While their shrieks and cackles still rang in the air, they heard another sound, one that made Bim stop and stare and the dog lift his head, prick up his ears and then charge madly across to the eucalyptus trees that grew in a cluster by the wall ... bellowed in that magnificent voice (6).

In *Baumgartner's Bombay*, Anita Desai has portrayed the alienation of Hugo through the image of the curtain :

> He felt his life blur, turn grey, like a curtain wrapping him in its dusty felt. If he became aware from time to time, that the world beyond the curtain was growing steadily more crowded, more clamorous, and the lives of others more hectic, more chaotic, then he felt only relief that his had never been a part of the mainstream (Desai 1989 : 211).

A depleted self, Hugo is enshrouded in his own isolation. Desai delineates the estrangement of Hugo through auditory images, especially the German songs, mostly nursery rhymes which occur only at critical moments when the narrative documents the isolation of Baumgartner from his parents or from his peers. They point directly to Hugo's socio-cultural roots and his psychic displacement that begins in early childhood as he flounders to acculturise and identify himself with the German milieu. The song of the rider imagistically portrays his childhood disappointment and his estrangement from his apathetic father :

> Hoppe, hoppe, Reiter,
> wenn er fallt, dann schreit et.

> Falt er in die Hecken,
> fressen ihn die Schnecken,
> fallt er in den Klee,
> Schreit er gleich : O weh... (35)

The verse "comments on young Hugo's inability to assume and act out a role of his own choice and refers this disablement to archetypal situations (encoded in the song itself) of frustration, impotence, and loss of self-identity" [Ho, WLWE (32), 98].

Hugo is disowned, rather rejected by his father and is tagged to his mother in a bond of subjection. With both, his is the pitiable plight of a prisoner : "He looked at her with the hatred of one prisoner for another" (Desai, Baumgartner's Bombay 35). In this context the observation of Elaine, Y.L. Ho is worth noting :

> The child's alienation is entered into German culture, while the narrative re-enacts the culture as the incidental experience of one of its subjects [WLWE (32), 98].

The song also expresses young Hugo's failure at establishing a cultural rapport with the milieu. It is these childhood experiences of frustration and failure that disallows him a secure social place and a concrete self-identity. Hence his alienation from the milieu.The nightmarishly pungent and redemptive world of contrasts in the following rhyme enciphers the polarities of integration and alienation. It also pictures the non-conformist child Hugo, who declines to sleep — an outsider and a prey to katabolic forces :

> Schlaf, Kindlein, Schlaf!
> Da draussen gehn zwei Schaf!
> Ein schwarzes und e in weisses,
> und wenn das Kind nicht schlafen will,
> dann kommt das Schwarz und beist es,
> Schlaf, Kindlein, Schlaf! (37)

A Jew in the German social milieu, the young Hugo lives like a 'prisoner' marginalised from society. Even the episode narrated through the German nursery rhymes point to young Hugo's sensation of being an alien in his own schoolroom. Ironically he is stigmatized in Jewish School and it is here that he becomes gradually conscious of the alienation that will soon become his identity. Hence his alienation is not an outcome of his ageing but it is the offshoot of the idyllic little happenings and affairs of his searing infancy.

Stellar imagery in Desai's fiction is a part of the synaesthetic imagery. Stellar images which follow one after the other focus on the obsessions and longings of the lonely self. In *Cry, the Peacock*, it illuminates the agonizing ""solitude" of Maya, the psychic "distance" between her and her elderly husband. It lays emphasis on Maya's deep obsession with death and desolation, separation and loneliness : Death lurked in those spaces, the darkness spoke of distance, separation and loneliness — loneliness of such preparation that it broke the bounds of that single word and all its associations, and went spilling and spreading out and about, lapping the starts, each one isolated from the other by so much (24). The stars isolated from each other symbolically suggest the gulf between Maya and Gautama, though it is mainly psycho-temperamental.

The lunar image, which is another part of the colour imagery, only emphasises the "morbid" and "etiolated" self of Maya chasing shadows and silences, but never meeting them. Always aloof, she grows into pale and melancholic feminine image of a housewife. The "pale, hushed glow of the rising moon .... her rim climbing swiftly above the trees, its vast pure surface .... waxen white, virginal, chaste and absolute white, casting a light that was holy in its purity, a soft, suffusing glow of its chastity...." (240) is but a reflection of Maya's gloomy, pale and virgin life. The "stark gaze of the moon" (97) in the waiting silence of the night conveys her hopeless predicament. The image of the moon assumes deeper significance with the death of Gautama at the hands of Maya towards the end of the novel.

In Voices in the City, colour imagery (especially images of light and dark) is functional. The image of darkness in Part-II of the novel projects the forlornness of Monisha's broken heart in the face of the dark and dangerous forces of life :

> I will have only the darkness. Only the dark spaces between the stars, for they are the only things on earth that can comfort me, rub and balm into my wounds, into my throbbing head, and bring me this coolness, this stillness, this interval of peace. Even sleep has not this sweet, swaying stillness as

> these immensities of night sky to which I top my face, allowing them to fall into my eyes, and fall. Sleep has nightmares. This, this empty darkness, has not so much as a dream. It is one unlit waste, a desert to which my heart truly belongs (140).

Light and dark imagery, an extension of colour imagery explores the dim and dark corridors of the souls of Nirode and Monisha. It suggests their emotional estrangement and their abortive desire for a life of detachment in the deafening cacophony of Calcutta. It also reflects the caged isolation, psycho-physical torture, phantasmagoric and paralytic life, bogged and defeatist attitudes and dim apprehensions of failures, of darkness and stillness of Nirode, the bohemian artist. Like Adit, Nirode is haunted by "the black sensation of not belonging" (205). He longs for "shadows, silence, stillness — and well, he told himself, that was exactly what he would always be left with. He remained in the half-dark — and each light on that street served to show up an expanse of wall, a doorway, a balcony that was darkly shadowed — and bled with longing to go" (8).

The image of the moon in *Bye-Bye, Blackbird* points to Dev's existentialist predicament and his feeling of silence and stillness, of estrangement and incertitude in England. The lunar image occurs with the botanical imagery forming a cluster image : "In the night, Dev lay on his back, smoking a cigarette and watching the moon fill the pool of the ceiling with its thin polar light in which the long weeds and fronds of garden shadows languorously swayed and danced. The rush of the stream, grown louder now in the stillness of night, added to the illusion of being afloat in a water world as a shadow island — light, unanchored, disembodied as the mere shadow of a round wet leaf" (169).

Shut in by the "barbed wire fence", Hugo Baumgartner wants to shut out both the human and natural incursions of all sorts. His longing for shadows, silence and darkness is an attempt on his part to shut out both the human and natural incursions : "Baumgartner lay with his arms across his eyes, shutting out the probing needles of sun and heat, wishing, there were some way of shutting out the voices as well ...." (118).

The landscape image occurs in *In Custody* to project Deven's dry and drab existence, his immured life : "..... the impassable desert that lay between him and the capital with its lost treasures of friendships, entertainments, attractions and opportunities. It turned into that strip of no man's land that lies around a prison, threatening in its desolation" (24).

The desolation and waste Deven sees outside is a projection of the dismay and void within him. "Deven stared out at the white dust and yellow weeds, the leafless thorn trees, the broken fences, isolated tin and brick sacks and the scattered carcasses of cattle that littered the landscape and yet rendered it more bleak and bare under the empty sky" (28). The landscape image stresses the psychic states of the protagonists and points to the bitterness and harshness on the milieu from which the self craves to withdraw. It mirrors their psychoscape.

Maya's impending doom and estrangement is communicated through the various dance images. These images of dance are the symbols of death and desolation, which obliquely connote isolation and separation. The dance image figures as an iterative image which emphasises an escalating sense of fatality and despair. The Kathakali dance that "rose out of realms of silence into one thunderous drumming" (28), suggests Maya's psychic journey from stillness and silence to chaos and confusion. The bear dance is related to Maya's past, her childhood experiences which drive her to near-madness and hysterical derision. Of all the dance images, the image of the dancing Shiva and the Peacocks is thematically linked to the centrality of Maya's alienated self. The dance of Shiva gains a new mythological meaning. It stands for "divine isolation", a way out of the existential predicament in which Maya is entrapped and encaged. It is the symbol of "escape" and "liberation" from death and despair. The dance of the peacocks, portrayed in Chapter 3 and later on referred to in Chapter 6, Part-II, is the most poignant of all the images used in the novel. The bacchanalian and frenzied dance of the peacocks at the advent of monsoon is pregnant with meaning. In Maya, despair becomes hysterical and neurotic : "Pia, pia", they cry. "Lover, lover, Mio, mio — I die, die .... like Shiva's, their dance of joy is the dance of death, and they dance knowing that they and their lovers are all to die.... Before they mate, they fight. They will rip each other's breasts to strips and fall, bleeding, with their beaks open and panting'' (95).

Like the peacocks frantically longing for sexual communion, Maya craves for the company of Gautama, his touch and tickle. The cry of the peacocks becomes the symbol of the pathetic cry of Maya's bruised soul. Her suicide at the end of the novel becomes an enactment of her long-cherished desire for isolation in death.

There are a number of stray images in Desai's novels. The image of the barbed-wire, an extension of the image of a caged bird, occurs in *Baumgartner's Bombay*, symbolising the desperate, deserted and isolated life of Hugo, whose life seems cobwebbed and unsightly, like the ''strands of — barbed wire wrapped around the wooden posts and travelling in circles and double circles around the camp'' (111).

The image of a rushing and whistling train ''leaving the small signalman waving a pointless flag, lonely and sad at the door of his whitewashed hut in the middle of the desert'' (56) in *Cry, the Peacock*, evokes the world of loneliness. So it does in Voices in the City. So it does in, *In Custody*, where the train whistle reminds Deven of ''Prisoners in their bars, mocked .... in their cells'' (132), condemned and subjected to death-like isolation.

The image of the island as an interface imagery in Anita Desai. Like the image of ''incarceration'' and ''entanglement'', it forms a common link between the different images of isolation. Each character in Desai's novels is an island unto itself. The image of the island mirrors the individual's alienated plight, its abandonment. The island of Manori in *Where Shall We Go this Summer*? is the symbol of Sita's marooned life. She returns to the island but its inhabitants go on, completely oblivious of her presence. She remains isolated from the island till the very end, an ''island on the island'' (Ram, ''Island on the Island'', WLWE 98).

Solar imagery alongwith the images of light and darkness forms a base to show the to and fro movement of the self from light to darkness and from sadness to happiness. It again becomes a part of the synaesthetic imagery.

In *Clear Light of Day*, the image of the morning sun is unlike the one painted in *Bye-Bye, Blackbird.* The former attracts and enlivens, but the latter repels and isolates. Tara bows her head to "the morning sun that came slicing down, like a blade of steel on to the beck of her neck" (1). The morning sun here is not homely but alien that acquires a brutal and harsh nature through the use of the words 'slicing down' and 'blade of steel'. It is not a playful and cheerful sun, it is formidable and intimidating. It triggers off the feel of alienation in Tara, who drops the screen and remains isolated from its ghastly sight : She actually got up and went to the door and lifted the bamboo screen that hung there, but the blank white glare of afternoon slanted in and slashed at her with its flashing knives so that she quickly dropped the screen (21).

In *Cry, the Peacock*, Maya's psychic estrangement is described in terms of the light pouring in from her window : The light from the open window was too bright : it hurt my eyes like a giant red thumb pressed into the sockets of my eyes, end bit up Gautama's face luridly (144).

In *Clear Light of Day*, Desai evokes, through Tara's reactions to the light of the full moon, a sense of the eerie : "Like snow, its touch was cold, marmoreal and made Tara shiver.... She could not free herself of them, of this shabby old house" (158-159).

The most striking and powerful image projecting isolation and estrangement is the image of the cow drowned in the well in *Clear Light of Day.* The cow was drowned but was never taken out. It becomes the symbol of nausea, Nausea generating isolation : "That looked like a tomb in the moonlight, a white-washed tomb rising in the midst of the inky shadows of trees and hedges, so silent — everyone asleep, or stunned by moonlight" (159). Again, in *Clear Light of Day*, the children, unlike their mother, who continually broke apart into violent eruptions of emotion, seemed rigid, encased in separate silences like larvae in stiff-spun cocoons.

In Desai's novels, one comes across a symbolic link between different images, which form an interface, a common bond. Imagery is primarily used to capture and crystallise a wide range of experiences. It lends clarity and vividness to the situation she describes, events she documents and characters she delineates. Most of the images are so sharply condensed and chiselled that they resemble a piece of painting.

The characters in Anita Desai's fictional world are victims of alienation. They experience a fragmentation and disintegration which is conveyed through images. Words like 'tunnel', 'net', 'cobweb', 'snare', 'hedge', 'cage', 'tomb', evoke a sense of incarceration and isolation in which the characters live. The images of isolation, at times, overlap adding to the lyrical and rhythmic splendour of her novels. They are simple but histrionically powerful. Highly functional, they form an integral part of the fiction. Seldom decorative or ornamental, they reveal a world inside, a world of the inner weather. Never otiose, they help maintain the dominant mood of the novel throughout the succession of parts, and set up a fundamental identity between the form and the content; the space and the time. They appeal to the poetry of life. These images, observes Amina Amin, "look contrived and far-fetched, a striving after effect for its own sake, without relevance to the emotions felt or the situations described" (Littcrit 36). And she is wrong. Desai's images are neither unnatural nor unrelated. In the words of Madhusudan Prasad, "Desai's imagery which is chiefly anticipatory, pre-figurative or demonstrative in nature is always considerably functional.... Lusciously lyrical, her image patterns are singularised by interrelatedness and continuity" (Perspectives on Anita Desai 76).

Unlike Narayan's fictional society, the isolation of Desai's protagonists leaves them bereft of control and protection other than what they can generate for themselves. Desai's writing functions through its orchestration of sensory images, while Narayan's operates through ironically counterpointed situations, characters and conversations. Nanda Kaul in *Fire On the Mountain* longs to be "a tree, no more and no less", and this sort of isolation leads the protagonist into a state of silent alienation. The images of destruction and violence portray the plight of the protagonist inexorably driven towards self-effacement and self-annihilation. Thus images of isolation in Desai's novels lay bare the dark passions and bruised emotions of the individual soul languishing in self-alienation and struggling for self-identification.

The simple but dramatically powerful images in Desai trace the growth of the self from a state of seething discontent and despair to a state of psychic submission and spiritual consolation. Images of anguish in the external world of sights and sounds mature to images of spiritual identification of the inner world of the psyche. Rhythmically condensed, subtly chiselled colour images are knitly woven into the characters to point out the emotional chiaroscuro through successive stages of alienation leading to self-identification.

REFERENCES

Amin, Amina. ''Imagery as a Mode of Apprehension in Anita Desai's Novels'', Littcrit, 18, Vol. 10, No. 1, 1984.

Desai, Anita, 1980. *Cry, the Peacock*, New Delhi : Orient Paperbacks.

— 1982. *Voices in the City*, New Delhi : Orient Paperbacks.

— 1982. *Where Shall We Go This Summer*, New Delhi : Orient Paperbacks.

— 1985. *Bye-Bye, Blackbird*, New Delhi : Orient Paperbacks.

— 1977. *Fire on the Mountain*, New Delhi : Allied Publishers.

— 1980. *Clear Light of Day*, New Delhi : Allied Publishers.

— 1983. *The Village By the Sea*, New Delhi : Allied Publishers.

— 1984. *In Custody*, London : Heinemann.

— 1988. *Baumgartner's Bombay*, Harmondsworth : Penguin.

(Citations from the text kept within parentheses in the paper are from these editions of Desai's novels.)

14

Alienation of Women Characters in Anita Desai's Novels

DR. C.V. GEORGE*

The author of this article, Dr. C.V. George is a post-graduate teacher in Maharashtra Udayagiri Maha-vidyalaya, Udgir. His research on "Alienation of Women Characters in Anita Desai's Novels" is considered to be a great contribution to the Indo-Anglian literature. This article is a humble attempt to reveal the meaning of alienation and the inner life of Desai's characters in her novels.

Anita Desai is a dominant figure in the twentieth century Indo-Anglian fiction. She deserves accolades for her remarkable literary output. Persisting in unravelling the mystery of the inner life of her characters, she shows her perpetual interest in their psychic life. Solitude and self-exploration are the recurring themes of her novels.

Women novelists necessarily have a special way of looking at things because they live in severely confined spheres. But that has neither distorted Anita Desai's vision nor made it inferior. It actually adds some more sharpness to it. In the novels where her protagonist is a woman, this vision focuses on the environment, perhaps shaped by the predominance of patriarchy. It is in the presentation of this confrontation of the female protagonist with the patriarchal oppressive environment that Anita Desai's feminism surfaces.

Anita Desai is a prolific living writer who has been churning out fiction with consummate skill. The relentless Anita Desai has

* Department of English, M.U. Mahavidyalaya, Udgir.

brought out ten full-length novels of varied length, innumerable short stories and a couple of write-ups. In a short period of time she has aroused a lot of critical attention; of late dozens of full-length critical assessments have been flooding the market.

The study of isolation experienced by women in a male dominated society is a significant modern trend. In the Indian society women are not allowed to play any active role in decision-making. They are ignored or brushed aside. In such a situation Anita Desai tries to focus on the predicament of women in the society.

Any attempt to analyse Anita Desai's feminine consciousness in her fiction should naturally consider her concerns and perspective. Looking at the sensitive portrayal of characters, it can be concluded that she cares for the individual human beings irrespective of their being male or female. Her characters appear to be exceptionally talented but constantly disturbed by family ties. As a result, they experience discomfort and feel trapped in an oppressive environment. In most cases the hostile environment frustrates the aspirations of the individuals either leading them to their annihilation or a humiliating compromise. The process of her character construction includes a soul-searching self-exploration — may be male or may be female, a struggle for realization and an exposure to agony.

In novels where Anita Desai delineates a female protagonist, the struggle against the oppressive environment assumes the form of a patriarchal domination in one or the other visage, revealing her feminist predilections. She cares more for the individual, in comparison to the plot as pointed out by many critics, with an amazing insight into her psyche. Not able to amalgamate themselves into the society around, her characters undertake an inner voyage for the purpose of discovering their own selves. She concedes that nobody is an exile from the society and the individuals should strive to integrate themselves and find fulfilment. Anita Desai differs from the other feminists in that she concentrates on the individual's salvation through self-exploration by depicting its motivation. Her novels do not, strangely, deal with the problems of the Third World feminism, though the setting is entirely in India.

The most significant social issue that Anita Desai focuses on is the institution of marriage — particularly in the novels where woman is the protagonist. When a woman is caught in the trap of marriage, she has only one way left, that is to languish in misery. Somehow she reveals an evident lack of trust in marriage and marital relationships. Every attempt the woman makes to redefine herself inevitably ends up in lack of communication. This leads to the theme of alienation. Each novel of Anita Desai is progressively a search of the self for a heightened female awareness.

Anita Desai, like most women writers, turns her eye inward and writes about the flickering psychic reactions. She remarks in the course of an interview that she has been making statements about woman-emancipation in the texture of her novels which is evident for anyone to see. Her themes are original and different from those of other Indo-Anglian writers as she is "engaged in exposing the labyrinths of the human mind and in indicating the ways to psychological fulfilment." She records the dilemmas faced by the Indian urban individuals. She portrays and analyses human relationships in the context of emotionally related kin which is a fertile area for exploration.

Anita Desai's treatment of her theme begins as a simple personal story of an individual woman gradually developing into a wider conflict for her identity and ends up exploring possibilities of transition in the tradition bound Indian society residing in metropolitan surroundings. She brings about a new dimension to the Indian novel by drawing upon the troubled sensibility of a woman in an absurd world. Desai finds the existentialist theories — so fashionable during the sixties — compatible to her themes. Her characters like Maya, Sita and Nanda Kaul are lonely, anxious and estranged, and suffer from a sense of alienation that is not merely physical but psychic. Their estrangement steams from a lack of companionship with which they could feel secure. Desai explores the inner working of her protagonists' minds unfolding the inner recesses and revealing the fundamental human condition by placing individuals in situations of extreme tension. She thus introduces the psychological vein and a dissociation of sensibility which are not entirely Indo-Anglian. Most of the women created by Anita Desai have some or the other trait which psychologists would love to analyse. They strikingly appear as individuals and gradually get subsumed as types of women in conflict with their environment. Such types of women are ubiquitous. Anita Desai thus has not simply created situations and characters to populate her pages but is seriously concerned with the predicament of an individual woman in each of her novels, trying to explore her inner self for realization.

Where Shall We Go This Summer?, a novel by Anita Desai has a female central character, Sita, who suffers from intense delusions of her being separate and different from others while leading an ostensibly normal life-living with her husband and mothering his children. Suddenly she finds reality unpalatable and decides to retire to Manori, an island where once her father lived like the legendary Prospero during her childhood. There she intends to freeze her foetus — neither aborting the embryo nor delivering the child. The process of her resolution, experimentation and restoration to the society are discussed in the novel.

Village by the Sea is yet another novel of Anita Desai. Here a frustrated brother rebels against the family and in consequence, a tender child Zila is forced into accepting the family responsibilities because of her mother's sickness and father's drunkenness.

Anita Desai's next novels are *Cry, the Peacock*, *Clear Light of Day*, *Voices in the City* and *In Custody*. In all these novels the women protagonists are put in urban locations. Maya, the protagonist in *Cry, the Peacock*, suffers from a type of Oedipus complex, idolizes her father but becomes miserable as her search for a father substitute in her husband does not measure up to her anticipation. Her barrenness coupled with an albino fortune teller's prediction of impending demise of one of the partners after her marriage agitates her mind, occupies her wakeful thoughts and precipitously pushes her towards her insanity.

Bimla in *Clear Light of Day* exults in a feeling of equality when she wears her brother's clothes and realizes how circumscribed the life of a female is. She suffers for her pride of being a woman and ultimately reconciles herself to reality. Monisha in *Voices in the City* encounters parental discord and suffers later the traumatic experience of barrenness. She feels a sense of liberation when left alone in a jungle where she could befriend the dark corners of the house in solitariness — rather than in Calcutta where the novel is set.

The protagonist Sarla of *In Custody* and Sofiya Begum, the

neglected wife of the poet both belong to the same category of illiterate, neglected wives. Devan the lecturer is a docile busy-bee, humming with activity whom success eludes, whereas the eminent poet Nur remains helpless under exploitation from his once ladylove Imtiaz Begum. All the characters in the novel are afraid of facing the reality and suffer isolation while living among a throng — Nur in Delhi and Devan in its vicinity at Mirpore.

The next novel *Fire on the Mountain* is exclusively devoted to the study of old age and the trauma that accompanies physical disorders and sickness. Living a vegetable life, removed from human hustle and bustle, licking her psychological wounds, Nanda Kaul is confronted by the reality of a great granddaughter who is as much a recluse and emotionless as the bitter grandmother. The novel *Fire on the Mountain* corresponds with the bonfire of emotions that Nanda Kaul is subjected to by the frail looking Raka who sets the mountain on fire — literally.

In the last three novels *Bye Bye Blackbird, Baumgartner's Bombay* and *Journey to Ithaca,* Anita Desai with aliens in India not in the normative context of East-West encounter but that of foreigners who live in India by choice. These novels are diverse in their themes as the protagonists are. Here she takes up male protagonists with rather shadowy female characters. Adit and Sarah, Hugo and Zolte, Matteo and Sophie shift from their original positions of understanding reality through conflict with the environments they are placed in following the psychological processes of alienation and realization.

To revolt against injustice is human and if the victim is hyper sensitive, the situations becomes sensitive enough. If the victim is a sensitive young woman, her reactions may rather be intense — alternating between the two extremes of resignation and rebellion. In either case, the victim, as in Anita Desai's fiction, is driven into herself in order to realize one's own self. Anita Desai's female protagonists perceive the psychic truth which is distinctly different from the reality they confront. They develop fears, obsessions, neuroses, paranoia or schizophrenia and gradually withdraw from the society including their families and husbands. They develop incommunication and tend to ponder over existential problems and end up in alienation.

Anita Desai has an innate ability to peep into the inner recesses of the psyche of her characters rather than the outer spectacle of action. She has enormously contributed to the growth of Indian fiction in English by incorporating psychic aspect of her female characters who have suffered privations and humiliations, neglect and silence, aloofness and alienation.

Alienation has been the thematic motif that organically connects Anita Desai's fiction. This makes her an exceptionally unique novelist.

15

Note of Existentialism in the Novels of Anita Desai

DR. S.P. SWAIN*

A modern philosophical movement, Existentialism deals with man's disillusionment and despair. Originating in the philosophical and literary writings of Jean-Paul Sartre, it was more an attitude to life, a vision, or what Kaufmann calls a "timeless sensibility that can be discerned here and there in the past" (*Existentialism from Dostoevsky to Sartre* 12). A philosophical idealism, existentialism, in due course of time developed into a powerful revolt against reason, rationality, positivism and the traditional ways in which early philosophers portrayed man. Man's autonomy, assertion of his subjective self, his flouting of reason and rationality, positivism and the traditional ways in which early philosophers portrayed man. Man's autonomy, assertion of his subjective self, his flouting of reason and rationality, his denial of traditional values, institutions and philosophy, his exercise of 'will' and 'freedom', and his experience of the absurdity and the 'nothing-ness' of life are some of the existential themes which are reflected in the writings of the exponents of existentialism.

Anita Desai's chief concern is human relationship. Her central theme is the existential predicament of the individuals projected through the problems of the self in an emotionally disturbed milieu. Delicately conscious of the reality around them, her protagonists carry with them a sense of loneliness, alienation and pessimism. Desai adds a new dimension to the genre of Indian fiction in

* Department of English, Rourkela Municipal College, Rourkela.

English by probing the unquestionable existentialist concerns of her protagonists. Toeing the line of the existential humanists, to Desai, existentialism means "the mad or bad....the shocking, the sordid or the obscene" (Grene 1950 : 01). Anita Desai is obsessively occupied with the individual's quest for meaning and value, freedom and truth that provide spiritual nourishment to the estranged self in a seemingly chaotic and meaningless world.

The search for identity on the part of the existential self in Desai assumes a socio-psychic dimension. The Desai protagonists do not shy away from the assaults of existence. Existential heroes, they face the problems of life single-handedly with courage and determination. Experiencing disgusting absurdity of the world, they discover meaning in self-immolation or self-affirmation in "a world irremediably absurd where one is a stranger to oneself as well as to other people" (Camus 1960 : 52).

Desai's novels from *Cry, the Peacock* to *Journey to Ithaca* are a study in the depth and persistence of human affliction, inexorably sensitive and loving and compassionate as her protagonists are. Existential conflicts in Desai spring from the self's craving for the fulfilment of certain psycho-emotional needs, from the desire to overcome the horror of separateness, of powerlessness and of listless-ness.

Cry, the Peacock depicts existentialism in its deep-seated morbidity through the neurotic and hysterical self of Maya pining for com-panionship. Hers is an explosive life of incommunication. Her lone-liness, her aching heart and the progressive disorientation of self make her an existential character. The loneliness corroding her heart and lacerating her psyche is existential in nature. It makes her aware "of the loneliness of time, and the impossible vastness of space" (Desai 1980 : 29).

All the three major characters in *Voices in the City* are tortured by their hollow existence. Nirode is a rotless character drifting directionlessly, shifting from one goal to another, finally faced with a void, a sense of emptiness. He quotes Camus : "In default of inexhaustible happiness, eternal suffering at least would give us a destiny. But we do not have even that consolation and our worst agonies come to an end one day" (Desai 1982 : 40). He experiments with failure like a true existential hero. Wearied by his own unsureness, "he swept back and forth like a long weed undulating under water, a weed that could live only in aqueous gloom, would never rise and spring into clear day light" (63). His existential search for meaning and value in life ends in emptiness and bankruptcy. Like Nirode, Monisha too looks for loneliness and longs for privacy. She prefers non-existence to a meaningless existence. She fails to relate to the reality of her life. She fails to hold in harmony all the varying yet vital demands of her life. Amla seeks to opt out of the absurd into a life of parties, dinners and dances. Yet hollowness dogs her. Nirode, Monisha and Amla are not concerned with simple problems of work-a-day existence since the journeys they make are essentially spiritual.

In *Bye-Bye, Blackbird*, we notice Desai's existentialist concern rooted in expatriate experience. Ostensibly concerned with the lives of Indian immigrants in England, the novel explores the existentialist problems of alienation, adjustment, rootedness and the final decision in the lives of the three major characters — Dev, Adit and Sarah. It is scattered in numerous symbols and images revealing Desai's ir-resistible existentialist musings.

The silence and emptiness of the houses and streets of London make Dev feel utterly uneasy. He feels a strange sort of schizophrenia, faced with the dilemma as to whether he should stay on in England or return to his homeland. The "bewildered alien, the charmed observer, the outraged outsider...." (98), he feels "a tumult inside him, a growing bewilderment, a kind of schizophrenia that wakes him in the middle of the night and shadows him by day, driving him along on endless tramps in all weathers while he wonders whether he should stay or go back" (99). He is caught in the ironic "double net" (141) of his existence. Fully conscious of his otherness, Adit is filled with a pass-ionate homesickness. Nostalgia in him acquires a dreadful dimension of an illness, an ache. Like an existentialist, he comes to consider himself to be a stranger, a non-belonger in England. He moves about in London in a kind of morbid search for belongingness.

Sarah has to play different roles — Sarah, the Mrs. Sen, Sarah the Head's secretary sending out the bills and taking in the cheques and when she has none to play, she feels she is nobody. Here is

Sarah an existential character grappling to grasp her real identity : "Staring out of the window at the chimney pots and the clouds, she wondered if Sarah had any existence at all..." (38).

Where Shall We Go this Summer? is Desai's "shortest existentialist novel" (Prasad 1981 : 60). As in *Cry, the Peacock,* here too, Desai very remarkably voices "the terror of facing single-handed the ferocious assaults of existence" (Dalmia, *The Times of India* : 13), through her recurrent, favourite existential theme of husband-wife alienation. An anguished soul, Sita is fed up with the dreary metropolitan Bombay. Her father fixation hinders her contact with her husband. She feels a frog out of water in her father-in-law's "age-rotted flat" (24) where they all live like pariahs "a life of subhuman placidity, calmness and sluggishness... She flouts the dehumanising and destabilizing norms and values of a society whose stranglehold it is difficult to escape (Swain and Naik, *JIWE* : 22). Through Sita, Desai voices the animal existence of human beings : "They are nothing...nothing but appetite and sex. Only food, sex and money matter, Animals" (47). Sita's desperate escape to the idyllic environs of Manori isle is another exercise in futility. Everything linked to her twilight existence betrays an ambiguity and ambivalence. She is uncertain of her own self little knowing which half of her life is real and which unreal.

Fire on the Mountain limns out the existentialist problems and predicaments of the middle class people, particularly women. Tired of a life of duties and responsibilities for so long, Nanda seeks refuge in the sequestered life of an undisturbed privacy, that of "a charred tree trunk in the forest, a broken pillar of marble in the desert, a lizard on a stonewall" (23). Nanda's problem is the predicament of one exposed to a protracted life of unrelenting routine. She is left with little nerve for anything save a wish to have a sigh of relief in peace. The image of the prey and predator (a hoopoe pouncing upon a grasshopper and stabbing it to death) projects itself to the human world through the rape and murder of Ila Das. Here, Desai repeats the animalistic existence of the contemporary society despite the progress of civiliz-ation, a theme which occurred in *Where Shall We Go this Summer*?.

Clear Light of Day breaks new ground in the sense that it dwells on an existentialist theme of time in relation to eternity. Time is treated as a fourth dimension depicting the unavoidable emotional turmoils in the protagonist. Unlike in *Baumgartner's Bombay* where Camus' influence on Desai is dominant, here the novelist has come under the impact of Kierkegaard, Bergson, Augustine, Pascal, Heidegger and Proust, especially in her treatment of time. Delineating the life of two brothers and two sisters who grew up in a house in old Delhi, the novel is about time as a destroyer and a prserver, and about what the bondage of time does to the smooth and unruffled existence of human beings. Tara's deep obsession with her childhood is suggestive of her initial inability to comprehend the passage of time. However, ultimately she realises the existentialist significance of time as she discovers a shocking, changed pattern of relationship and an economical way of living in her old family.

In *Village By the Sea* existentialism occurs rather thinly. Here, through the life of a young village boy Hari, Desai captures the existential predicament of the ruralites undergoing the pangs of a society in transition. The existentialist theme in this novel takes on a Marxian undertone. It is not so deep and profound as in the other novels of Anita Desai, but has been used only in a limited sense as in *In Custody.*

Existence in *In Custody* is viewed as an eternal trap — the epitome of pessimism reflected in the character of Nur who finds it very difficult to escape from his cage — "... a cage in a row of cages. Cage, cage. Trap, trap" (131). This is the existential search for freedom — the human quest for liberty : "Then where was freedom to be found? Where was there fresh air to breathe? (131). In a limited sense only the novel is open to interpretation of existential philosophy.

Baumgartner's Bombay belongs to the genre of the novel of the 'absurd'. Baumgartner is a wandering Jew in quest of roots. the bitterness of a neglected childhood, the horror of being hunted and hounded out of his own country, exposure to an outlandish ambience in an alien land, forever condemned to the life of an exile, he moves from one existential dilemma to another. The novel focuses on the absurdity of his existence both in Germany and India. In Germany he was a Jew, alienated from the mainstream of life. In India he is dubbed as a Firangee, unwanted. There is no resolution to his crisis. Like the fall of Hitler, "Defeat was heaped on him, whether he desrved it or not'' (135). This is an existential fact which assumes the proportion of a cosmic truth as Baumgartner realises that life is nothing but an ironic dilemma of pointless activity. This realisation leaves him aimless and absurd. He breaks away from the Kantian notion of a designed universe. ''He was nobody, an old man with an empty bag'' (10). His existence is an absurd odyssey from nothingness to nothingness, fron nowhere to nowhere. Forever condemned to the life of an exile, he moves from one existential dilemma to another. Mrinalini Solanki attributes Baumgartner's existential problems to his immigrant experiences. But I would rather say that Hugo's isolation avers the importance of his ontological need. It is related to his spiritual and existential evolution in an alien milieu.

Desai's *Journey to Ithaca* is a compassionate portrait of people struggling to find a spiritual home. It delineates Matteo's alienation and the concomitant quest for spirituality. Like Hugo, he is the 'nowhere man' and like Arun Joshi's Sindi Oberoi, he is a 'perennial outsider'. He has come to India in search of spirituality. ''It is the spiritual experience'', he tells Sophie, ''for which you must search in India, nothing less'' (36). Disgusted with the drab and mundane reality of familial and conjugal life, he is all out for the life of a sage in an ashrama. His quest for eternal truth is a struggle for spiritual sustenance. The sight of an old man worshipping a stone makes him realize the muddle of existence and the complexity of the universe: ''The stone glowed now, became brilliant in Matteo's eyes ... he felt certain divine light'' (68) — a light which brings him an existential realisation of the conundrum and muddledom of human existence. A split self, Matteo's existential suffering springs from his constitutional inability to adjust to his self-created situations and the challenges of spiritual life. Unable to balance the claims of his body and his soul, his personality undergoes gradual disintegration. With the death of the Mother, his quest for spirituality comes to a halt. Alienated from the milieu, he neglects his duties towards his family, the society and even towards his own self. His is a case of double alienation — alienation from the self as well as the society. His existential contradiction results in a state of constant disequilibrium. Always 'on the run', Matteo emerges as a restless, seeker of his 'spiritual self'. He begins his journey with romantic dreams and spiritual ideals, but utilimately they prove to be mere illusions that define man negatively. When he faces the naked reality of his existence, he emerges as a disillusioned romantic, an existentialist. Thus, "while depicting the conflict-ridden existence of Matteo, Anita Desai is dealing with the predicament of the modern man caught in the contrived dialectical opposition between 'what is' and 'what ought to be' [Solanki, Kumar (ed.) *New Perspectives on Indian Writing* 96]. A disintegrated and fragmented being, Matteo's endeavour all through has been to attain integration of being and wholeness of personality.

Critics like Solanki and R.S. Sharma have often observed that the Desai protagonist is a psychologically fragmented individual who relies chiefly on indirect methods of coping with a stress situation which ventilates through various survival strategies. Escape, withdrawal and a denial of reality seem to be prominent primitive survival strategies among the Desai protagonists. But is the self only psychologically fragmented? I would rather attribute the laceration of the self in the Desai protagonists to their emotional shocks which manifest in various modes of psychological observations. Hence, the individual in Desai novels is both emotionally and psychologically disturbed. But can human existence be solely identified in terms of intellect only? It would be better to call the Desai characters emotionally malaformed and socially isolated. Unreason, in Desai, manifests in the world of absurdity. Ujwala Patil attributes Ila Das's rape and murder in *Fire on the Mountain* to Preet Singh's desire to humiliate her for the injury she had caused to his male ego; but it is rather a manifestation of an individual's cannibalistic and canine existence. It is an assertion of male chauvinism on the part of Preet Singh. In many of the Desai novels the language and imagery have a subjective existential tone. Most of the protagonists adopt the existentialist, heroic posture necessary to face the ordeals of life. Anita Desai adopts the decadent type of existentialism that borders on nihilism. The existentialism in Desai's novels is not philosophically disturbing as in the novels of Raja Rao. It is intellectually engaging and poetically captivating as in the novels of Shashi Deshpande.

WORKS CITED

Cruickshank, John, *Albrt Camus and the Literature of Revolt* (London : Penguin Books, 1960).

Dalmia, Yasodhara, *The Times of India,* April 29, 1979, p. 13.

Desai, Anita, *Cry, the Peacock* (New Delhi : Orient Paperbacks, 1980).

Voices in the City (New Delhi : Orient Paperbacks, 1982).

Bye-Bye, Blackbird (New Delhi : Hind Pocket Books, 1971).

Where Shall We Go this Summer? (New Delhi : Orient Paperbacks, 1982).

Fire On the Mountain (New Delhi : Allied, 1977).

Clear Light of Day (New Delhi : Allied, 1980).

Village By the Sea (New Delhi : Allied, 1983).

In Custody (London : William Heinemann Ltd., 1984).

Baumagartner's Bombay (London : Penguin Books, 1988).

Journey to Ithaca (London : Heinemann, 1995).

(All citations from the novels of Desai are from the above editions of the text).

Grene, M. *Introduction to Existentialism* (The University of Chicago, Chicago Press, 1950).

Kaufmann, Walter, *Existentialism from Dostoevsky to Sartre,* Cleveland and New York, Meridian Books, The Word Publishing Company, 1968.

Patil, Ujwala, "Sexual Violence and Death in Anita Desai's *Fire On the Mountain*" in G.S. Balarama Gupta (ed.) *Studies in Indian Fiction in English* (Gulbarga : JIWE Publns., 1987).

Prasad, Madhusudan, *Anita Desai : The Novelist* (Allahabad : New Horizon, 1981).

Sharma, R.S. *Anita Desai* (New Delhi : Arnold - Heinemann, 1981).

Solanki, Mrinalini, "*Baumgartner's Bombay* : An Attempt to Survive", in K.N. Awasthi (ed.) *Contemporary Indian English Fiction* (Jalandhar : ABS Publns., 1993).

— "Anita Desai's *Journey in Ithaca* : A Quest for Integrated Being", V.L.V.N. Narendra Kumar (ed.) *New Perspectives on Indian Writing,* New Delhi : Prestige, 1997.

Swain, S.P. & Nayak, P.M. "*Where Shall We Go This Summer?* : Sita's Incarcerated Self", *The Journal of Indian Writing in English (JIWE),* Vol. 22, Jan-1994, No.1.

16

Anita Desai : "A Grain of Sand in an Oyster"

DR. O.J. THOMAS*

Anita Desai brushed aside the conventional themes, techniques and narrative patterns prevalent in India with the publication of her first novel *Cry, the Peacock*, published in 1963 and introduced a new idiom and direction to Indo-Anglian novel and literature. Indo-Anglian literature has provided Indian writers a golden opportunity to swim across the much abused murky waters of domestic fiction and move closer to the global trends and tendencies. Anita Desai has done just that. She has added a new dimension to Indo-Anglian fiction by concentrating on the exploration of the troubled sensitivity of her characters, especially, the women in particular. N.R. Gopal has rightly mentioned,

> "In contrast to her in (Ruth) Jhabwala's work the social background is rather more important than the characters, in Kamala Markandaya's works the emphasis is as much on the principal characters as on matters economic, political, social and cultural. Nayantara Sehgal while dealing with social problems, confines herself to a particular social class, namely the upper class and the aristocracy."[1]

Indo-Anglian novelists continued to go round the treadmill, with out-dated material and the orthodox eighteenth century techniques, feeding heavily on sentimentalism and cultural hyperboles. It is, infact, gratifying on the one hand and quite interesting on the other

* Head, Department of English, J.N. Govt. College, Port Blair.

hand that the women writers in Indo-Anglian fiction have shown greater understanding and verve to delve deep into the psyche of the Indian characters. N.R. Gopal has gone into the details thus,

> "Fortunately this movement from the outward gross realities to inward complexities found as its mouth-piece a number of women novelists who by the peculiar situation of their existence have been able to see the Indian complexities from close quarters, when constraints of varied hues and shades work upon the sensitive individuals. Of these women novelists, Anita Desai happens to be the leading voice. We may miss in her fiction the customary strains of rural poverty, caste and class conflicts, but she has fascinating stories to tell about individuals who have to traverse a ground too tricky and treacherous to handle smoothly."[2]

She has no doubt championed the cause of women in her works. But what distinguishes her from the rest of Indo-Anglian writers is her pre-occupation with the individuals and their inner world of sensibility and the resultant chaos inside the mind."[3] Doing so she has attracted the attention of the intellectuals of Indian Academic field. More and more research scholars are working on her novels, these days, fascinated by her poetic language, greater understanding of the characters, their alienation, existential qualities, and exploring and understanding the complexities that often tempt characters to commit suicide or even murder, while they appear normal and affable to others.

It is not out of place here to know a few points regarding her life before going deep into her novels by way of analysis. She was born in Mussoorie on 24th June, 1937, of a Bengali father and a German mother. This amalgamation of diverse elements of cultural backgrounds and experiences, within the family itself might have helped her in formulating her ideas in *Bye, Bye Blackbird.* She had her education through Queen Mary School in Delhi. Later she did her B.A. in English literature from Miranda House, New Delhi University. She was married to Ashvin Desai. They have four children. Inspite of being a reputed writer, she has taken good care of her children.

It may appear incredible to believe that even such a gifted novelist had her problems and difficulties in getting her novels published in the beginning years. In reply to Ramesh K. Srivastava's question whether she found any difficulty in finding a publisher she said, "Yes, I faced some difficulty in finding a publisher for my first novel. From 1963 till 1978, I had more rejections than acceptances. I experienced very little acceptance or recognition for the first fifteen years...."[4] The type of the novels that she writes, certainly might not have gone down attractive with the publishers then. It was of a different kind. Indian public had not been properly exposed to certain techniques and ideas which had become hall marks of the modern age in Europe and America. Literary terms like psycho-analysis, alienation, existentialism had not come down to common use in India. Many people then had not heard about Franz Kafka, Freud, Camus and Kierkegaard. While the novels of English novelists like James Joyce, D.H. Lawrence and Virginia Woolf were overshadowed in India by Victorian Novelists. But the new writers in India exerted their pressure and got slowly accepted, when elements like alienation, loneliness, and the pressure of work and urban urgency percolated into the Indian psyche. As anybody can guess she was influenced by some of these writers and their techniques. She admits it in her interview with Ramesh K. Srivastava when she states, "In my twenties when I first began to work seriously and consciously on my novels, it was D.H. Lawrence, Virginia Woolf, Henry James and Proust that influenced me more strongly."[5] Further, she says, "...the novels of the Japanese writer Kawabata and more and more, modern poetry — particularly that of Rimbaud; Hopkine and Lawrence"[6] influenced her in later stages.

Once she made her presence felt, she established clearly a new type of novel in Indo-Anglian literature. Her novels are under careful critical evaluation. Some have praised her as the most successful of the Indian novelists who write in English, while some others have summarily dismissed her as an aberration on the Indo-Anglian firmament. Darshan Singh Maini has stated after a detailed evaluation of her novels,"... She is somehow unable

> to invent events and episodes that may bring out the dramatic potential of her *donees*. There are,

> therefore, no great scenes in her, but moments of lyric, beauty and intensity. So long as her moral vision remains subservient to the poetic and metaphysical urges of her imagination there cannot be much hope for her development."[7]

While some Western critics have praised both her language and her artistry; some Indian critics have found fault with both. It is interesting to go through the *Times Literary Supplement*, *Spectator*, *The Observer*, *Illustrated London News in England* and *New York Time Book Review*, *New Yorker* and several other newspapers and journals which have reviewed her works favourably. It is interesting to go through a sample of such criticisms before going into a critical analysis of her novels. Victoria Glendinning writes, "She writes an extra-ordinarily delicate, lucid English which puts many English writers to shame."[8] While Hermione Lee is of opinion, "Absolutely first-rate. As finely written 'atmospheric' piece alone, the stories would be memorable."[9] Such diverse opinions are generally expressed about writers who are really talented and enduring. It is worthwhile to know about the different aspects of her novels.

II

It is simply because of a "complex" that we continue to discuss whether English should be used as a medium for expression of our ideas in India. Firstly, as I do not subscribe to the idea that English is a foreign language to educated Indians. In fact, many of us find it extremely difficult to express ourselves completely in our own mother-tongue, though many are not prepared to accept the truth publicly. As R. Parthasarathy has clearly stated, "It is nearly one hundred and fifty years since Indian poets gathered under the common umbrella of the English language."[10] It is more or less to speak about English fiction in India. But still, "There are many, both

> in India and in the West, who believe that Indian writing in English is at best a hot-house plant, a contrived thing which may for sometime attract attention by its novelty, illustrating the logic of Dr. Johnson's famous example of a woman's preaching being 'like a dog's walking on its hinder

> legs'. It is not done well but you are surprised to find it done at all."[11]

It shows the arrogance of English speaking people, not all of them, but a minority, who still considers Indians as second-rate stuff, good to be used as clerks but not as officers. This colonial mental set up in the English people and its reactions in India under the garb of patriotism, some people have tried to denigrate Indian writing in English. In this write up, I do not see the scope and relevance to go into a detailed study of the uses of Indian English, and its literature. Sri Aurobindo has rightly answered his critics through his writings in English language in his own words, "It is not true one can't write first-rate things in a learnt language."[12] Joseph Conrad's example is often pointed out to demolish the senseless criticism against Indo-Anglian literature. He learnt English at the age of twenty six to become one of the best writers in that language. He once wrote, "My faculty to write in English is as natural as any other aptitude with fiction I might have been born.... If I had not written in English, I would not have written at all."[13]

Anita Desai, has clearly given expression to her reasons for selecting English as the medium. The Indo-Anglian writers, according to her, "...meet with an almost hysterical derision from Indian critics and either outright dismissal by English critics or, at the most, a condescending curiosity as though one were Dr. Johnson's dog."[14] At least, in her case, the reason is genuine. This is the only language in which she has ever written down her ideas. As stated earlier her father was a Bengali and her mother a German. English is the language through which she got her education and as such she is better equipped to write in English. She sarcastically expresses her problems when she writes,

> "According to the rules laid down by critics, I ought to be writing half of my work in Bengali, the other half in German. As it happens, I have never written a word in either language...that I did not choose English in a deliberate and conscious act....I'd say perhaps it was the language that chose me. But I am not aware of any act of choice. I started writing stories in English at the age of seven,...."[15]

It is, therefore, clear that English is just like her mother-tongue. In fact, she has expressed her pleasure in selecting this language for her writing career. She writes,

> "...I am very glad to be writing in a language as rich, as flexible, supple, adaptable, varied and vital as English. It is the language both of reason and instinct, of sense and sensibility. It is capable of poetry and prose. I do believe it is even capable of taking on an Indian character, an Indian flavour, purely by reflection."[16]

She has quoted Henry James to establish the usefulness of English. He once wrote, "One's own language is one's mother but the language one adopts as a career, as a study, is one's wife, that one sets up house."[17] Writing according to her, "...is not an act of deliberation, reason and choice. It is a matter of instinct, silence and waiting."[18] In order to explain her position on the language she quotes four lines from "Poet, Lover, Bird-watcher", by Nissim Ezekiel,

> "The best poets wait for words
> The hunt is not an exercise of will
> But patient love relaxing on a hill
> To note the movement of a timid wing...."[19]

This topic has lost the edge of its earlier criticisms, as Indo-Anglian books have been selected for International awards. Arundhati Roy's *The God of Small Things* is the latest in the series. International Community has finally and also, repeatedly accepted Indo-Anglian writings, as genuine ones in English. Majority of Britishers still have an interest in India and its literature. In America there is a lack of understanding about Indian situations as there is a gap of information and knowledge about India. But slowly this curtain is being raised as a result of Indian fiction in English.

III

Anita Desai, is often considered as a lyrical novelist. *Cry, the Peacock*, is considered as lyrical novel as the language used is of a special type. In *Bye, Bye Blackbird*, Anita Desai has written and quoted poems in several parts. B. Ramachandra Rao is correct when he writes about the poetic quality of her novels and their perfect harmony in form and the unity of various elements. He writes, "Each novel of

> Mrs. Anita Desai is a marvel of technical skill. Everything irrelevant or superfluous is pruned out. So carefully is this pruning done that we have little masterpieces, which possess formal perfection and poetic richness. This perfection is not mere skill of a novelist obsessed with technique. It is the product of a mature artistry which fuses the different and differing elements into a remarkable unity."[20]

After an in-depth comparative study of the novels of Mulk Raj Anand and Anita Desai, O.J. Thomas has commented, "Anita Desai's

> novels depict therefore, a poetic depth that is often lacking in Indo-Anglian literature before she started writing. In the novels of others one comes across the outside world, but she likes to delve deep into the unsolved mysteries of her characters...."[21]

Darshan Singh Maini is of the opinion that Anita Desai is struggling "...to bend, if not subvert, a genre to its own purposes...." But later he defends poetic novels and says,

> "It has a visionary aesthetic which makes it a spiritual experience. What is more important, a poetic novel is, first and foremost, a work of fiction a fabulist's handiwork. Its poetry is a matter of vision, tone and atmosphere. It's note there to sabotage the story, but to take it to the farthest reaches of imagination and thought."[22]

Poetry is used by Anita Desai as a technique right from the beginning of her career as an author. She has used lyrical language in all her novels. This quality of her novels, often, separates her and her identity from other Indo-Anglian writers. N.R. Gopal reiterates this point when he writes, "Another important technique that she uses is use of poetry, unlike in *Bye, Bye Blackbird*, here [*Where Shall We Go This Summer*] the poems quoted are more serious."[23]

Several critics have tried to suggest that Anita Desai has tried to compensate for the lack of action in her novels with the help of her lyrical language. B. Ramachandra Rao has also expressed this opinion while he analyses *Fire on the Mountain*,

> "They are equally poetic descriptions of sandstorms and rain, the forest fires, the birds and the animals, the snakes and the lizards, the langurs and the butterflies and of the grotesque revellers at the Kasauli Club. There is, however, very little action in the novel."[24]

The predominance of 'lyricism', according to some critics have marred the effectiveness of her first novel *Cry, the Peacock*. She has changed the trend in her second novel. D.S. Maini writes on this point,

> "In her second novel, "*Voices in the City*, Anita Desai has sought to break the strangle hold of lyricism which threatened to become ingrown and autophagous in *Cry, the Peacock*. Obviously, she realized the need to subordinate it to the discipline of events, and work it out rather than allow it to feed upon itself. Also, she appears to have realized the point that her first novel, despite its power and poetic appeal, was deficient in the sense of history and the sense of place."[25]

It need not have been a turn around as he has pointed out. An author, as a rule goes on experimenting with his/her techniques and also changes them to suit new characters and situations. It is foolish to expect of a writer to continue with the same technique in all the novels.

Poetry, when it is used in fiction, should supplement and support action. According to Darshan Singh Maini great writers like Melville and Faulkner have turned to the help of rhetoric, but for them as he says, "...rhetoric is not a mere ploy, it's the condition of their kinetics."[26] Further, he says about *Cry, the Peacock*, "[It] remains a splendid piece of writing but not a great work of fiction."[27] But he has also said later in the same paper, "...Anita Desai's *Cry, the Peacock* which, undoubtedly, is next to Raja Rao's book, *The Serpent and the Rope*, the most poetic and evocative Indo-Anglian novel.

Poetry divorced from time and action cannot raise the stature of a novel; but considering the themes of Anita Desai's novels, it can be safely said that she has used this technique effectively. Her novels, may have several other defects, but poetic language has enriched all her novels. In fact, the first impression that a reader gets when one reads them is the poetic quality in them, than anything else.

Time Literary Supplement, has recognized her novel the *Cry, the Peacock* as a lyrical novel. The novel is not an ordinary one based on the critical evaluations of the readers. The readers, no doubt, would have found it difficult to digest as the time sequence and space sequence were not followed in it in the Aristotelean sense of a proper beginning, middle and end.[28] But the general acceptance of the novel tells its own story.

IV

Anita Desai is broadly labelled or in certain places being accused of a "feminine novelist". It is true that she shares some of the qualities which made Jane Austen famous and special, so far as the handling of characters are concerned. She has depicted through her characters feminine personality and feminine psyche better than most other Indo-Anglian novelists. Anita Desai's characters are not all the time searching for a life partner or are they after the glamour or outward show of the society ladies. Hers is a world of the mental preferences and dislikes. D.S. Maini has rightly said it when he writes,

> "*Cry, the Peacock* is typically a feminine novel, a novel of sensibility rather than of action. It has the quality of an orchid and of a flute about it. Its concern is almost wholly with the terrors of existence, and it achieves its effects through a series of exploding and multiplying metaphors."[29]

"Sensibility rather than action" is not an accusation that she alone has acquired as a novelist. From Jane Austen onwards most of the women are branded with the same kind of criticism. Women novelists, often have deliberately tried to paint different pictures, which men seldom understand.

One of the most important point in the life of a woman is her sense of vulnerability. From childhood she is taught repeatedly by parents and also they learn by themselves that their life is vulnerable. Always there is the risk of running into problems, wherever, they go or live. Maya is an embodiment of this feminine sense of vulnerability, which indirectly prompts her into actions which in turn may appear as 'feminine' or female oriented. D.S. Maini writes in this connection,

> "Perhaps vulnerability is of necessity tied to Maya's extreme sensibility; she who notices, and even sensually experiences, the colour of every sunset, the scent and shape of every blossom, attributes to these things a uniqueness and value which others would not observe, much less cherish."[30]

Her heroines often play safe and keep their ideas to themselves. It would have been impossible for Maya to open up her mind before Gautama. Her ideas about him are always kept as secrets from him. She has her own battles to fight and scores which are not very clear are to be settled. Maya's anguish and her feminine ideas often find expression to our utter dismay,

> "He is the one responsible for this for making you believe that all that is important in the world is to possess, possess riches, comforts, posies, dollies, loyal retainers all the luxuries of the fairy tale you were brought up on. Life is a fairy tale...." (p. 115).

In another sentence she passes the death verdict on Gautama,

> "The man who had no contact with the world, or with me. What would it matter to him if he died and lost even the possibility of contact? What would it matter to him? It was I, I who screamed with the peacocks, screamed at the sight of the rain clouds...." (p. 175).

In *Voices in the City*, Anita Desai narrates the story of a Bohemian brother (Nirode) and his two sisters (Monisha and Amla). They had another brother Arun, who went to England for higher studies. The parents are separated and the father is a drunkard. N.R. Gopal says, "In this novel also Anita Desai has portrayed feminine psyche mainly through the character Monisha...."[31] "Monisha is similar to

Maya in that she is also childless, sensitive and a victim of ill-matched marriage."[32] Her own ideas and her vulnerability are noteworthy. She lives in her husband's family with too many members. Though she has a room of her own, her sisters-in-law without hesitation barge into her room discussing her sarees and her blocked fallopian tubes, leading to sterility. She says,

> "I think that what separates me from this family heaving and rolling beneath me in its dreams of account books, pensions, examination results, stores, rooms, births, marriages, ovaries, wombs, dowries, locks, keys, property, litigation, wills, bequests, orphans, adoptions, relations, marriages, birth and property."[33]

She feels cut off and vulnerable and her actions are defensive and often calculated to protect her interests. In *Fire on the Mountain*, Nanda Kaul, the wife of Prof. Kaul, the Vice-Chancellor, in her later life :

> "... treasures her privacy and the care and concern with which she guards it give the impression that it is her defence against the intrusion of some unhappy experiences of life which still haunt her and which she wishes to ward off."[34]

Nanda Kaul also feels vulnerable here.

Women writers, everywhere, have preference to write about women characters and often such preferences are seen as limitations of their creative abilities. Some critics have gone a step further and said that Anita Desai's novels are written around women characters whose marriages are broken or ill-matched. But this does not pause a problem for her to explore the feminine preoccupations in the lives of the characters. Most of her characters (heroines) are important for their extreme sensitivity, especially against a male dominated society and also for their neurotic behaviour patterns. A daughter-in-law like Monisha in *Voices in the City*, stands against the normal picture of a domesticated one who sacrifices her life for the family. In this novel she finds herself at odds and commits suicide.

"Motherhood is the ultimate objective of the woman and that

is why the importance of and craving for children,''[35] play a very important role in her novels. Anita Desai started with the character of Maya, a childless woman. She continued this theme with Monisha in *Voices in the City*. But she has presented women in her novels who are mothers. But her portrayal of women who are childless are more effective and far-reaching. The sensibilities of women who crave for children and their passion for the normal type of life, even when outwardly kept under wraps, betray their feminine feelings. In *Where Shall We Go This Summer* and in *Fire on the Mountain*, she has portrayed women with children. In *Where Shall We Go This Summer*, Sita is perturbed by the idea of giving birth to a fifth child. N.R. Gopal logically argues in this connection,

> ``Against all sane advice she goes to the island in an advanced stage of pregnancy. She lives in the world of Fantasy thinking that going to the island and thereby to the world of childhood she could prevent the biological process of delivery.''[36]

In Anita Desai, the feminine characters suffer a lot for not having children but those characters who have children are also not normal in their behaviour patterns. Both are neurotic.

> ``The debunking of the myth of motherhood runs a continuous thread in Anita Desai's novels. The mother in *Cry, the Peacock* is acerbic, and too involved in the social welfare, activities pay much attention to the travails of children in the family. She is running creches, she is keeping track of her husband who is a freedom fighter and she has little time or patience to render help to the distraught Maya.''[37]

Some critics have gone deep into psychology of some of these writers and their heroines. The educated independent women who brush aside the male dominated world as silly and meaningless, have gone ahead as insurgent and have raised a literature of protest. She has cited the examples of George Eliot, Virginia Woolf, Jane Austen and the Bronte sisters. Anita Desai joins this illustrious company of female authors who have created memorable heroines and other characters who continuously fight for their rights, and assert their individuality. They are often faced with a choice between conviction and conformity. They always choose the former though they have to face the violent tides of the society against them.

It is interesting to note here the meaning of such delineations of characters. What do they contribute to the society? Have they served their families or their children? By failing in every field and by showing their rebellion only, what has the author succeeded. Does it mean that modern day family life in India is nothing but a Wasteland, where no drop of rain falls, even in the end? Such questions remain unanswered. The heroines don't show any sign of reforms. Can they betray all norms and family life. How many women in Indian set up are ready to carry on a gossip and discussion on blocked fallopian tubes openly in such an age of science and technology. But as Shanta Krishnaswamy points out in Anita Desai,

> "Being a woman is problem. All the rules and restrictions against which little girls chafed and women grumbled about were designed only to block all routes to escape from the conventional mode of living, from 'society that beastly tamer'...."[38]

Anita Desai has taken pains to depict women of all ages and groups. Maya is a married woman, Raka a child growing into girlhood. Nanda Kaul and Ila Das are old women. Among them one comes across women of different types. Maya is hyper sensitive and neurotic, Monisha an intellectual type and Sarala (In Custody) a woman who cannot see life beyond the four walls of the house. There are women presented as keeps (Lotte in *Baumgartner's* Bombay) and women who enjoy overt or secret relations with men of their choice, without bothering about the rules of the society. According to N.R. Gopal, "In different novels Anita Desai has portrayed different facets of human feminine psyche."[39] Thus, she has succeeded in presenting the feminine psyche with all its variety and shades. How far such characters have succeeded in their lives is another point altogether. It is also not clear how their rebellions or self-assertions are going to correct the aberrations which have crept into the society. If such characters stand simply for themselves and for the sake of feminine psyche only what contribution they make to the onward march of the human race is not clear. A Wasteland is not important to Man. But if such presentations of characters can help in the better understanding and correction of some aberrations in the society it will serve some purpose. Anita Desai's characters are not important in themselves. But if men understand the suppression and oppression of women in the society, it will serve to correct certain attitudes. On such a term it is important.

V

Anita Desai's novels are studied and researched today not so much for the outward action but for the psychological treatment of the themes. The title of 'psychological novel' was applied to the fictional works of a group of novelists like Mrs. Gaskel, George Eliot, George Meredith, Joseph Conrad and Henry James in the beginning. The term got its real meaning and purpose when Marcel Proust, Dorothy Richardson, James Joyce contributed their works to the movement. Virginia Woolf and William Faulkner wrote novels about 'moments of feelings' rather than 'matters of fact.'[40] Such novelists have internalised action going by the sensibility and experiences. Henry James writers about experience and memory,

> "Experience is never limited and it is never complete; it is an immense sensibility, a kind of huge spider-web of the finest silken threads suspended in the chamber of consciousness and catching every air-borne particle in its tissue. It is the very atmosphere of the mind; and when the mind is imaginative much more when it happens to be that of a man of genius — it takes to itself the faintest hints of life, it converts the very pulse of the air into revelations."[41]

This kind of novels became famous as 'Stream of Consciousness' novels or as 'interior monologues'. Shri Ramesh K. Srivastava defines it as,

> "The Stream of Consciousness novel usually connotes uninterrupted, ceaseless, disordered and chaotic flow of the consciousness of its characters including their varied sensations, disjointed thoughts, memories, associations and reflections which find

> expression in a stream of words, symbols and images corresponding to the pre-speech, non-verbalized disjointed, illogical levels of mental-emotional life."[42]

Anita Desai considers the outside world and action only as a tip of the ice-berg, the bulk of which remains submerged. Through her novels, she tries to bring about the submerged portion of it. *Cry, the Peacock*, is considered to be the first psycho-analytical fiction (novel) in Indo-Anglian Literature. Anita Desai has succeeded in bringing out the mental fulminations and unhindered thought processes of its heroine, Maya, who is revealed as a hypersensitive and neurotic female character, who causes a lot of harm not only to herself but also to a host of others including her husband. Ramesh Srivastava is right when he says,

> "Desai has skillfully given an elaborate description of Maya's mounting agony which makes to the novel a fascinating psychological study of the protagonist's neurotic fears and throbbing anxieties. Maya's nervous imagination magnifies everything out of proportion — a petty remark, a trivial situation, an insignificant thing or an unimportant incident — and these evoke in her a neurotic response reminding her, by association of ideas, of her approaching death."[43]

Thus, the Rangoon creeper appears to her as a snake, the shadows of trees move towards her with terrible speed and remind her coiling snakes. The hill orchids, appear to her as a symbol of death, as they have very short lives. Her neurotic personality creates and recreates frightening images and she becomes convinced that she has been caught in the net of the inescapable and there was no possibility of mercy.

Maya suffers from "father obsession" or what is known as 'father-fixation' which prompts her to marry Gautama, a man twice as old as herself. In spite of such a marriage she is able to switch her love and affection to her husband. "But Maya still hooked on to the past, clawing on to her rosy memories, refuses to grow with the passage of time and her changed circumstances."[44] Added to this the temperamental differences in their personalities play very important roles. Maya gets pleasure from her sensations and emotions while Gautama is intellectual, systematic, and rational and pragmatic. These temperamental differences are the main reasons for the communication gap that develops between the two of them.

Maya becomes alienated and lonely. It is in such a state of her mental set up that the prophesy of the albino priest that one of them would meet with death quite early in life switches on her thoughts. "Death! he finally, admitted, in one such moment, 'to one of you, when you are married — and you shall be married young' " (p. 30). The death of Toto affects her so badly as it,

> "...could warm, passionate, faithful, uncomplaining, unphilosophizing, intimate and closely attached to her. For her Toto represents everything that Gautama is not."[45]

The call of the Peacock itself is a symbol of love and death: The cry of the peacock haunts her nights.

Anita Desai's preoccupation with women of disturbed mental status often takes us to the level of subnormal and women nearing the border of lunacy. N.R. Gopal has correctly pointed out in this connection,

> "Anita Desai not only explores and portrays the feminine psyche of a common woman but also of the subnormal bordering on abnormal women. These are the women who because of various factors are under so much of mental stress that they cannot be called insane but then certainly they are not normal."[46]

Voices in the City, (1985) is specially noted for the similarity of its title with that of her novel, *Cry, the Peacock*. The titles are based on sounds or noises coming from a distance, which disturb the characters. The locale for this novel is Calcutta, with which Anita Desai was familiar. The novel is divided into "Nirode", "Monisha", "Amla" and "Mother". These titles explain the importance of the characters in this novel. N.R. Gopal has stated in a nutshell the story of the novel when he writes, *Voices in the City* is "The unforgettable story of a Bohemian brother and his two sisters caught in the cross currents of changing social values.''[47] Monisha is presented in this novel by Anita Desai as an intellectual woman who is suffocated in congenial atmosphere of her in-law's house. She just like Maya finds herself unhappy in the house of her husband. She is also alienated from him. Religion does not give her shelter as she is an intellectual woman. Her loneliness and her unhappiness drives her to commit suicide by fire.

Another character developed by the novelist in contrast to Monisha is Sarala a well-to-do lady and wife of a friend of Nirode. She is fond of drinks and Anita Desai has developed her as a woman of questionable character.

Monisha's mother is a very beautiful lady, polished and somewhat level headed. She is also refined and sophisticated with good tastes. After the death of her husband she develops an affair with one retired Major Chadha, which created a rift between her and other family members. Anita Desai has explored the minds of ``unwomanly'' women to show that they don't want to have children or that they are barren. This is true in the case of Maya (*Cry, the Peacock*), Monisha (*Voices in the City*), Sita (*Where Shall We Go This Summer?*), and Nanda Kaul (*Fire on the Mountain*). Sita shudders at the idea of giving birth to her fifth child and she withdraws herself into an island of her choice. Earlier she tries to settle scores with Raman's family by smoking openly, while even men of the family do not do so. She gets upset by trivial things in the novel.

Anita Desai is not simply satisfied with the portrayal of young and middle aged women alone. Radha in *Fire on the Mountain* is a girl who is placed by the side of Nanda Kaul in the novel. The title of the novel is specially connected with her as she only starts the fire. The traumatic childhood of this girl upsets her life and she is turned into an introvert. Her refusal to play with toys, in fact, makes her a special child, who is different from others.

In sexual matters also characters like Maya and Sita have different ideas. Maya feels deprived of such pleasures, while Sita considers it a quality nearer to beasts and hates it.

It is interesting to go through the different novels of Anita Desai. They are not narrated in a chronological order. Her novels are reflective and past and present, childhood experiences and those of later life intermingled and carefully mixed up in such a way, that one feels obliged to Wyndham Lewis for his comments on a "Stream of Consciousness" who, "robs work of all linear properties, whatsoever, of all contour and definition."[48]

Anita Desai stands tall as the pioneer in the field of Indo-Anglian novels. Ramesh Srivastava has summarised her role in the field when he writes,

> "It is not only in the subject matter, characterisation and in presenting the atmosphere of mind but also in the use of narrative technique, symbols, images and the disturbed time-scheme that Anita Desai deserves to be called a psychological novelist."[49]

VI

Anita Desai's characters are all lonely and haunted by various obsessions. The story-line is, often, limited and helps in the vindication of the characters, through analysis of their psychic disorders. Her works are now categorised along with existential ones. N.R. Gopal's comments are worth quoting when he writes,

> "Aspects of Existentialism are in evidence in the total framework of her stories. Its emphasis on the alienation of man from an "absurd" world, his consequent estrangement from 'normal' society, and his recognition of the world as negative and meaningless — presents the sensitive individual, fragmented and spiritually destroyed by the particular social conditions of life, a life complex enough to make him obsessed."[50]

Individuals who feel segregated through their thinking process alone form the backbone of her novels. Individuals strife not only with the social customs, the feeling of isolation and meaninglessness also play an important part in her novels. According to N.R. Gopal again,

> "Maya, Nirode, Amla, Monisha, Sarah, Sita, Nanda Kaul — all suffer from a sense of isolation that is not merely physical but also psychic. What is more, their respective personality traits and attitudes

> also determine the mental and emotional effect on their isolation. This estrangement from which they suffer is, in fact, the consequence of the absence of desired relationships rather than the absence of contacts, the lack is not of company but of companionship. They find themselves alone and anxious in a world in which they are unable to establish emotionally satisfying social affinities."[51]

Ramesh K. Srivastava is right when he says,

> "While most of the women characters are sensitive, the male characters are not and as such, they often aggravate, even cause, the problem of women characters. Gautama is detached, philosophical and rational and even inconsiderate....In *Bye, Bye Blackbird*, Adit is insensitive to the sufferings of Sarah, ... Raman in *Where Shall We Go This Summer*, fails to understand the problems of Sita.... Preet Singh in *Fire on the Mountain* rapes and kills Ila Das very brutally."[52]

There are several such characters in her novels who are self-centred and insensitive to the requirements of women characters, which push them to the background, forcing them to suffer loneliness, neglect and frustration. It is a real fact as Ramesh Srivastava says,

> "Some of Desai's characters suffer from various complexes and psychic diseases. Therefore, some traits in their temperaments which, when developed out of proportion with the rest, check the healthy growth of personality. Anita Desai shows her depth in human nature by depicting the gradual conversion of a trait into characters neurotic."[53]

The most famous examples are Maya's father-fixation and Nirode's claustrophobia. They finally feel lonely, helpless and hopeless. The existential qualities appear clearly in them.

Western writers like Rimbaud, Hopkins, Lawrence, Virginia Woolf, James and Proust influenced her. According to N.R. Gopal, "These Western novelists and poets suited her purpose and she makes, like them, the use of flashbacks and stream of consciousness technique in some of her novels.''[54] It was easy for her to move from psycho-analysis to existential elements. According to Ramesh K. Srivastava, ''It is obvious that existential predicament — the fact of death as the ultimate condition of man and the resultant sense of despair — is the aesthetic centre of Desai's fiction.''[55] In *Voices in the City*, the author tries to bring out the ''dark domains of the psyche of three characters, Nirode Ray and his sisters, Monisha and Amla.''[56] The city itself is a spirit dark and evil in the novel. ''...brutal voices and manifold demonic voices assumes the role of a 'living spirit'.''[57] The author has used many words and phrases to refer to the evil nature of the spirit of the city like, ''beastly blood thirsty Calcutta,'' ''the devil city'', the ''monster city'', ''the city of Death'', ''the City of Kali'', ''Goddess of Death'', and as such the symbol of death is woven into the story neatly and unobstrusively. G.S. Balarama Gupta while analysing her *Fire on the Mountain* has stated, ''Philosophically, Anita Desai's *Fire on the Mountain*, is a lyrical fictionalisation of the quintessence of existentialism.''[58]

According to Anita Desai, though art is like life, and reflects it, it is not life. According to her, ''...life is reality you see on the surface — the visible world while literature plunges the depths below that lie hidden and need to be explored and described.''[59] Therefore, she is correct in her approach and through psychological analysis of her characters, which often resulted in the depiction of frustration, rootlessness, hopelessness and longing for death as an ''orifice'' to escape from all the tensions of life.

VII

Anita Desai, has come in for criticism regarding the structure of her different novels. Often there is a criticism that her novels do not conform to any particular structure. Darshan Singh Maini calls her first novel *Cry, the Peacock*, a novelle, and says,

> ''The fact that Part I and Part III of the novel are a 3 page and 7 page affair respectively will show the ambiguity of the exercise. As Prologue and Epilogue, these pages may be justified, but they are too thin to carry conviction as 'parts of a novel'.''[60]

Part 1 and Part III are third person narratives while the second Part is a first person narrative from the mouth of Maya, the heroine. It means the beginning and the concluding parts are the versions given by the author herself. He further writes, "The middle story with its wave like, sinuous movement is, thus, best rendered through her own consciousness and in her own agonised idiom."[61] In Indo-Anglian literature what distinguishes Anita Desai, is her preoccupation with the psycho-analytical method, adopted for her novels. Unlike other Indo-Anglian writers like Kamala Markandaya, Nayantara Sahgal or R.P. Jhabwala, she is not interested in the social, political and economic aspects of life. Shyam M. Asnani has correctly pointed out,

> "Her forte is the exploration of the interior world, plunging into the limitless depths of the mind and bringing into relief the hidden contours of the human psyche. This main thrust on the inner life of the individual, on myriads of inner impressions, passing fancies, and fleeting thoughts, together with her razor-like sharp awareness of the futility of existence is perceptible in each of her novels."[62]

Such being the compulsions of her art and her priorities, naturally the structures of her novels suffer and the psychology aspects dominate in her novels. Still, it is not necessary that a writer has to divide her novels into such outward divisions.

Anita Desai, is not a creative writer and a critic at the same time as had been the case with Edgar Allan Poe, Nathaniel Hawthorne, Henry James, T.S. Eliot and E.M. Foster. But it is not fair to accuse her of ignorance as far as the principles guiding fiction as such. Through various articles and interviews she has revealed a good part of her artistic approaches and compulsions.

Anita Desai has already made it clear that the external action constitutes very little while we consider the ice-berg as a whole. It is simply one tenth of it. What she tries to do is to discover the nine tenth of the life, which lies hidden underneath. Her pre-occupation is with truth. The discovery of it. The unravelling of its meaning and interpretation of it. Anita Desai has expressed her opinions clearly on this point when she says that the novels of Dostoevsky, Henry James or Proust,

> "...When one reads such novels one realizes the power of a novel to convey truth far more vividly, forcefully and memorably than any number of factually correct documents, exhaustively detailed histories or excellently documented biographies."[63]

The external structure of her novels, what we call the physical structure of it, is not the actual structure that she intends to give to her novels. "The centre of the fictional construct becomes some dominant consciousness artistically realised."[64] If we understand this consciousness, there is no difficulty in understanding the form and construct of her novels. The critics who find fault with the external structure of her novels, actually do not remember this fact. She does not lay any emphasis on external plot construction. She does not like to impose a story over the character, or else the stream of thoughts or consciousness is lost for ever disturbing the form and action of the character. Asnani says in this connection, "Whatever action there is in her novels is part of the integral whole composed of the human psyche, the human situation, the outer and inner rhythms."[65] Therefore, the arguments that her novels have no proportionate sections or proper plots are made on the basis of pre-conceived ideas. Her novels are to be studied and evaluated on a different plane. Conventional methods and scales cannot be applied to her novels. Ramesh K. Srivastava writes about *Cry, the Peacock*,

> "The story of the novel operates on two levels : factual or the surface level, as seen by Gautama, the fancied as experienced by Maya. The reader has the advantage of knowing both."[66]

Anita Desai has variety in her plots. It is a truth that her themes, characters and plots are not repetitive. N.R. Gopal has rightly pointed out, "Each book has an individual structural pattern of its own. However, all the mechanisms she employs tend the work a unique harmony where incidents, people, situations combine to produce an artistic whole."[67] But it is difficult to believe his assumption that her plots are, ...not so much deliberate contrivances but outgrowths of the themes and the slow movement of the story. Anita Desai's own admission that she starts writing without having very much of a plot in her mind or on paper, need not be taken for its face value. The plots in her novels are connected with the vision of the whole action and its harmony in its totality. In fact, Anita Desai herself admits, "One should have a pattern and then fit each piece, in keeping with the others and so forming a balanced work."[68] This "pattern" wherein, she fits in the pieces is exactly what we call a 'plot'. Therefore, one has to admit that she imposes a level of form on her novels. N.R. Gopal has also stated that her novels have proper style and design. He, further, writes, "All the components of the novel *viz.* plot, characterisation, description and setting, the narrative method and style are subject to its shaping pressures."[69]

After a survey of her different novels one gets the impression that her works are not architectural marvels, as far as their structures are concerned. But certainly she has succeeded in blending her themes with characters and situations. As such, for the purpose of special effects for her psychological novels she has used her design in a special way, so that the purpose of Unity is achieved, though not outwardly or physically but through proper amalgamation of her themes, characters and incidents which take place in her novels.

She herself has explained how she gives shape to her novels, "I believe the idea — which may be no more than a leaf dipping under a rain drop, a piquant scrap of news casually read, a face seen in a bus — comes into being as silently and unconsciously as a grain of sand inside an oyster. There it grows and develops, silently and almost unconsciously. ...Eventually this grain grows into such a mass that it begins to exert a pressure. It no longer resembles a pearl that has come to birth in silence and secrecy and lies pale and lustrous inside a closed oyster, but becomes like a monster that one has inadvertently brought to life and that is now bursting and clamouring to be let out."[70] She further says that she has no control over it and it grows of its own volition. Only when it is out on paper she has any semblance of control to domesticate it. Thus, her novels are just like in their origin and development.

REFERENCES

1. N.R. Gopal, *A Critical Study of the Novels of Anita Desai*, Atlantic Publishers, New Delhi, 1995, p. 4.
2. *Ibid.*, p. 2.

3. Shyam M. Asnani, "Desai's Theory and Practice of the novel" in Ramesh K. Srivastava (ed.), *Perspectives on Anita Desai*, Vimal Prakashan, Ghaziabad, 1984, p. 5.
4. Ramesh K. Srivastava, "Anita Desai at Work : An interview" in *Perspectives on Anita Desai*, Vimal Prakashan, Ghaziabad, 1984, p. 213.
5. *Ibid.*, p. 217.
6. *Ibid.*
7. Darshan Singh Maini, "The Achievement of Anita Desai", in K.K. Sharma (ed.), *Indo-Anglian Literature : A Collection of Critical Essays*, Vimal Prakashan, Ghaziabad, 1977, p. 229.
8. Evelyn Damashek Varady, "The West Views Anita Desai : American and British Criticism of Games at Twilight and Other Stories", Ramesh Srivastava (ed.), *op. cit.*, p. 195.
9. *Ibid.*
10. R. Parthasarathy, *Ten Twentieth Century Indian Poets*, OUP, New Delhi, 1976, p. 1.
11. M.K. Naik, *op. cit.*
12. *Ibid.*, p. 3.
13. *Ibid.*
14. Anita Desai, "The Indian Writers Problems," in Ramesh K. Srivastava (ed.) *op. cit.*, p. 1.
15. *Ibid.*
16. *Ibid.*, p. 2.
17. *Ibid.*, p. 3.
18. *Ibid.*
19. *Ibid.*
20. B. Ramachandra Rao, *The Novels of Anita Desai*, Kalyani Publishers, New Delhi, 1977, p. 62.
21. O.J. Thomas, "The Enslaved and the Unsolved : The Characters of Anand and Anita Desai", *Quest*, Vol. 12, June, 1998, p. 42.
22. *Ibid.*, pp. 216-17.
23. N.R. Gopal, *op. cit.*, p. 83.
24. B. Ramachandra Rao, "Technique in the Novels of Anita Desai", in Ramesh K. Srivastava (ed.), *op. cit.*, p. 89.
25. D.S. Maini, *op. cit.*, p. 221.
26. *Ibid.*, p. 217.
27. *Ibid.*
28. Som P. Sharma and Kamal Awaste, "Anita Desai's *Cry, the Peacock*, A Vindication of the Feminine", in Ramesh K. Srivastava, *op. cit.*, p. 138.
29. *Ibid.*, p. 220.
30. Ann Lowry Weir, "The Illusions of Maya : Feminine Conscienceness in Anita Desai's *Cry, the Peacock*", in Ramesh K. Srivastava, *op. cit.*, p. 153.

31. N.R. Gopal, *op. cit.*, p. 24.
32. *Ibid.*
33. *Voices in the City*, pp. 138-39.
34. Harish Raizada, in Ramesh K. Srivastava (ed.), p. 44.
35. *Ibid.*
36. N.R. Gopal, *op. cit.*, p. 27.
37. Shanta Krishnaswamy, *The Women in Indian Fiction in English*, Ashish Publishing House, New Delhi, 1984, p. 258.
38. *Ibid.*, p. 213.
39. N.R. Gopal, *op. cit.*, p. 31.
40. *Ibid.*
41. Quoted in Ramesh K. Srivastava, *Six Indian Novelists in English*, Guru Nanak University, 1987, p. 277.
42. *Ibid.*
43. *Ibid.*, p. 282.
44. *Ibid.*, p. 284.
45. *Ibid.*, p. 292.
46. N.R. Gopal, *op. cit.*, p. 22.
47. *Ibid.*
48. Wyndham Lewis, quoted in Ramesh Srivastava (ed.), *Perspectives on Anita Desai*, op. cit., pp. xxv-xxvi.
49. Ramesh K. Srivastava, *Ibid.*, p. xxvi.
50. *Ibid.*, p. 5.
51. N.R. Gopal, *op. cit.*, p. 5.
52. Ramesh K. Srivastava, *op. cit.*, p. xxlx.
53. *Ibid.*
54. N.R. Gopal, *op. cit.*, p. 6.
55. Ramesh K. Srivastava, *Perspectives on Anita Desai*, *op. cit.*, p. 185.
56. *Ibid.*, p. 36.
57. Anita Desai, *Voices in the City*, p. 44.
58. G.S. Balarama Gupta, in Ramesh K. Srivastava, *Perspectives on Anita Desai*, *op. cit.*, p. 185.
59. Anita Desai, *Ibid.*, p. 218.
60. Darshan Singh Maini, Ramesh K. Srivastava, *Perspectives on Anita Desai*, *op. cit.*, p. 120.
61. *Ibid.*
62. Shyam M. Asnani, "Desai's Theory and Practice of Novel" in Ramesh K. Srivastava, *op. cit.*, p. 5.
63. Anita Desai, *Kakatiya Journal of English Studies*, Vol. 3, No. 1, 1978, p. 1.
64. Shyam Asnani, *op. cit.*, p. 9.
65. *Ibid.*, pp. 9-10.

66. Ramesh Srivastava, *Six Indian Novelists in English*, *op. cit.*, p. 295.

67. N.R. Gopal, *op. cit.*, p. 8.

68. *Ibid.*, p. 8.

69. *Ibid.*, p. 13.

70. Anita Desai, ''Anita Desai at Work : An Interview'' in Ramesh K. Srivastava, *Perspectives on Anita Desai*, *op. cit.*, p. 214.

17

The Ironic Presence of Nature in the Novels of Anita Desai

DR. SANDHYARANI DASH*

Nature plays a significant role in Anita Desai's fiction. In the stark, barren and lifeless lives of the protagonists Nature acts both as a metaphor of hope and life and as an ironical presence that sharpens the awareness of a grim existence in the hollow metropolis. Desai's perception of the city is deeply interfused with a subtle awareness of Nature in all its diversity — the flower and the grass, the seasons and the hills, the animals and the birds. While Desai's perception of Nature is in itself quite delightful, Nature also provides a symbolic dimension to the total meaning of her fiction and thus becomes a shaping element of her form and style. Nature in Anita Desai's novels appears basically in its two perspectives: (a) as tamed and enclosed, perceived through the metaphor of the garden, and (b) as open and benign, perceived through sights and sounds.

"I was drawn away from pain into a world that knew no pain" (*Cry, the Peacock* : 21) says the morbid and morose Maya in the presence of the flowers in the garden. Her sad mood mingles with the mood of the flowers as she inhales their scent :

> I bent upon them, inhaling that mist of sad maidenly scent feeling mood merge into mood, sensation into sensation, till there was nothing left but that mist (21).

The spring season comes with the long insistent call of the brain fever bird. The spring is combined with the qualities of the autumn as the trees shed their leaves and new leaves about to

* Lecturer in English, V.N. College, Jajpur Road, District Jajpur.

appear in them. The silk cotton trees are first to flower, "their huge, scarlet blooms, thick petalled solid podded, that made blood-blobs in the blue" (34). The spring in her garden reminds Maya of another spring — the spring of her childhood which was "far more idyllic one" (36) when she had been strolling amidst the vegetables with her father. The Paradisal state of innocence of the garden of her childhood is glorified by Maya when she remembers the breakfast in the garden with her father which was like a feast or a revel of the elves and fairies who "feast on melons and syrups by moonlight". The garden has an element of fantasy attached to it. Maya remembers :

> Our table is laid beside a mandarine orange tree — there is one it each corner of the garden — a little faery tree, with its glossy leaves, and an overload of small, bright miniature lanterns on a carnival night (44).

When Sapru's wife comes to the garden with her loose, straggling hair, sobs and complains against the irresponsibility of her husband, Maya's father feels agitated. He says to Maya, "It is remarkable what a magnet human nature can be for disorder and failure" (45). He cannot tolerate disorder of any sort. He is a man of orderliness, and is systematic like a Mughal garden, "gracious and exact where breeding, culture, leisure and comfort have been brought to a nice art" (45).

The garden of Maya's childhood and the garden at present intermingle as the flow of thoughts cascade down from past to present. Her memory stretches towards the single white blossom outside her room, and the garden strikes her as a symbol of symmetry, pattern and order that are absent in her own life. She finds these values in her father's character and also in the lives of other people, her neighbours whose gardens are well protected whereas her own garden has been neglected. She goes upstairs to the roof and gazes into her own little garden, leaning over the parapet. She also gazes at the gardens of others and searches for a pattern and a design that has "deserted her own life". She soon realises she has failed to take care of her garden; "I have failed to care for my garden for so long now, and the gardener has neglected it" (180).

In Maya's garden of Eden, the snake enters in the guise of the albino astrologer. Maya lies in her chair waiting for somebody she does not know : "I lay back in my chair and breathed deeply, lay there waiting — for summer? for snakes? for the moon? I did not know" (12). She has the vision of the snake in the form of a "giant physical shadow", the shadow of the astrologer and his prophecy. She feels as if in the thick blades of grass, the snake reaches her, lapping her feet. She leaps from her chair in terror "overcome by a sensation of snakes coiling and uncoiling their moist length about me, of evil descending from an overhanging branch of an insane death, unprepared for heralded by deafening drum beats" (13). The seasonal flowers are not there but there are still some beds of petunias which are "sentimental, irresolute flowers" which emanate fragrance that matches her mood to perfection and she stares at them "with the embrace of recognition" (19).

The garden of Kalimpong is Monisha's abode of peace into which she escapes through memory to forget the violence, the crowd and lack of privacy in the city of Calcutta. She experiences a deathlike stillness in the city and most of the time she thinks about Kalimpong and about Jiban's last posting in a district away from the city and the family. She is delighted by the solitude of the jungles; "the aqueous shadows of the bamboo groves and the earth led with great fallen leaves" (*Voices in the city* 116).

In her letter, Monisha's mother refers to the profusion of spring in the garden of Kalimpong. Monisha's dull existence in the house and the lack of any communication with others drive her towards an inner garden, a garden of her own creation. Amla reflects :

> This sister had wandered away, into some unholy garden of her own, stood there now like one of those lifeless statues, on the brink of the stone fountain was dry and what confronted her was no ripple and tickle of cool water but only dry hard flagstones (149).

Aunt Lila's garden is sharply contrasted with the garden of Kalimpong. The "bird of paradise" has long flown from this garden. It is a "dark, unbreathing garden" where "unkown grass housed singing swarms of mosquitoes and spider webs alone multiplied and reproduced amidst the leaves of the plantains and mango trees that had years ago surrendered the desire to propagate and fructify" (148).

Dharma's paintings seem to be the "studies of the finer secrets of nature". Looking at the still pond where the white geese swim silently, Dharma says to Nirode : "So it has, Nirode, like you, I find myself inexorably drawn away from my island back to the main land again" (224).

Nature acts as the agent of change in the taste and attitude of Dev. His strong resentment turns to appreciation as he wanders through London enjoying its natural scenery. The beautiful daffodils in the parks the patches of bright sunshine, the grass under the green canopies of the Kew Garden have a great impact on him. He is intoxicated by the beauty of the countryside. The fields of tall, ripe hay and wheat and barley swaying in the gentle breeze look luxuriantly green and golden. There is no speck of dust, no patch of arid earth, no sign of blight" (*Bye Bye Blackbird*, 126) for miles together.

The island of Manori with the vast smooth sea all around it symbolises Sita's lonely life amidst her own family and the society. The sea is "silk-smooth" which bounds with enthusiasm and sparkles with hope. But the island concretises Sita's feeling of isolation. It "primarily exists in its 'full reality" only in her mind and no more than a "projection of her inner psyche" says Vimala Rao (*Commonwealth Quarterly,* 46). Nature thus presented through the metaphor of the island is closed and cut off from all outside relationships. But presented through the sea it is open, benign and wide. The sea stands between the two polarities of the city and the island. Sita's return to the island suggests both renewal and regeneration as well as alienation. To the island where Sita's father had created a distinct social identity for himself and his followers, Sita comes back in search of her personal identity.

The final section of the novel *Where Shall We Go This Summer?* presents Nature in its colourful variety. The description of the monsoon is indeed lyrical :

> The monsoon flowed-now thin, now dense; now slow, now fast; now whispering, now drumming; then gusting. There was never silence — always the roar and sign of tide, the moan of casuarinas in the grove below, tossed and hurled about in grey, tattered billows, the clatter of palm leaves that hung their ragged fingers down and made channels for the rain to spout down onto the roof (*Where Shall We Go This Summer?* 102).

Nature provides joy but it is also an ironical reminder of the grim realities of life. Sita tries her best to forget her sorrow and agony in the island of Manori but the rain persistently revives her memory. "Usually she repressed them with an agonized determination but the rain drumming, thrumming, pouring all about her locked her in, locked her up, forced her to turn on herself" (112).

As the monsoon breaks Sita and her children stand on the terrace to watch the clouds. The clouds are "Kohl-black floating and shifting, and casting a shadow over the "slaty sea" changing it into green-black colour. A shaft of white sunlight is reflected upon the dancing waves of the sea. The clouds remain loose and buoyant. From the terrace Sita and her children watch the sails move in and out of the islands of light.

Sea and water are two dominant symbols in *Where Shall We Go This Summer*?. In the presence of the island and the sea Sita never feels alone :

> She never felt alone. She felt surrounded by presences — the presence of the island itself, of the sea around it and of the palm trees that spoke to each other and, sometimes, even to her. They were so alive (126).

Sita discovers, in the sea, the ultimate intangibility of life. She identifies herself with the jelly fish stranded on the sand bar "washed up by the waves". Sita feels :

> Perhaps I am only the jelly fish washed up by the waves, stranded there on the sand-bar. I was just stranded here by the sea, that's all. I had not much

> to do with it all she sadly admitted, with that black, stripped truthfulness that she could never colour or coat (152).

After her reconciliation with Raman, she realises that "her time on the island had been very much of an episode on a stage" (152) and that she must go back to her routine life of duties and responsibilities.

Nanda Kaul, the protagonist of *Fire On the Mountain* moves away from the mainland and is drawn back to the hills of Carignano for privacy, solitude and tranquility. As the Vice-Chancellor's wife and the head of a large family she had a hectic and disturbed life. She had longed for privacy all through her life and at last got it in the hills of Kasauli :

> Here on the ridge of the mountains in this quiet house. It was the place and the time of life, that she had wanted and prepared for all her life — as she realized on her first day at Carignano, with a great, cool flowering of relief and at last she had it. She wanted no one and nothing else (*Fire On the Mountain* 3).

The garden of Carignano is a projection of Nanda Kaul's yearning for loneliness and privacy. The fresh fragrance of the flowers refreshes her as she walks across the lawn. She enjoys the sight of the phlox bloomed in a border edging the lawn. They are close, white and fresh giving out a scent of "freshness and cool". The garden of Carignano is also a projection of Nanda Kaul's self that is bare and empty. She does not wish to plant a tree in it like any other owner but enjoys its bareness. The garden is as lonely as its owner :

> No she revelled in its bareness, its emptiness. The loose pebbles of the garden pleased her as much as rich turf might another. She cared not to add another tree to the group of apricots by the verandas or the group of three pines at the gate (31).

Through age and experience the garden has arrived at a state of elegance and perfection like Nanda Kaul. The garden is exact and beautiful in its present state and needs no addition. It is made of a very few elements but they are exact and "germane as the strokes in a Japanese scroll" (31). Nanda Kaul does not want any addition to it as she does not wish to add to her own "pared, reduced and radiantly single life" (31). She thinks Raka is an intruder "a mosquito flown up from the plains to tease and weary" (39). Looking at her Raka thinks of Nanda as another pine tree. Her grey saree, a rock, "all components of the bareness and stillness of Carignano garden" (40). Nanda Kaul is surprised to discover that Raka has the gift of disappearing suddenly and silently for hours together. She finds Raka the "perfect model" of what she herself is merely a "brave, flawed experiment". If Nanda is a "recluse of vengeance", her great grand child Raka is a recluse by "nature by instinct". Raka is "born to it simply" (48). Solitude never disturbs her. She never asks for anything. She is very different from other children. She has come to Carignano for nothing else but to be alone, "stubbornly to be alone". Her intense love for Carignano makes Nanda think that Carignano belongs to none else but to Raka :

> Certainly it belonged to no one else, had no meaning for anyone else. Raka alone understood Carignano, she alone valued that, Nanda Kaul knew (80).

Coming home, Tara finds the garden of her childhood neglected and abandoned. The rose walk is a strip of grass, still streaked green and grey which lies between two beds of roses at the end of the lawn. There is a line of trees like silver oak, mulberry and eucalyptus at this place of the garden. Tara thinks probably this is the only place where "bit of cultivation left", everything else, even the papaya and lilies seemed abandoned to dust and to neglect, to struggle as they could against the heat and sun of summer" (*Clear Light of Day* 1).

The rose walk takes Tara back to her childhood. She remembers how as a child she has followed her mother to the garden when her mother was expecting her last child and was advised by the doctor to take some exercise. Tara while walking beside her mother used to scream at the sight of a snail in the garden. Now as she shouts at the sight of a snail, Bim is surprised to see "a grown up woman" playing with a snail. Through the snail, Tara tries to capture the feelings and experiences of her childhood. Her reluctance to accept the passage of time is further reinforced by the image of the monotonous sound produced by the coppersmiths beating on the metal in the sleeping garden symbolising the fleeting Time : "In the sleeping garden the coppersmiths beat on and on monotonously like mechanics at work on a metal sheet tonk, tonk, tonk. Tonk, tonk, tonk" (23).

Their garden is neglected like those of their neighbours which are also "still, faded and shabby as theirs". These gardens are overgrown and teemed with "wild, uncontrolled life" (34). But in the garden of Hyder Ali there are roses of different variety. Tara wonders, "Why could they not have such roses too".

Thus, in Desai's novels garden signifies privacy, security and pattern. It is polarized against the city which stands for human vulnerability, insecurity and violence. In the chaotic and ambivalent world of the protagonists it is the only benign presence which seeks to strike a harmony between the past and the present. It symbolises the soothing experiences of the past as well as the unhappy predicament of the present. It is in this respect that the garden becomes an integral part of the form of Desai's fiction.

A sense of insecurity, horror and bareness pervades the landscape of Delhi in the novel *In Custody*. When Deven comes to Delhi for an interview with the poet Nur, he perceives the landscape of Delhi in terms of "white dust and yellow weeds, the leafless thorn trees, the broken fences, isolated tin and brick shacks and the scattered carcasses of cattle that littered the landscape and yet rendered it more bleak and more bare under the empty sky" (27).

The neem tree which has grown outside the wall of Deven's house has branches spreading out to the courtyard. Deven's wife Sarala wants the branches to be cut down as they keep out the sun, but Deven forbids her to do so as the tree gives them shade during summer. Deven feels caged by marriage, family and job. He spends the life of a prisoner and does not find freedom anywhere. He looks up at the sky to find out some chink that could promise or assure an escape from his present state of existence. But Nature does not provide him any solace. He finds the stars "smothered and murk". They do not promise any hope. The "nocturnal breeze" brings no message. The leaves of the neem tree are dry, still and lifeless. The starkness and lifelessness in nature reflect the drab and unexciting nature of life :

> Out in the lane a bullock cart creaked by the wooden wheels lacking oil and shrieking dismally. Across the canal a stray dog barked in a long monotonous howl of protest. Then there was silence. A long while later it was broken by the sharp shrill whistle of the Janata Express from Assam clattering down the railway line (131-132).

When Deven visits Delhi again in the summer he finds the entire plain laid waste by "months of devastating heat". There is nothing to see except the "sulphur yellow dust". There is not a single crow or vulture to be seen. He observes : "Bushes and grass all appeared to have died; the land was shorn, or shrouded" (187).

The starkness and bareness in Nature correspond to the pattern of life the protagonists lead. In Anita Desai's novels the trees, birds, seasons, hills and gardens symbolise hope, regeneration and freshness as well as the grim reality of existence.

Nature in Anita Desai's fiction plays an important role in shaping the spirits of the protagonists. Violence, murder, madness also occur in the world of Nature. Through its different moods and elements Nature casts a deep shadow over the spirits of these characters who are but helpless victims of a cruel, indifferent and malignant Nature. The elements of violence in Nature are presented through different sights and sounds.

Amidst the flowers and trees in the garden, under the starry night, Maya is conscious of some evil, an indefinable unease. She feels the presence of a "truly physical shadow" like the shadow of a giant tree approaching her, spliting across the leaves and grasses. She feels snakes coiling and uncoiling and lapping at her feet. It is the figure of the astrologer in her subconscious and his prophecy which has been revived in her memory by the death of her pet dog Toto. Maya anticipates another tragedy about to happen.

The blossoms of the lemon tree are stronger, crisper as if the petals are cut out of "hard moon shells" by a sharp knife of mother-of-pearl into curving, scimitar petals" that guarded the heart of fragrance'' (*Cry, the Peacock* 19). But the fragrance and the flowers have no meaning for Gautama. He has always shrugged off Maya's words as superfluous and trivial. Instead of the flowers, Gautama looks at the night sky. Maya sees the stars surging towards them. The stars are bright. They symbolise hope. But in the midst of their shining beauty, Maya is also conscious of the ``still spaces of darkness'' above and around them. She feels as if Death is lurking in these spaces. The darkness speaks about the ``distance, separation and loneliness''. Maya is drawn inward to herself, to her own situations. The sky looks intensely black and soft. The deep dark night always looks beautiful. Maya smells a ``foreign odour'' amidst the scent of the lemon blossoms. She stretches for the stars unhappily, fearsomely as if they communicate an important message to her in a language which she cannot read, ``it was as though I were faced with an important message in a language I could not read'' (27).

The message comes at last; not through the stars but through the moon. The moon, vast and ``ghost white'' casts a shearing shaft of ``stark white'' over Maya's body. The moon is not the benevolent moon of the love ballads and fairy revels but a fearful moon ``demoniac creature'', ``the fiercer dancer'', the ``mad demon'' of the Kathakali dancer heavily masked with skirts swirling and stamping his feet and with eyes shooting ``beams of fire''. The moon brings to Maya's mind the sound of deafening drum beats as if ``it was a phantom gone berserk'' (28).

The spring season begins with the mournful cry of the brain fever bird upsetting Maya violently. It is the spring in Gautama's garden in the metropolis of Delhi which makes her sad and insomniac. In contrast to this, the spring of Maya's memory, the idyllic spring of her childhood is quite different. The spring in her father's garden is full of blossoms in their colourful variety. She sees through them the sky and the vast lawn stretching out towards the creeper-hung bungalow. The garden is full of butterfly, grass, green foliage and flowers. The bare neem tree very carefully conceals the nests of the birds and children throw stones at them. They send pariah kites high up to the sky that pale from the cold weather's intense cobalt to an ``effete milk washed blue''. Children pick up the radiant billows of the pods of the cotton tree and blow them up in the air and women collect them to sell to the manufacturers of pillows and babies quilts. The pigeon's nests on the verandah are filled with babies who twitter and mutter all day.

The loneliness and insanity in Maya are suggested through several images taken from Nature — the wind, the dust storm, the snake, iguanas and the desert. Maya remembers the beautiful white flowers like tuberose and queen of Night. But all these chaste white flowers lure snakes to their "hearts of scent". The snakes come slithering towards these "virgins of the night" and with their forked tongues "lash and lash again at the heart of innocence" (126). The rats with their young suckling them also spread plague. The vision of the desert makes Maya conscious of her loneliness. The lizards are bleached into albinos by the desert sun. The rats are also a sort of albinos because they live in the dark and hardly expose themselves to the sun. The rats, the lizards, the snake and the desert all intensify Maya's sense of loneliness and an approaching death. She cries out in agony : "The desert is waiting, the rats and the lizards. They will claim the flesh, the winds will carry the bones away. Mind the wind shut the windows. Hide, hide" (127-128).

As storm approaches, Maya turns restless. The description of the cloud is lively and metaphorical :

> In the east the sun glared, one eye glared, so white, so hot, that before its gaze each object, dead or alive, cringed : the white bones on the desert shrank, split and crumbled, and in the jungles, green leaves curled, withered had dead. In the west hung dust clouds, sulphur-yellow, iodine tinged, heavy, gloomy, loaded with the respite that comes before storm, violence, murder (181).

The storm comes at last after a long waiting. The servants run shouting through the rooms. They are wildly excited and run here and there to see whether the doors and windows are locked. Maya feels like a dancer who, waiting to go on stage, "pounds the earth with uncontrollable feet once the hypnotic drumming begins" (187). She experiences an agony in ecstasy" a "pain in magnificence". Nature becomes violent, becomes "red in tooth and claw" and tells upon the spirit of the protagonist, Maya. She experiences a similar storm inside her : "Here was a turmoil a wild chiaroscuro of oven hot colours that churned over and over in a heat swelled bubble around me. It revolved around *me* about *me*, it was *mine. mine.* this was *mine*'' (*Cry, the Peacock* 188).

The rush and whirl outside provide Maya with the feeling of being lifted off the earth into the sunset, as if released from bondage, fate, death and dreariness and from unwanted dreams and liberty. She runs from room to room laughing. Then the storm abates. The wind drops and the evening comes. It is a strange evening as the atmosphere is still, the wind has dropped, ''tired of storming'' and Maya's thought of Arjuna, her long lost brother brings a faint touch of nostalgia to the evening air.

While the storm reveals the violent and malignant aspect of Nature and its impact on the spirit of the protagonist corresponding to a similar storm inside her shattering the balance of her mind, the cry of the peacocks has an element of pathos in it which sharpens Maya's sense of loneliness, separation and death : The death cry of the peacocks is ''blood-chilling''. Their shrieks of pain ''Pia-Pia-Lover, lover. Mio, mio — I die, I die'' is a cry of agony in the force of approaching death. They fight before they mate. Their dance is a dance of liberation like the dance of lord Shiva. Thus, ''living, they are aware of death. Dying they are in love with life'' (95-96). Their cry reminds Maya of her Death-in-Life existence : ''I heard their cry and echoed it. I felt their thirst as they gazed at the rain-clouds, their passion as they hunted for their mates, with them I trembled and panted and paced the burning rocks'' (96).

She is carried back to her childhood through memory, to the wild tracks of land which remain eruptions of rock and wilderness to her. She remembers the majestic peacock, trailing over a bronze boulder its ''long, burdensome'' tail glittering and gleaming in a '' thousand shades of carbon blue and green and lamp black''. Through the death cry of the peacock, Maya hears the call of the albino astrologer. She identifies herself with the peacocks : ''Now that I understood their call, I wept for them, and wept for myself, knowing their words to be mine'' (97).

The decisive year has come. Maya does not know whether it is she or Gautama, who is to die the fated death. She spends sleepless nights in the moonlight, that ''bland white eye that watched and waited''. Gautama and Maya walk up the stairs to the terrace. Maya feels Gautama's words lost to her in the presence of the moon's vast, pure surface which looks like a "great multifoliate rose, waxen white, virginal, chaste and absolute white, holy in its purity, a suffusing glow of its chastity, casting, its reflection upon the night with a vast, tender, mother love'' (208). Gautama's figure seems to her a "crooked grey shadow'' that "transgressed its sorrowing chastity'' and she pushes him down to the very bottom.

Sita's desire not to give birth to her fifth child is in itself a transgression of Nature. She is afraid of the bloodshed and violence that go with the process of creation. She stands all day on the balcony keeping away the crows that attack a wounded eagle on the roof top of a neighbouring house, "who winced dreadfully every time she heard a child cry''. In that city of flats and "alleys'' crows form a shadow civilization. The crows hop clownishly about the rock, on which the sea breaks "scrambling to catch a rotten fish or scraps of edible flotsam left by the waves to stink in the sun'' (*Where Shall We Go This Summer*? 38). They also sit outside on the ledges and balcony rails of the flats, waiting for the lazy cooks to throw out the kitchen garbage into the alley. They catch them in the mid-air. These "tatterdemalions'' are experts ; in all evil practices that go on in the civilized society like murder, infanticide, incest, theft and robbery, everything is "much practised by these rough, raucous, rasping tatterdemalions'' (38). They whistle in ecstasy and wave their wings as they find a wounded or a baby eagle. They laugh and rasp as they whip it with their "blue-bottle wings'' and tear into it with their "Scimitar beaks''. The eagle tries to crawl into the shelter of the wall's shadow and its "leaf-red'' wings scrape the concrete and then its "Gold-beaked'' head falls to one side. Sita shouts for a stick and stones. But the crows are indifferent. They are used to a certain amount of opposition and aggression from the human population of the city; they could tackle it, ignore it, choking with laughter'' (39).

Sita watches disbelievingly at Menaka when she crumbles a sheaf of new buds on the small potted plant that Sita had grown on the balcony with much labour. Menaka had painted a monsoon scene by using a number of colours and had given an "authentic rendering of rain''. Sita looks at the painting admiringly and then finds Menaka tearing it into pieces because she thinks "they are not worth keeping". All these acts of violence lead Sita to think that "destruction may be the true element in which life survives, and creation merely a freak, temporary, and doomed event" (56). Sita leaves the island and goes with Raman to the mainland, to the city which seems to her a place of solidity and security, "the solidity of streets and the security of houses". But she is disappointed with life in the city", a crust of dull tedium, and she decides to turn back once again to the island, where she would hold her baby safely unborn by magic. The sea would wash the frenzy out of her life : "Perhaps the tides would lull the children too, into smoother, softer beings. The grove of trees would shade them and protect them" (101).

But in the island Sita finds the opposites happen. The children do not enjoy the island. There is always the 'roar' and 'sigh' of the tide. The children are scared of the moaning sound of the casuarinas in the grove, the clattering of the palm leaves hanging over the roof making chinks through which the rain spouts down on to the roof. She finds them "staring at her, watching her as though waiting for her to breakdown and admit failure" (103). It seems to Sita as if to her children life in the city on Napean Sea Road is "right and proper" and this so-called "escape" to the island is madness. Sita does not find the island any more romantic or magical. If it had any magic in the past it is now buried beneath the "soft grey-green mildew of the monsoon, chilled and chocked by it" (103). Sita finds her children moving round and round the ruined house in rain and "whenever their paths crossed every half hour or so, they accused her in silence and she pleaded with them in silence too" (103).

Nature does not remain benign, pleasant and jocund for Sita in the island. It repeatedly reminds her of the futility of her existence and her vain attempts to forget the grim realities of life. The monsoon in the island continues like an "unceasing burial", she finds the children getting bored in the island. Menaka is eager to join the medical college. Karan does not find any game to play in the island. Sita realises that by escaping to the island, she cannot escape life. The children are excited and delighted at the news of their father's arrival. This leads Sita to think of her children as being disloyal to her, disloyal to the island and its wild nature. She feels ashamed of herself. When Raman comes Sita has a heated discussion with him. When Raman finally decides to go out of the island Sita feels herself free and released, like the free sea-bird at evening which "wheeled around and began to circle about and then dropped lower and lower towards her home" (150). She follows the footprints of Raman. She sees on the sand a chain of footprints, one following another precisely, logically. Then together they walk up the stone steps to the grove. Standing on the step, Sita sees the rope dangling from the old *figtree* which the young Moses had tied in the long past when she was a child. She realises that the island belongs only to her father. It does not belong to her. On the eve of her leaving the island the habitants remember her father :

> "Let her go. who cares? We will only remember him, the father. How he lived, and his magic. The island is his, it is really his" (157).

The barren rocks and hills of Carignano becomes the projection of Nanda Kaul's self. She is herself lonely, has kept herself aloof from relatives and the society to spend a life of seclusion in the quiet house at Kasauli. The barren landscape, the lonely pine tree, the rocks and hills of Carignano do not provide her the absolute tranquility of her dreams. It is Raka's intrusion on the one hand and the consciousness of the grim realities of life on the other come on her way.

The screams of the hoopoes are shrill and maddening. Nanda Kaul rushes to pick up a bright apricot which falls down from the tree and is squashed by its fall. Suddenly she finds a bright hoopoe coming down and tearing at its bright flesh and flying off with a lump in its beak. The sight "did not fill her with delight" (*Fire On the Mountain* 4).

The house at Carignano has a history of violence, murder and death. Nanda Kaul had come here with the desire to enjoy the "stillness and calm" but the letter from her daughter Asha perturbs. She leans over the wooden railing at the back of the house where the yellow rose creeper had blossomed "so youthfully" last month but now reduced to an "exhausted mass of grey creaks and groans" again. Her desire for privacy and freedom, which she could never get as the Vice-Chancellor's wife and for which she has come to the hill side is suggested through the image of the eagle :

> An eagle swept over it, far below her, a thousand feet below, its wings out-spread, gliding on currents of air without once moving its great muscular wings which remained in repose, in control. She had wished, it occurred to her, to imitate that eagle gliding, with eyes closed (19).

She watches a lapwing in the mustard fields beyond the garden hedge, "its uneven flapping flight through the funeral moon light". The cries of the nervous bird sharpens her sense of loneliness :

> Herself a grey cat, a night prowler, she watched it till it disappeared in that direction of the river, its cries growing fainter. Then rubbing her foot in the grass, she relished the sensation of being alone again (26).

The garden in the Vice-Chancellor's quarters that was full of trees. Full of too many marauding parrots and squirrels and also too many children who "raided them for fruit" is an extended metaphor of the busy and hectic life of Nanda Kaul among children, relatives and guests. In contrast, the garden of Carignano is an image of bareness and emptiness. She does not want any addition to the garden, which like herself has arrived at a state of "elegant perfection", through a process of age, withering away and elimination. She also does not want to add anything to her own "pared, reduced and radiantly single life". When Raka comes she explores the hills and rocks of Kasauli and gets merged with them for hours together. Like Nanda, Raka wants only one thing; "to be left alone and pursue her own secret life amongst the rocks and pines of Kasauli"(48). She has all the "jealous, guarded instinct" of an explorer.

The destructive aspect of Nature is suggested by images of violence and destruction. The Pasture institute is an image of violence where the doctors make serum for injections for dog bites. They kill the mad dogs and use them for tests. They throw the bones and ashes of dead animals into the ravine and jackals come at night to that place to chew the bones. The "forest fire" is a threat to the quiet and undisturbed lives of the people of the hill side. Nanda Kaul tells Raka that a whole village may burn in a fire that big. Raka hears the cries of animals and birds burning that fire. The next morning she finds "a cindery smell" and a layer of ashes that is deposited on Kasauli like a "grey pelt".

The group of langurs with their destructive habits attract Raka. She runs towards them with Ram Lal yelling and waving her arms as they tear leaves off the apricot trees in search of fruit, pluck the flowers and destroy them, dash into the kitchen and grab at potatoes, "baring their teeth and gibbering at whoever came in the way". The sight of destruction fascinates her. The single house on the hills and another unbuilt one attract her like a "strong sea current". There is something "illegitimate, uncompromising and lawless — that made her tingle. The scene of devastation and failure somehow drew her, inspired her" (90).

Through the image of prey and predator Desai depicts the violence in Nature. The hoopoe catching the 'moths' in the mid-air and 'ragging worms out of earth and fighting with the bulbuls are a few instances of such images :

> .... Closer to closer, the hoopoe promenaded under the apricot trees, smartly and unfurling the striped fan on top of its head. Its young had flown and it appeared to be celebrating, even flounting it's independence, its new youth and freedom. It pounced upon a grasshopper and stabbed it to death with its victorious beak (103-104).

When Illa Das telephones Nanda and informs her of her arrival in Carignano, Nanda Kaul becomes distracted for some time. She babbles on the telephone and Nanda turns her head the other way in an effort to escape but she finds a white hen dragging out a worm "inch by resisting inch" from the ground till it "snapped in two". Nanda feels herself like the worm. The violence in the animal world is slowly transferred to the human world. The boys tease Illa Das like langurs. They swing about her long arm and hoot at her little grey top knot and wobble on top of her head, "whooping and hooting, munching and mooing, they ran to the right and left of her, suddenly swearving to bumb into her small, brittle person, to send her crocheted and moth eaten shoulders bag flying or her umbrella spinning..." (108).

These acts of violence at last culminate in the rape and tragic death of Illa Das by Preet Singh and his gang. In the evening when Illa Das comes through the forest path Preet Singh behaves roughly with her. The figure of Preet Singh emerging from the rocks is a ghastly sight in the still quiet hillside :

> Just then a black shape detached itself from the jagged pile of the rock, that last rock between her and the hamlet, and sprang soundlessly at her. She staggered under its weight with a gasp that ripped through her chest. It had her by the throat. She struggled, choking trying to stretch and stretch and stretch that gasp till it becomes a shout, a shout that the villagers would hear, the red dog would hear, a shout for help (142).

But nobody comes to her help. The fingers of Preet Singh tighten and Illa Das lies dead; "crushed back, crushed down into the earth, she lay raped, broken, still and finished (143).

The news of the tragic death of Illa Das shatters Nanda Kaul's world of reverie into pieces. The illusory world which she had created as on emotional shelter completely breaks down :

> She had dropped the telephone. With her head still thrown back, for back, she gasped : No, no it is all lie! No, it cannot be. It was a lie — Illa was not trapped, not dead. She had lied to Raka, lied about everything (145).

She realises that all the "graces and glories" with which she has tried to captivate Raka are only a fabrication, tranquillizer pills, which helped her to sleep at night. Nanda Kaul's attempt to escape reality like Sita's escape to Manori in *Where Shall We Go This Summer*? is an exercise in self-deception. Complete involvement in "undiluted illusion represented by Illa Das or "undiluted illusion" like that of Nanda Kaul, both eventually spell tragedy (Prasad M., *Anita Desai : The Novelist* 102).

The fire that Raka sets to the forest is expressive of her resolve to destroy Nanda Kaul's world of make-believe. It is not merely an act of violence as Francine E. Krishna says, but also "an act of purification as if she might burn away the lies and deceit of

Nanda's portrayal of her childhood as well as the violence of her own'' (Krishna F., *Indian Literature* 169).

There is always an interaction between the human and the non-human world as much of the imagery this novel deal with the animate non-human features of Nature and the landscape like animals, birds and insects. These images are not static rather they change according to the change within the characters. For example when Raka is strolling with Nanda Kaul and happens to see the langur they seem to her funny creatures but after the traumatic experience in the club with people under masks resembling langurs when she meets the langur for the second time they seem to her like pierrots, clowns and bandits.

The animals and birds which are described in connection with Nanda are benign like domestic hens, house flies or the animals of her imaginary world such as the Himalayan bear, crocodile or leopard. But Raka is described as a wild animal, ``as secretive as a little wild bird, or an insect that hides''. She is also compared to a jackal; ``Raka no more needed or wanted, a house than a jackal did or a cicade. She was a wild creature — wild, wild, wild, thought Nanda Kaul'' (*Fire On the Mountain* 103). Violence emerging out of the human world preys upon all the three major characters of this novel. Nanda Kaul is a victim of the violence of indifference of her husband, Illa Das is a victim of rape and murder, Raka is a victim of the world of her parent that she is born to. All the violence of the human world correspond to the violence in Nature that are expressed through the images of the hoopoes, the hen dragging out the worm, the destructive monkeys, snakes, night jars and jackals. Everything is engulfed by the forest fire at the end suggesting the ``funeral fire'', the fire of purgation :

> Lately her great-grandmother had bored her with it, played it with such threatrical ardour as to make it as unreal as theatre. It made her ache for the empty house on the charred hill, the empty summer-stricken view of the snakes, bones and smoking kilns — all silent, and a forest fire to wipe it all away, leaving ashes and silence (120).

The same image of birds and insects are also significant in *Clear Light of Day.* Tara finds no change in the garden of her parents' house. The gardener has planted jasmines in the garden and of green parrots come to the garden shrieking and settle on the sunflowers and "rip their black-seeded centres to bits" while mynahs hop up and down on the lawn "quarrelling over insects" and Bim's cat gets annoyed when the mynahs' shriek. The scent from the flower garden, a "scent of spider lilies" resembles the fragrance of "ladies newly bathed powdered and scented" for the evening. The uncared for and teeming gardens outside resemble the lack of orderliness in the lives of the neighbours :

> On either side of their garden were more gardens, neighbours' houses, as still and faded and shabby as theirs the gardens as overgrown and neglected and teeming with wild uncontrolled life (*Clear Light of Day* 23-24).

The garden, though a symbol of pattern and order, also turns malevolent sometimes. The experience of Bim and Tara in the Lodi garden in *Clear Light of Day* is ironical reminder of this. The experience is symbolic of the sacrificial life of Bim. It also reveals the escapist in Tara. Tara and Bim visit the Lodi garden with the Mishra family in the spring time. While strolling in the garden, Tara descends down the grassy slope and sees Bim still standing at the top, attacked by a swarm of bees. She is in their midst as if she is their "chosen queen made prisoner" :

> It was a bees festival, a celebration, Bim their appointed victim, the sacrificial victim on whom they had dropped the ceremonial shawl drawing it close about her neck as she stood dropping, shivering under the weight of their guazy wings, their blue-black humming (135).

When Bim is attacked by the bees, Tara escapes from that place frenziedly running to the Mishras for help. She is scolded by Raja for her escapist nature as she leaves Bim alone and helpless.

The thirst of summer, the parched and barren atmosphere of summer correspond to the dry and parched existence of the protagonist Deven in *In Custody*. When Deven returns to Delhi, he stands near the doorway and sees the sparrows nesting in the skylight twitter and quarrel, scattering twigs as they rustle about their nests, somebody outside shouting Su-ra-hi keeping the earthen jars on the back of his donkey. The coming of the devastating summer announced by the 'Surahi' hawker outside is already a felt experience for Deven :

> The call that had seemed to announce summer, heat and thirst — but summer was already here, devastating everything, laying waste his life, like this desolate room (*In Custody* 170).

There are references to "temperature", "heat", "thirst" and summer throughout the novel *In Custody* which are suggestive of the "parched" dry life of the protagonist Deven :

> The temperature that day was a hundred and fourteen degrees. The neem trees along the street dropped stricken, encased in dust. The horses between the shafts of the old tonga stood with their legs sloping under them, their necks swaying between their knees. Even the flies that adhered to their muzzles and flanks had ceased to buzz and crawl and appeared to be stuck on with glee (190-191).

Deven enters a park and sits on an empty bench. He sees the dome and the eastern wall of the mosque. The sun is very bright, almost dazzling his eyes. The enormous arched doorway that soares upwards to the dome looks like a vast bubble. It looks absolutely still, silent as if it is the silent answer to his questioning :

> Since it was silent, he could not hear it, but he felt it impress its shape upon his eyelids, very gently, very lightly, and like fingertips pressing them down to sleep (192).

But the summer with its dryness, its heat and thirst is not going to continue for ever. When the heat becomes unbearable for Deven, he hears thunders in the distance, perhaps, announcing that the monsoon is drawing closer. Deven thinks it has come because he cannot endure the heat and waiting any more.

When Deven receives the letter from Nur, he realises that the relationship between them, between art and the artist, is still inextricable in spite of occasional misunderstanding. Deven has a vision of Nur's bier, heaped with flowers and women in the family crying and wailing around. He hears the funeral music. He imagines that when Nur's body would be placed inside the grave, he would be incharge of the widows and his son. Deven looks at the whirlpool in the water. Nature takes a different colour with the change of outlook of the protagonist. The sky is gradually filled with a grey light. It Is no longer dark. The grey light slowly dissolves the "dense blackness" of the night. It "glistened" upon a field of white pampass grass which wave in the slow breeze. Deven feels that he has already become the custodian of Nur's very soul and spirit by accepting his poetry, which he cannot abandon under any pressure. The novel ends with an optimistic note: "soon the sun would be up and blazing" (204). The possibility of brightness, freshness and regeneration suggested by the sunlight, is also indicative of a possible change in the present condition of the protagonist.

In her latest novel *Baumgartner's Bombay*, the different aspects of Nature are so influenced by the life in the city that they lose their inherent charm and turn insipid, blank and colourless like the lives of the characters. As Lotte observes out of her window: "Right at the top, a layer of sky. A blank sky, as always with neither colour, nor form. Empty, after noon light. Daylight, perpetual light and blankness" (4).

Life in a busy metropolis like Bombay is always on the go, always brisk. People seldom find time to look at Nature during day time. It is also due to the hot sun and the busy life of the day that they come to the sea shore in the evening to spend some time away from the hurly burly city life: "Baumgartner did not turn towards the sea. That was for the evening, when the breeze came up with the tide and the sun fell headlong into the waves, livid and melodramatic in its orange and purple flames and people strolled, for pleasure buying themselves peanuts to eat or coconut to drink from, and one was no conspicuous if one loitered too" (8). But for the protagonist Baumgartner, Nature loses all charm when he finds her mother playing a duet with the young Friedmann : "She smiled at Hugo when he came in but did not stop playing" (41).

Nature becomes a metaphor of indifference; his mother's indifference to his father and his family. Instead of acting as a benign shaping spirit the garden turns out for Hugo to be a disturbing presence. Being too small though he could not discover a meaning in his mother's indifference but surely he felt something for which he did not like to stay in that place for long.

The human world always interacts with the world of nature in the novels of Anita Desai. Nature in her novels acts both as a consoling agent and also as a disturbing presence. It provides solace to the characters by taking them away from the world of pain and suffering and at the same time makes them conscious of the grim existential realities. There is a constant interaction between the inner world of the protagonist and the outer world of nature and in the process of this interaction, an intense vision of the ambivalence of life is projected. In the novels of Anita Desai, Nature thus appears as an ironic presence that pervades life in terms of both its materiality and spirituality.

WORKS CITED

Desai, Anita, *Cry, the Peacock,* Orient, New Delhi (1990).

—, *Voices in the City*, Orient, New Delhi (1982).

—, *Bye, Bye Blackbird,* Orient, New Delhi (1985).

—, *Where Shall We Go This Summer*? Orient, New Delhi (1985).

—, *Fire on the Mountain,* William Heinemann, London (1977) .

—, *Clear Light of Day*, William Heinemann, London (1980).

—, *In Custody*, William Heinemann, London (1988).

—, *Baumgartner's Bombay*, Penguin Books (1989).

Krishna, Francine E., "Anita Desai : *Fire on the Mountain*".

—, *Indian Literature* 25.5 (Sep.- Oct. 1982), 169.

Rao, Vimala, "Anita Desai's *Where Shall We Go This Summer*? An Analysis." *Commonwealth Quarterly* 3.9 (Dec. 1978)

Prasad, Madhusudan, *Anita Desai : The Novelist*, New Horizon, Allahabad (1981), 102.

18

Time as Narrative Device in the Novels of Anita Desai

MS. JAYITA SENGUPTA*

In Desai's novels,

> Thoughts come, incidents occur, then they are scattered and disappear. Past, present, future, Truth and Untruth. They shuttle back and forth, a shifting chiaruscuro of light and shade, of blood and ashes.
>
> (*C.P.*, p. 179)

To match the disconnectedness of thought and sudden shifts of perspective, Anita Desai's method is to 'connect'. The writer's task, according to her is to 'connect' and 'all the time connect' in a process 'that does employ language but also transcends it'.[1] The apparently disparate blocks of narrative find meaning in the novel in the ultimate vision of life where time is at once duration and flow. It is both the life giving and the life destroying force, depicting the idea of Time as the destroyer and the preserver.

The concept of Bergsonian duration is prevalent in all the novels, and in some novels, Desai shifts blocks of time from chapter to chapter. While one chapter would be narrated in the acting present, the next chapter would depict the past in the present tense. This is also to suggest the flux and reflux of the consciousness, where past, present, future lie all mixed together.

The idea is to present time, not measured by clock. Duration or "pure time" is at work, which the consciousness grasps as a "flowing irreversible succession of states that melt into each other

* Lecturer, Rabindra Bharati University, Calcutta.

to form an indivisible process."[2] The novels where the narrative shifts blocks of time are *Baumgartner's Bombay, Clear Light of Day* and *Where Shall We Go This Summer*? The use of flashback and montage in these novels not only act as a narrative device to unravel the past and explore consciousness but also contribute to the narrative pattern in the novels.

In *Baumgartner's Bombay*, the novel opens with Lotte just returned from the scene of Hugo Baumgartner's murder. The novel closes with Lotte again trying to solve the mystery of Baumgartner's life and find meaning in human existence. It is within the framework of the living present that the story of Baumgartner is told in flashback. After the first few pages of Lotte episode, the narrative shifts from Lotte to Baumgartner in 'omniscient narration' shifting now and again to "third person narrator participant" method. As Baumgartner hobbles down the road to fetch something 'tasty' for his cats, his mind cuts back and forth from present to past scenes on the streets. The woman's automatic gesture of edging saree over her face, the straw haired child and the street family busy in the daily chores create the idea of time in its perpetual flow. Baumgartner's mind flits across time and he recalls an incident and his reactions to it. The murderous look of the husband when he had unknowingly intervened in the couple's quarrel leaves an imprint of fear in his mind. The very memory makes his hair stand on end and he hurries past the streets to his destination. Fear as a motive occurs again and again in this novel to 'connect' Baumgartner's past with his future. As Baumgartner reaches Cafe de Paris, the narrative records his introduction to the German drug addict. He recognises the youth to be a Nazi and the discovery recalls to his mind his horrifying past. His instinct is to run and the narrative adequately portrays his fear flowing back from his past in the lines :

> The Camp fire and the beer. The beer and the yodelling. The yodelling and the marching. The marching and shooting. The shooting and killing. The killing and the killing and killing.
>
> (*B.B.*, p. 21)

The force of the stream of consciousness narrative here reveals Baumgartner's consciousness jerking back to past. One thought leads to another in the chain of consciousness to end in an ultimate scream "Killing". While the word symbolizes Baumgartner's most secret fear, it also effects a prolepsis.

As Baumgartner runs away from his fear, the narrative in chapter II moves further back into past. The horizon of analepsis expands to bring the reader into direct contact with the character's history. The narrative technique is cinematographic in its use of flashback from the first chapter to the second. As Baumgartner breaks into a run, in his endeavour to escape from his fear the past sweeps over his consciousness to drown his present. Chapter II, hence, records in the stream of consciousness technique his childhood and his early youth. Here time moves more or less chronologically as Baumgartner relives his past in his memory. However, sometimes blocks of memory cut across one episode to another. The narrative records his disappointment, anguish and shame in the lines :

> You came so late and then 'You don't look like everyone else's mother', he complained. Why don't you look like the other mother's?
>
> (*B.B.*, p. 33)

This is followed by the passage :

> Left alone with her, left behind by his father, he kicked at her with savagery. He blamed her, blamed her entirely.
>
> (*B.B.*, p. 33)

The sense of disappointment here brings to his mind in a flash, two episodes one after the another, overlooking the chronological pattern of events. Thereafter the chapter chronologically portrays the events taking place, like his change of school and home, change in fortune with his father's imprisonment, return and death. Baumgartner boards the ship to Venice and then finally to India and the flashback temporarily ends here.

However, the closing lines of chapter II ".... the boat had arrived ... packing his valise he ran out into the moist dark" (*B.B.*, p. 64) finds connection with the present in chapter III. "But the light was different here" (*B.B.*, p. 68). Baumgartner wipes his eyes with his handkerchief as if awakening from a dream. The narrator once again records Baumgartner trotting down the road to Lotte's house. Through their conversation past once again creeps into the present. Lotte retells and in a way reshapes her past, while Baumgartner listens on, contributing to it from time to time. The past in this novel exists not just as a memory of certain events back in time. The recollection of past here is the revitalising force for the characters to continue with their living in the present. In spite of the differences that may exist between the two, circumstances draw Lotte and Baumgartner together to relive their past with a sense of joy and togetherness. Time appears to be in a sense of arrest as they go through their early days in India. At the same time, their comments on their past appear to give a new ardour to their bygone days. To sum up in Ritcher's words,

> Not only is the past always with us but consciousness is forever changing, and so our memories redefined each moment by the present self and coloured by fresh perceptions are in a state of continuous alteration.[3]

The sleep of exhaustion overtake both as the strain of recollection to carve out joy in their otherwise hapless life drain them out. Baumgartner's mind once again flits back to the past in his dreams. The next chapter takes over from where chapter II had ended in the montage technique. The narrative portrays Baumgartner's experiences, feelings and thoughts on his entry to India. Time and again Baumgartner's recollections of his own opinions on his first encounter with India or his recollections of Lotte's comments on his Indian experience intercede the narrative. Take for example the passage : "What on your very first day you ate curry? And you did not get food poisoning? ... Baumgartner laughed rather proudly" (*B.B.*, p. 88). Such intrusions suggest that these recollections are repetitive in Baumgartner's memory. They flow in and out of his mind and shape his very existence in the present.

Otherwise the narrative in the flashback here records chronologically Baumgartner's experiences in India in the city of Bombay and Calcutta. The reader learns of Baumgartner's acquaintance with Lotte at Prince's and their casual friendship. The details of Baumgartner's luxurious stay at Middleton Row in the Park Street area of Calcutta and of his uneasiness at receiving his letters to his mother returned back to him stamped "Addressee unfound" are also narrated. As the historical happenings overtake once again Baumgartner's train of life, he loses touch with his mother and all his acquaintances in India. The narrative further moves on to report to the reader his experiences in the military Camp. However, the memory of his childhood in Germany remains eternalised in his mind and the narration reveals his intense longing :

> he would crouch and hide, holding him to a desperate wish that Germany were still what he had known as a child and that in that dream country his mother continued to live the life they had lived there together.
>
> (*B.B.*, p. 118)

Chapter V, once again reverts back to present to find Baumgartner awakening from his sleep in a panic. The chapter narrates Baumgartner's walk back to Cafe de Paris for lunch and his second encounter with the German youth. This time on Farokh's, the manager of the Cafe's, insistence he is compelled to bring the German with him to his apartment in Hira Nivas. The unnerving conversation between Baumgartner and the German youth records the latter's experiences in the country. But the German's life being so utterly different from Baumgartner's, exist in the novel only as a prolepsis. The youth's greedy observation of Baumgartner's few precious belongings act as a connecting link for the flashback in the next chapter.

Chapter six records Baumgartner's life after the war and his employment with Chimanlal. After his few horrifying experiences of killing and riots that overtake Calcutta in 1940s, he escapes to Bombay. The narrative for once records his somewhat settled life under Chimanlal's employment. Baumgartner nostalgically recalls his friendship with Chimanlal and their visits to the race course. The mystery of the trophies won in the races with his partner in the preceding chapter is solved here. His first entry into the race course recalls his disappointment, as a child mentioned earlier, on his father not taking him to the race course. The memory of anguish in his childhood flits over time as Baumgartner silently wishes to shout, "Papa, what do you think?... Papa, do you see me here, at the races" (*B.B.*, p. 193).

Here the past once again overlaps with the present in the flashback. While in chapter II the incident was presented in flashback scarcely, the other half is sketched in this chapter. The rhymes in German flow into Baumgartner's mind as he recalls his mother trying to pacify him with a baby game. He had struck out at her in his hurt pride, and the shocked and hurt expression of her mother at his violence, lingers in his memory forever.

The narrative thereafter in this chapter moves on to reveal what prompted Baumgartner to choose cats as his companions and how he finds Lotte again. The movement of time is felt with Chimanlal's death and the son's throwing out Baumgartner from his father's office. The chapter ends with a sense of nullity as if Baumgartner has finished with his life's activity. The sense of nullity cuts across the narrative to meet Baumgartner's ineffectual life of the present.

The concluding chapter closes the story of Baumgartner with his murder. The narrative reverts back to the actual present with Lotte musing over the cards on the table. The novel ends with the suggestion of time moving on and the continuation of life in Lotte. While the alternating chapters in montage technique reveal durational time, the idea of Time as the preserver and the destroyer take over. Durational time exists in the mind of man and the clock time moves on with life in its flow. A narrative pattern is discerned in the novel depending on duration and temporal time. While the beginning meets the end, in between, the chapters in flashback alternate with present and past to suggest flashback within flashback.

In *Clear Light of Day* too, Anita Desai is not interested in mere chronology. Her intention in this novel is to discover "the final pattern of meaning that emerges out of the apparent meaninglessness of life in a small family."[4] This she achieves, by using time as "an elastic medium capable of expanding according to the emotional 'breadth' of the moment."[5] As R.S. Sharma notes, "The four sections of the novel suggesting the four dimensions of time record the transitions that take place in an Old Delhi family.[6] The novel contains in its four dimensional structure, the four aspects of time that is, the passing moments or hours, the durational time, the voyage from youth to age, and the historical time.

The novel begins with Tara awakening to the call of koels in her ancestral home. As She runs down the garden path, the memories of her girlhood years flit past her mind. She recalls her mother pacing up and down the rosewalk and herself chattering and prancing up and down behind her till a snail under a fallen rose petal catches her attraction. Take for example the lines :

> As the stared, a petal rose and tumbled onto its back and she saw uncovered the gleam of a — a pearl? a silver ring? Something that gleamed something that flashed then flowed — and she saw it was her childhood snail
>
> (*C.L.D.*, p. 2)

The passage reveals that the childhood delight and illusion has remained eternal in Tara's mind. She has moved back into past to recapture her feeling as a child.

Memories haunt Bim's mind as well. That even a simple gesture of tugging at her hair can recall an episode from the past is evident here. The lines,

> Bim stood tugging at the hair that hung loosely about her face as she had done when she had sat beside her brother's bed that summer that he was ill...
>
> (*C.L.D.*, p. 2)

are true to Proustian observation of involuntary memory which can be trigged off by even trivial sense experiences. A similar such instance true to Proustian observation follows a few pages later as Tara surveys her room where she had spent her childhood. The sight of parrot bitten guava fruit brings to her mind how as a child she would run to pick up the fruit. The urge remains in her and her "mouth tingled with longing to bite into that hard astringent flesh under the grind hind" (*C.L.D.*, p. 11).

Memories of past cut back and forth into the narrative as Tara muses on the unchanged nature of her ancestral home. The monotony and dullness of the home impinges on Tara's consciousness as she feels the very spirits of her parents in the house. The old long notebooks "with which her parents had sat day after day, year after year ... playing bridge with friends" (*C.L.D.*, p. 22), conjures up in her mind a host of past incidents. One thought leads to another. Tara remembers Raja's anguish and his angry decision to set fire to the cards and the book of bridge records and Bim's desire to snip all the cards. The agonising scene of her father sticking needle into her mother's arm remains eternalised in her memory. The feeling of insecurity and fear remains in the dark recesses of her mind.

As the narrative moves on, the reader is able to grasp certain missing links about Raja and Bim's relationship. Bim's producing of Raja's letter answers the query in Tara's mind and the reader's mind as well about their strained relationship. However, the letter instead of impressing Tara with its obvious implications brings to her mind a fresh set of memories about Raja and Hyder Ali. While these memories along with conversations serve as a source of knowledge to the reader about the characters background, they also reveal a passage of time from the characters' childhood to youth. But memories in this novel like life with its hurdles, do not flow like a river. They move in jumps, as if they were 'held back by locks that are opened now', to let them 'jump forward in a kind of flood' (*C.L.D.*, p. 42). Bim recalls the historical past of the summer of 1947 giving another dimension to the sense of time in the novel. She reflects,

> There are these long still stretches, nothing happens and then suddenly there is a crash . . and then life subsides again into the back waters till the next push, the next flood.
>
> (*C.L.D.*, p. 42)

The chapter ends with the historical time meeting the personal time. Tara crouches against the pillar as if to run away from her youth, Bim too wishes never to be young. The human misery over partition mingles with their personal misery of wasted. The wailing of the cricket in the background echoes the mood of sadness. The lyrical setting of the novel with cricket wailing, Koels calling, Badshah barking, Baba's gramophone roaring lend a musical structure to the novel and suggest a passage of time.

The analepsis expands into the next chapter in a cinematographic technique with the riot in the background. The narrative records Bim's endeavours to pacify Raja's anxieties about Hyder Ali's family and continues to unfold Raja's college days and his associations with Hyder Ali. Slowly the attention of the reader is reverted back to the happenings in the family like mother's illness and death and then swings back to Raja's college days in Hindu College and his fascination for Hyder Ali. The narrative here proceeds chronologically measuring time temporarily with the course of events in the past. The interesting details include Baba's acquiring of gramophone and records from Hyder Ali's deserted house and Begum, the dog's coming into the Das household. Badshah's existence as being Begum's offspring is clarified at this point of the novel. The chapter closes with Bim's ridiculous romance with Mr. Biswas, the doctor, Mira Masi's death and Raja's departure to Hyderabad. With Bim and Baba left alone to fight their fate, the past mingles with the present. However, the next chapter does not pick up threads from this one to swing back into present. Instead, the flashback continues from Tara's point of view.

The narrative in this chapter begins with Tara's impressions of her childhood and Baba's infancy. It moves on to inform the reader of Mira Masi's arrival and the children's encounter with her. The narrative moves on to depict the childhood of Bim, Raja and Tara shared with Mira Masi. While the narration chiefly from Bim's point of view records the later days of Mira Masi, this one records the earlier days. Tara's impressions of fear and horror in the first chapter are expanded in this part of the novel. The episodes of father injecting her mother and her expression, of Tara leaving Bim alone to suffer the stings of the bees are depicted more clearly. However, Tara's memories of childhood also contain some pleasant details. The narrative unfolds Tara's experiences of growing up with her brother and sister. Slowly the chapter reveals over the pages the passage of time with Tara wearing her first silk saree. The chapter then closes with Bim's affirmation of remaining unmarried, to look after the rest of the family.

The flashback ends here and the narrative reverts back to present in the concluding chapter. While Tara for once develops an objectivity to see things and judge them from her point of view, Bim too makes her decision. The complexities and the tangles of the past are somewhat unknotted. However, certain things remain unresolved and Tara's confession does not make much sense to Bim. Tara is relieved only to discover that time as the great healer has made Bim forget the subtleties of the bee incident. Past creeps into their conversations at the mention of Dr. Biswas, yet it is only for the sake of giving a final shape to the present. The most part of this chapter is geared to present and attempts to resolve the complications of the past to move on to future. As the accumulated hurts and insults gather momentum on Bim's mind, she struggles finally to find her way out to solve her entangled emotions in clear light of reasoning. She realizes that no other love had started as far back in time and had "so much time" in which to "grow and spread" (*C.L.D.*, p. 182).

The novel ends with the promise of reconciliation. However, past can never be forgotten. With the instance of Bim giving a start on hearing Mira Masi's name, there is evoked a sense of warning. Bim in her being an example to her nieces should not allow herself to suffer Mira Masi's plight. Listening to Mulk's voice and comparing it with his Guru's, Bims memory harks back to the lines in Raja's copy of Eliot. 'Time the destroyer is time the preserver' is what she realizes. With the stings of Raja's letter being washed out from Bim's mind the favourable part of her memory remains dominant and she awaits future with longing.

In *Where Shall We Go This Summer*? the visit to the island itself is like revisiting the past. Sita's remembrances of her childhood days creep into the text now and then in the first chapter. The narrator observes that, "Sita's feet seemed to remember instinctively, the path that led through them form Moses' small kingdom..." (*W.S.*, p. 16). However, the present experience of the island sharply contrast the past experience. In Sita's memory, the house had white walls, which gleamed chalkily above the waves. But Sita reaches there to find it pitch dark. Even the light of lanterns cannot redeem the darkness and Sita finds the house as "ashes white and waste". But the past that generally creeps into this chapter is a recent one. The narrative here chiefly unfolds the reason for Sita's journey to the island, and in the process reveals the incidents which preceded it. The incidents are narrated in a way to suggest that they are arranged in an order in Sita's mind to clarify to her ownself her decision.

With the concluding passage in omniscient narration about Manori and its symbolical significance the next chapter moves back to the winter of 1947. The narrator records Sita's father's entry into Manori to create his paradise there. The passage like this one :

> She saw the island as a piece of magic, a magic mirror... it took her some time to notice that this magic, too cast shadows
>
> (*W.S.*, p. 46)

sums up·Sita's past and onlooks her future. The narrative thereafter records Sita's days in the island with her father. However, the future and the recent past keep creeping into the narrative and the lines, "Only connect... So she had spent years connecting link by link, this chain" (*W.S.*, p. 68) suggest to the reader's mind that this chapter is not a mere flashback. It is symbolic of Sita's sea of unconscious mind. Her father's shady nature impinges on her consciousness and she fretfully tries to grasp the mystery about his life. Past and recent past cut across the narrative as the narrator hastens to add that "She had to struggle to free herself from the chain or she might have spent her life in the cold meshes" (*W.S.*, p. 63). The story continues to inform the reader about the passage of time with Jeevan's disappearance, father's death and Sita's marriage. The narrative then swings back to present with Sita's planning to visit Manori.

The concluding chapter records Sita's stay in the island and proceeds to contrast it with her fantastical remembrances of it in the style in which the first chapter had hinted on. The novel moves more or less chronologically here depicts temporal time as Sita battles with her conscience to face reality. Incidents from Sita's life in Bombay find way into the narrative. Her casual mention of her dying with one of Miriam's cigarettes in her mouth makes Menaka smirk in distaste. This makes Sita think back in time She recalls an incident from Menaka's childhood when the girl would lie in bed scared about her mother's death. The clock time operates in this part of the novel with the passing of strenuous moments and strained conversations between Sita and her family. The recollections of her life in Bombay creep into the narrative to clarify the present situation.

In *Cry, the Peacock*, past creeps into the present in the shape of Maya's memories of the albino astrologer and of the bear dance chiefly. The writer here, does not shift blocks of time in the flashback or montage technique for long periods. The narrative technique at work is that of stream of consciousness where past intermittently exists with the present. For example, in the Part II of the novel, the passage narrating Maya's conversation with Gautama about the Kathakali troupe in Delhi leads Maya to think of her father. There is flashback within flashback :

> When with my father, even breakfast in the garden becomes a party, as good as revel of elves and fairies .... (As a child, I enjoyed princess like .... the glories and bravado of Indian mythology...)
>
> (*C.P.*, p. 89)

Then suddenly with the memory of peeling oranges, Maya's mind jerks back to the present : "No one, else,... loves me as my father does" (*C.P.*, p. 89).

Time in this novel is at once 'polytemporal' and 'barrier time'. Durational time or polytemporal time operates in Maya's consciousness where past, present and future lie inseparably. 'Barrier time' is at work as Maya believes in the albino astrologer's prophecy of death of either her husband or herself within a span of four years. The concept of time as the preserver and destroyer, is the principle narrative vision in the novel. The look at the end of the novel is described thus :

> Such storms had blown since the time when the earth was desert.... Such storms would sweep the earth and the last traces of these huge masses of creeping, crawling, toiling struggling cell conglomerations that now wracked the earth when the time came for annihilation.
>
> (*C.P.*, p. 187)

Gautama too explains to Maya something similar to the above observation :

> This life you speak of, this little flash-in-the-pan, how insignificant and trivial it appears when compared with the immortal cycle to which all humanity is bound.
>
> (*C.P.*, p. 127)

In *Fire on the Mountain* too time does not flow in a forward sequential movement. There are constant references to the past, as R.S. Sharma notes :

> Nanda Kaul unconsciously seeks to freeze time into a motionless constancy, but time keeps moving through her past which she recapitulates as she reacts to her present surroundings.[7]

Hence, in this novel also, inner time flows independently of the clock time. But psychological time for its existence often depends upon the stimuli from the external world of objects and images. As S. Anant notes, Desai explores the psychological processes of mind, to discover its significance by plumbing depths, "then illuminating those depths till they become a more lucid, brilliant and explicable reflection of the visible world".[8] True to this observation a passage records Nanda's life in these lines :

> ...the yellow rose creeper had blossomed so youthfully...but was now reduced to an exhausted mass of grey creaks and groans...
>
> (*F.M.*, p. 17)

Part I has Nanda Kaul hovering between past and present. Future obtrudes in the shape of a letter announcing the impending arrival of an unwanted great-grand child. Part II is devoted solely to Raka's arrival and her sojourn at Carignano. Here, Desai, very subtly depicts the change in Nanda Kaul's attitude to Raka. In the IInd Part, Raka's gruesome experiences of her days with her parents time and again, surface her consciousness, and she is overwhelmed with fear at the sight of any cruelty. Her visit to the Pasteur Institute to find human beings wearing masks of animal heads shocks her and she runs away from it. Again the charred house on the hilltop which she runs to, on hearing of her mother's fresh illness hold subtle connections with her past. While the past never surfaces clearly as in the other novels, it is subtly hinted at here. The only time it really comes to the surface is with the Pasteur Institute incident, as Raka recalls vividly her father's cruelty to her mother and her.

In Part III, the scraps of Ila Das's conversation with Nanda Kaul however recall the memories of their earlier days. While Ila records their past honestly Nanda pushes it away from her mind to fictionalise it. The agony of her past days find outlet in her groans all alone in the house. It is only in the concluding portion of the novel, she admits her past. "It was all a lie, all. She had lied to Raka, lied about everything. Her father had never been to Tibet" (*F.M.*, p. 145). As her consciousness is unable to bear the strain of accepting Ila's murder and the truth of her futility of existence she collapses to death.

Time in this novel has been unkind to all the characters. With the passage of time, life in *Fire on the Mountain* merely dwindles to decay and death. The archetypal fire of cremation sweeps over the ravines to suggest the ruthless nature of time as the destroyer. However, the ambiguity remains, as the conflagration could also be the symbol of the wrath of Nature to destroy evil in the world. The idea of time as the destroyer in the immortal cycle of destruction and preservation is hinted at in the conflagration.

In *Voices in the City* and *Bye Bye Blackbird*, time is not preponderant as in the other novels. Memories flow from Nirode's mind about his mother's seductive ways in Kalimpong and find symbolic representation in his dreams. His mind revolves round this bitter memory and brings a sense of nullity in his life. With Monisha's death, he strains to solve the riddle of life and sort out his feelings about his mother. In the other novel, *Bye Bye Blackbird,* time follows a chronological pattern. Psychological time manifests itself in the feelings of nostalgia over India or England. As Desai herself admits, this is a very straight cut novel. She remarks that :

> *Bye Bye Blackbird* is the only book I've written that is truly about objective world, objectively observed characters — hence, the lightness of it.[9]

In Custody is the only novel, where Desai does not use the flashback or memories to depict psychological time. However, there is an interesting phenomenon at work in the novel with regard to time. Desai attempts to use here spatial time in some of the scenes in the novel. The idea is to represent in words as in an impressionistic painting the simultaneity of perception. An illustration from the novel will help to qualify this observation.

> ... 'Yes, yes, yes — Murad bhai — is he coming?
> I sent him an invitation too'

> 'He didn't tell me', Deven cried....
> 'Yes, Yes, Yes — I told him to bring you along...'
> 'Imitiaz Begum', called a voice from the audience, 'You are like a star fallen into the well of the courtyard from which we have come to fetch water... Will you give us star poems tonight?'
> 'I can recite nothing — nothing...' 'So had you last drop to help your survive this evening?' She teased them.
> Someone brought a silver box of betal nut and leaves — the smile Imitiaz Begum gave was as sudden and shift as if scissors had cut it through her face, snip, snap....Her audience tittered and she threw them a contemptuous look. Her mouth trembled with tension.
> Deven looked anxiously at the poet who was shifting uneasily about in the cane chair making it creak.
>
> (*I.C.*, p. 80-81).

The passage moves on to narrate Deven's reverie which is broken by 'Wah! Wah!' to continue again. It is interesting to note that Desai is not merely presenting a scene comprising a mass assembled in a situation as in *Madame Bovary*. While "everything sounds simultaneously here"[10] the reader also has access to Deven's mind. The simultaneity of perception is not just external but internal as well. Desai's style hence in this novel in her use of spatial time is peculiarly her own. To recall her opinion on the art of writing mentioned at the onset of our discussion on her technique, "A writer does not create a novel by observing a set of theories — he follows flashes of individual vision."[11]

To conclude briefly, referring to her statement mentioned above, it is the vision of the novelist which underlies the stylistic pattern of her work. The theoretical aspects of time in narrative are used in the novels to reveal the submerged self in human consciousness. Sometimes the author presents dramatically the external occurrences alongwith internal workings of mind at the same time, to achieve simultaneity of perception. Again sometimes the narrative merely depicts the ticking of the hours, minute by minute, or encompasses the idea of the ambiguous nature of time as the destroyer and preserver in her novels.

REFERENCES

1. Anita Desai, "The Indian Writer's Problems", *Language Forum*, Vol. 7., Nos. 1-4, April 1981-March 1982, p. 226.
2. P. Edwards, ed. *The Enclopaedia of Philosophy* (London : Macmillan, 1967), p. 288.
3. Harvena Ritcher, quoted by Asha Kanwar in *The Novels of Virginia Woolf and Anita Desai : A Comparative Study* (New Delhi : Prestige Books, 1989), p. 44.
4. R.S. Sharma, *Anita Desai* (New Delhi : Arnold Heinemann, 1981), p. 130.
5. L. Ruddick, *The Seen and the Unseen* (Cambridge : Cambridge University Press, 1977), p. 14.
6. R.S. Sharma, p. 120.
7. *Ibid.*
8. S. Anant, "Anita Desai's, Fire on the Mountain", *Indian Writing in English,* Vol. 19, No. 1, Jan. 1981.
9. "Anita Desai at Work" : An interview with R.K. Srivastava, *Perspective on Anita Desai,* Ed., R.K. Srivastava (Ghaziabad : Vimal Prakashan, 1984), p. 221.
10. Flaubert, quoted by Joseph Frank, "Spatial form in Modern Literature", *Essential Theories of Fiction,* ed. Michael Hoffman et. al. (Durham and London : Duke University Press, 1985), p. 107.
11. Anita Desai in "An Interview with Anita Desai", by Atma Ram in *World Literature Written in English,* Vol. 16, No. 1, April 1977, p. 100.

19

Multiple Meanings of Marginality in Anita Desai's *Baumgartner's Bombay*

J. WILSON*

The term 'post-colonialism', like 'post-modernism', has become so heterogeneous and diffuse that it defies any clear-cut definition. Over the years it has undergone near-protean transformation as more and more colonial-conscious writers have published powerful works that resist easy generalization by any theoretical parameter ushering in the necessity of encountering them in their own innovative contexts and perspectives. For instance, Frantz Fanon analyses works in the multiple contexts of gender and sexuality, nationalism and hybridity. There are also aspects of post-structuralist, Marxist, feminist and post-modern issues which have become important, often controversial in relation to post-colonial issues. Literature, on the other hand, reflects the long-term effects of the irreversible, complex changes permeating colonised cultures long after the imperial phase ceased. They may be projections of the political scene, as in Raja Rao's *Kanthapura*, racial as in George Lamming's *In the Castle of My Skin*, or seen in the linguistic manipulations as in the works of Raja Rao, Achebe, Naipaul and Lamming.

In India, as elsewhere, the shift from the limited concerns of coloniser-colonised exemplified in Prospero-Caliban complex to a more diversified and complicated idiom relevant to the twentieth century is evident. Today, when the world has become a global

* Reader, Department of English, Sarah Tucker College, Tirunelveli, Tamil Nadu.

village, the Jewish diaspora has given way to a common experience of migration or exile generating fissured identities and hybridities alongside problems of dislocation and dispossession and a larger problem of a lost centre. In the words of Ania Loombia, "the migration of peoples is perhaps the definitive characteristic of the twentieth century, and in crucial ways diasporic identities have come to represent much of the experience of 'post coloniality' (Loombia, 180)." Nabakov, Borges and Beckett deal with the figure of exile in their works. Many Asian writers in England and America like Dilip Hiro, Jamila and Reginald Massey, Hanif Kureishi, David Henry Hwang discuss different aspects of the problem, as have Kamala Markandaya in her *The Nowhere Man* and Anita Desai in *Baumgartner's Bombay* taken up the problem of the 'permanent refugee'. In *Baumgartner's Bombay*, Anita Desai pursues the solitary life of Hugo Baumgartner as he flees Nazi Germany and tries to find a home in a politically-torn India struggling to carry on after British rule.

Anita Desai has made a place for herself in immigrant writing too. Born of a German mother and Bengali father, and currently settled in the U.S., her cross-cultural background added to her first hand experiences as an 'outside' or the 'marginal' in another dominant society account for the unmistakable stamp of authenticity in her novels. Even in her use of the English language where other writers like Raja Rao, Rushdie and Naipaul mould the language to convey a sense of ethnicity, she is, as Meenakshi Mukerjee calls her, "a rare example of an Indo-Anglian writer who achieves that difficult task of bending the English language to her purpose without either self-conscious attempt of sounding Indian or seeking anonymous elegance of public school English" (Dash, 158). With the same sense of detached charm she uses autobiographical material as base for her multi-dimensional novel, *Baumgartner's Bombay*. Asked why she chose to write a novel about a German in Bombay, in an interview, she replied :

> ...And it was when I saw this Austrian Jew in Bombay — I actually saw the man pottering around the streets picking up scraps for his cats — that I began to imagine his past. And that gave me the key to open that German world. And I was able to

> use my mother's memories of pre-war Germany and our own perception of the war far away from India simply as a set of rumours and news that came to us (Libert, 54).

Similarly she was given a cache of real German letters for translation and because they had been so empty they teased her mind. "I had to supply the missing history to them" (Robinson, 42), she says. Hence, Hugo, the protagonist of *Baumgartner's Bombay* emerges as the *Billewallah Pagal*, the Madman of the Cats, whose tragic history inspires yet a flicker of hope in a chaotic world full of sound and fury signifying nothing.

That Hugo was an alien in a strange land, came from a foreign country, was of a different colour, spoke a different language, had a different religion is established early on in the novel. To the couple living on the platform, themselves refugees from a drought hit village, Hugo was a mere non-entity. The woman, as she scourged vessels by the roadside, thought of Hugo simply as "a lump in grey pants" (6), a "nobody, an old man with an empty bag" (8). The watchman generally ignored him or had only a faint smile "but with a twist of distaste at the corner of his mouth" (6). After fifty years in India, the land was familiar to him, but "the eyes of the people who passed by glanced at him who was still strange and unfamiliar to them, and all said : *Firanghi*, Foreigner." (19) The authorial voice sums up his life in four words — "Accepting — but not accepted'' (20). In Germany, his dark complexion marked him for a Jew; in India, he was fair, therefore, ostracised in both countries. Paradoxically, even his cats knew he did not belong — he was not feline — but they accepted him. Lotte, like Hugo, also feels like an exile in Bombay : "Mostly I am alone. All all alone" (203).

All our ideas, our awareness, our self-conceptions are collected from the world around us. As Marx and Engels emphasised, "It is not consciousness that determines life, but life that determines consciousness." Hugo's consciousness of continued rejection and 'otherness' began with his childhood in Germany. The cruelty of racial discrimination dawns on him only after a series of subtle forms of rejection have been forced on his childish mind. Why his mother arrived later after all the mothers had left, with the coveted bourbon after school, why he alone missed his Christmas present, and what the word 'Jude' printed in red across their shop window implied were mysteries; however, ironically, it was in his first Jewish school that he meets with rudeness and the need to learn survivability although this still does not make him feel 'different'. The hero of Joseph Heller's *Good as Gold* states about his Jewishness, "I never realised I was Jewish until I was practically grown up. Or rather, I used to feel that everybody in the world was Jewish, which amounts to the same thing." Likewise, Hugo is almost grown up when he realises the extent of his marginalisation in a land that hated Jews and sought to exterminate them.

Anita Desai employs a distinct narrative strategy that not only enforces rhythm and pattern to her story but also marks the regular alternating from past to present in a zig-zag movement that inscribes time not as linear or circular but as the swing of the pendulum. Metaphorically it is emblematic of the passage from childhood to adulthood, from colonisation to decolonisation, from trauma to creativity. This is further reinforced by her use of German nursery rhymes and English songs.

The German songs belonging to childhood, by remaining untranslated, suggest a further distancing in the minds of the readers with significant gaps and imprints to be later developed in his adulthood. They also have a strong undercurrent of ironic commentary on the dissolution of Hugo's childhood security crumbling down around him as the horrors of Nazism overtake his family reducing him and his mother to a state of uncertain dependency on their former German partner, Herr Pfuehl. The song "Es tanztein Bibabutze mann" (a bogeyman dances in our house) refers to Herr Pfuehl, who later cunningly appropriates their business; and "Fuchs, du hast die Gans gestohlen" (Fox, you have stolen the goose) is appropriately used when Frau Baumgartner is forced by circumstances to hand over the business to Herr Pfuehl.

By interiorising the feelings of a marginalised person in Hugo, Anita Desai portrays him not just as Gramsci's simplified 'subaltern' but as a complex victim of multiple marginality. As a Jew, Hugo is dispossessed in Germany. His predicament is poignantly projected in the lines of W.H. Auden's "Refugee Blues" :

Say this city has ten million souls
Some are living in mansions,
Some are living in holes :
Yet there's no place for us, my dear,
Yet there's no place for us.

Once we had a country and we thought it fair
Look in the atlas and you'll find it there :
We cannot go there now, my dear,
We cannot go there now.

* * *

Stood on a great plain in the falling snow;
Ten thousand soldiers marched to and fro :
Looking for you and me, my dear, looking for you and me.

Even after the war, Hugo cannot entertain hopes of returning to his homeland because of his race. His bitter experiences in Berlin and later with fellow Germans in the internment camp had even killed his desire for the language and gradually he found 'the language slipping away from him' (150) replaced by English and Hindustani.

Driven by harshness of racial prejudice to seek refuge in India, he is once again hounded by British soldiers — his colour cannot save him and he spends six years of captivity among other Germans where the cycle of fear-hate syndrome is repeated. With frayed, troubled roots Hugo's life's journey literally turns out to running in circles, like the circular tracks of the race course, never arriving, because in India he is unaccepted and betrayed to the state of a permanent refugee.

He is marginalised as a child back in Germany. In the Christmas celebration at school, he feels agonising shame that he did not 'belong' to the picture book world of the fir tree, the gifts and the celebration. More than that he worried whether he did not "belong to the radiant, the triumphant of the world" that it symbolised. Yet he privileges the 'step down' and preserves his individuality over the 'step up' and compromise on his self-respect. Later, or another occasion, Hugo pleads with his father to take him to the races. All the magic that he knows — 'Mick-muck-mo, Make-it-so' or praying to Lieben Jesus — does not work. As the grown up world of his father eludes him, he looks at his mother : with the hatred of one prisoner for another" (35), clearly revealing his preference for his father's world of action to his mother's world of poetry and ideology. Years later, interestingly, when Hugo feels life has regressed to childhood with the mechanical routine at the war camp, he secretly looks up to Julius as his surrogate father.

In India, the 'immigrant-resident' syndrome takes over. From a consciousness of race, Hugo is made painfully aware of the difference in colour and language throwing him out of the orbit of normal existence. "Most people" as RD Long expresses it,

> most of the time experience themselves and others one or another way that I shall call egoic. That is, centrally or peripherally, they experience the world and themselves in terms of a consistent identity, a me-here over against a you-there, within a framework of certain ground structures of spaces and time shared with other members of their society (Critical Responses, 210).

This sense of 'ontological security' is destroyed when there is a drastic change in the existing order, and corresponding modification of this defined image or identity or self usually takes place. This reshaping happens through the use of reason or the exercise of choice resulting in a new awareness of oneself and of one's surroundings, and a flexibility to adapt to a changing order. Hugo also undergoes a metamorphosis in India, incidentally, his growing into adulthood — from a state, where at one level, even after fifty years he is unsure which language to employ to communicate, mumbling, 'Good morning, *Salaam*' to the watchman and a stage when he feels rejected even by the gods — "The gods spat him out. *Raus*, Baumgartner, out. Not fit for consumption, German, Hindu, human or divine" (190) — to a stage when India becomes "his country, the one he lived in with familiarity and resignation and relief" (219) and when he voluntarily chooses to stand apart from the crowd — "If he became aware, from time to time, that the world beyond the curtain was growing steadily more crowded, more clamorous, and the lives of others were hectic, more chaotic, then he felt only relief that his had never been a part of the mainstream. *Always*, somehow, *he had escaped the mainstream*" (My emphasis, 211). In this way, Hugo works his way through his psychic tensions and conflict by self-realisation and self-assertion.

There are other voices from the periphery as well that cannot be overlooked. There is a complex positioning of the ambivalent female subject as strong or weak, successful or failures determined by their power to confront challenges meaningfully. Hugo's mother, Frau Baumgartner embodies a fragile beauty that is readily consumed by the fiery Nazi extermination campaigns. Here is a world overflowing with poetry, violets and books. Sadly deficient in her capacity to comprehend the precarious conditions surrounding her and lacking the courage to take the 'leap of faith' and move to a safer corner of the world with her son, her fate correspondingly fades with her sentimental song :

> The sweetness always ended in a quaver. It drew and produced a teardrop. The teardrop hung suspended, glinting in the light from the window and Hugo watched, mesmerised, waiting for it to explode and drop. Tear — drop, pear drop. Silver — light, gold — fresh. And then — the fall (29).

Her life becomes as ineffectual as her letters — cryptic, stereotyped and failing to 'communicate' passes into oblivion.

Gisela and Lotte were twin dancers at Prince's in Calcutta when Hugo first meets them. Gisela claims her roots were in Russia, 'a czarina fled from the Reds' as Lotte sarcastically pokes at her credentials. First as the Lily of Shanghai and Singapore and later as 'Prima ballerina', whose performance of the Dying Swan would have raised Pavlova from her grave in horror, Gisela possesses indomitable resilience and enterprise that points her out as one of fortune's favourites. During the war she vanishes with a Raja 'to collect some real furs and diamonds.' She makes a dramatic reappearance with Julius, now turned Julian von Roth and herself as Gala exploiting the vulnerable Indian artists promising them international fame. Even when the 'Art Gallery' closes down, Gala continues on her inexhaustible resources to somehow thrive, as Lotte predicts : "Of course, they will somehow live. You think our Lily will let him sit and do nothing — like you?" (211).

Lotte's 'multicoloured history' includes her incarnation as a memsahib, as Mrs. Sethia the wife of a nondescript Marwari businessman from Calcutta. Better a dubious marriage with an old man with material comforts than the internment camp. Lotte's choice of her survival over quality of life, of myopic practicality over the visionary makes her a spiritual drifter, happy to cling to passing straw to keep her afloat; Kanti first, and Hugo next, after Germany could no longer be 'home' to her. Her philosophy seems suspended on the one word 'compromise' for life otherwise becomes appallingly unbearable to women like Lotte in a society split by the gender difference, where men are centralised, marginalising women to the zone of non-existence. Moreover,

> In patriarchal society, women are split subjects who watch themselves being watched by men. They turn themselves into objects because feminity itself is defined by being gazed upon by men (Loomba, 162).

Lotte succumbs to her lot submissively accepting the existing order of things in society. Gisela, on the other hand, is the 'empowered' female dominating the male, thereby subverting the social order. Significantly, the 'cat' figure pervades the whole novel unmistakably in some form or other, what with its proverbial nine lives, emphasising the concept of survivability as one of its themes.

The 'hermit', the 'solitary individual' has always interested Anita Desai. In an interview she remarks : "Well, I think, solitary and introspective people are always very aware of living on the brink...but perhaps my introspective characters are more aware than others of what lies on the other side" (Dash, 10). In the eyes of the world, Hugo is a massive failure, schizophrenic, a man who had withdrawn from life after a temporary spate of success at business and the race course, to turn into a 'crustaceous crab', 'ungainly turtle'. Disillusioned, tortured, and emotionally isolated, Hugo turns inward to realise his true self and this self-knowledge extricates him from ultimate extinction.

Hugo becomes one of society's "self-impelled isolates" because it is a matter of survivability as when he deliberately avoids British soldiers recognizing in them a threat to his identity or when he makes silence his natural condition in the internment camp or when he built a new language using English or Hindi or Bengali in the India he was making out for himself; however, more than the mere need to survive, Hugo had carved out for himself the mental picture of the kind of life he wanted to live. Venice, the city of his dreams, a land where East meets West becomes his ideal and he learns to cross man-made borders and accept life and humanity for what they are and on their own terms. Thus, an unambitious life with his cats, caring for them and finding comfort and companionship in return, and taking the risk in helping his Aryan 'enemy' which finally cost him his life, are all in keeping with his strange philosophy of life : to build and not destroy; to save, not kill; to give, not expect in return, although he himself had met with nothing in life except defeat, betrayal and rejection.

It is with people like Hugo on whom defeat is heaped upon defeat that Albert Camus identifies, as in the words of Dr. Rieux in *The Plague*, "I feel more solidarity with the vanquished than with the saints". Hugo is a mixture of silent strength and deafening ego. He may be called the 'daring failure' as preferred to the 'safe success', daring because of his escape from fixity and the ordinary, and he becomes irredeemably an individual. It is here that the author goes beyond ethnicity and moves on to universal issues that concern humanity such as consciousness Vs. conscience, Hugo choosing the former and Chimanlal's son the latter as he casually terminates Hugo's partnership without compunction considering all relations ended with his father's death, while at the end of the novel, he takes charge of disposing Hugo's body matter of factly by the same dictates of his conscience, Hugo being his father's friend.

One can also discern three responses to society and to life (a) the victimisers, the exploiters, always on the hunt craving interminably like Kurt, the young German or on a mad rush for 'success' like Gala, the fortune-hunter, (b) those who compromise as an escape from problems, like Lotte who marries an old Indian merchant to escape the discomforts of wartime camp and (c) the non-conformers like Hugo, those with the courage to say 'no' to society's hypocrisies and superficialities. Hugo also faces Sita's dilemma in *Where Shall We Go This Summer* : "To certain people there comes a day / when they must say the great Yes or the great No," and Hugo's choice is the great No. Given a post-colonial reading Hugo, instead of regression grows into adulthood and maturity, overcomes his èxistential predicament of dislocation, and interprets the reality he confronts creatively albeit unconventionally.

Hugo's life, therefore, communicates directly to our own age of catastrophic upheavals and of ugly, squalid defeat. Anita Desai, like Melville, found human dignity in "little dark corners of life; not among the powerful and successful, but among the oppressed, the defeated; among the victims of God or of nature or of man or, simply of 'things' " (Lewis, 12). As expressions of marginality, and in the author's words, as "a certain psychology of the individual," Hugo's experiences point to the real centre of life !

WORKS CITED

1. Loomba, Ania, *Colonialism/Post-Colonialism*, Routledge, London, 1998.
2. Prabakhar, T. ed., *The Indian Novel in English*, Phoenix Publishing House Pvt. Ltd., New Delhi, 1995.
3. Lewis, R.W.B. ed., *Herman Melille*, Dell Publishing Co., Inc., New York, 1962.
4. Department of English, Osmania University, *Critical Responses*, Sterling Publishers, New Delhi, 1995.
5. Dash, Sandhyarani, *Form and Vision in the Novels of Anita Desai*, Prestige Books, New Delhi, 1966.
6. Libert, Florence, "An Interview with Anita Desai," *WLWE*, Vol. 30, No. 1, Spring, 1990.
7. Robinson, Andrew, 'Out of Custody,' *The Observer*, 3 July, 1998.

20

Victims and Survivors in the 'Sugar-Sticky Web of Family Conflict' : A Reading of Anita Desai's *Fasting, Feasting*

PAMELA OLIVER*

Anita Desai's latest novel *Fasting, Feasting* makes a return to her earlier subject of the family, "the role it plays in perpetuating a patriarchal society and the way it can blight the lives of its members both women and men" (Chew 23). An intellectual, unfeeling husband and his over-sensitive wife in *Cry, the Peacock*, two sisters and a brother struggling to find a meaning in their existence in *Voices in the City*, a sensitive woman sick of her humdrum family life in *Where Shall We Go This Summer* ?, dissatisfied sisters growing apart in *Clear Light of Day* and an isolated, old woman and her wild great-grandchild in *Fire on the Mountain* are all vividly presented in Desai's familial canvass. *Fasting, Feasting,* as the editors' blurb points out, "cuts right to the heart of family life in two different cultures" — an apparently close-knit family living in a provincial town on the gangetic plains and a plastic representation of it in the suburbs of Massachusetts.

The first part covers the family of MamaPapa and though it is a third-person narrative, we see things through the eyes of the plain, older daughter Uma. The parents lead a "Siamese twin existence" on a sofa — swing on the veranda overlooking the

* Lecturer, Department of English, Sarah Tucker College, Tirunelveli, Tamil Nadu.

garden, rhythmically swinging back and forth, "presenting the same indecipherable face, to the world". (13)

> MamandPapa, MamaPapa, PapaMama. It was hard to believe they had ever had separate existence, that they had been separate entities and not MamaPapa in one breath. (5)

Between the two, whose identity has been deleted or drowned in the other? Who is the victim and who the victimizer? Nevertheless it is also not a simple story of a traditional wife being relegated to the background by an over domineering husband.

> When visitors came and enquired after their health, one of them would reply in the first and sometimes third person singular, but the answer was made on behalf of both of them. If Papa gave his opinion of their local member of parliament or the chances of the government in the next election, Mama said nothing because he had spoken for her too. When Mama spoke of the sales at which she planned to buy towels or of the rise in the price of silver that made her wonder if it was time to sell her plate, Papa made assenting grunts because his thoughts were one with hers. Their opinion differed so rarely that...there was no point in appealing to the other parent for a different verdict : none was expected, or given. (13-14)

There are times when they do voice different opinions. If it is a matter of ordering meals for the day, it is Mama who stands her ground. But when Mama wants to terminate her unwanted late pregnancy, Papa sets his jaws, because he wants a son (to perpetuate his race, probably). When the long-awaited son is born, the son "appeared to be the glue that held them together even more inextricably". (30)

> He [Papa] had not only made her his wife, he had made her the mother of his son. What honour what status.... She had matched Papa's achievement, you could say, and they were now more equal than ever. Was this love? Uma wondered disgustedly, was this romance? (13)

In his review of the novel, Andrew Robinson comments thus :

> In Papa and Mama, the Indian parents, she [Anita Desai] creates two monsters of almost Gothic proportions, locked into inseparable marital disharmony, determined to inflict on their two daughters and only son every ounce of the prejudices and disappointments of their own lives, as a respectable barrister and his wife in an undistinguished town. (39)

Uma, the older daughter, is a dismal failure in whatever she puts her hands to. Though she loves school, she fails in all her exams. She is quite unable to master the art of housekeeping, and keeps dropping and breaking things. She is plain, short-sighted, clumsy and a terrible embarrassment to her family. She has to face terrible humiliation in the sphere of her marriage too. In fact, the first suitor in her life prefers her younger sister Aruna. The second one goes through with an engagement, but breaks if off and refuses to return the dowry. At the third attempt, Uma is married, only to find out later, that he is already married. So she returns home in permanent disgrace, with another dowry lost, and hereafter her existence is confined to the verandah, bedroom and kitchen of her parents' home, to be tethered at home so as to be at their beck and call. Even when there is a chance of escape, in the form of a job offered at the local hospital, she is not permitted to take it up. Yet in spite of all this dullness in her life, Uma displays an astuteness and understanding that none of the other characters is capable of. As the children grow up and grow apart, she senses :

> The tightly knit fabric of family that had seemed so stifling and confining now revealed holes and gaps that were frightening — perhaps the fabric would not hold, perhaps it would not protect after all. (86)

Uma's younger sister Aruna, who has developed a 'determined self-assertion', 'a kind of steely determination and 'a dogged ambition' offers a striking contrast to Uma "...no one had to teach her how to make samosas or help her to dress for an occasion. Instinctively, she knew" (85). She brings off the marriage that Uma has dismally failed to make.

> As was to be expected, she took her time, showed a reluctance to decide, played choosy, but soon enough made the wisest, most expedient choice — the handsomest, the richest, the most exciting of the suitors who presented themselves. (100)

True to her expectations, Aruna is whisked away to a life that is 'fantastic', which is 'like a dream.' "...such words, such use of them did seem to raise Aruna to another level — distant and airy..." (103). Every trace of her provincial roots is obliterated and she is overlaid by "the bright sheen of the metropolis".

However, Uma sees though the hollowness of Aruna's life and feels pity for her. Aruna has a vision of a perfect world and is constantly uncovering flaws which she has to correct. This eventually lands her in an uncomfortable household. Seeing Aruna vexed to the point of tears over trivial matters, Uma reflects :

> ...was this the realm of ease and comfort for which Aruna had always pined and that some might say she had attained? Certainly it brought her no pleasure; there was always a crease of discontent between her eyebrows and an agitation that made her eyelids flutter, disturbing Uma who noticed it. (109)

Arun, the boy who comes late into the family, bringing a lot of elation and pride into it, is the darling of the family, who has to be brought up with 'proper attention'. But Arun proves to be a disappointment in many ways. He is a vegetarian in his tastes.

> Papa was confounded. A meat diet had been one of the revolutionary changes brought about in his life, and his brother's by their education. Raised among traditional vegetarians, their eyes had been opened to the benefits of meat along with that of cricket and the English language, the three were linked inextricably in their minds....
>
> Now his own son, his one son, displayed this completely baffling desire to return to the ways of his forefathers, meek and puny men who had got nowhere in life. Papa was deeply vexed. (32-33)

He suffers from an endless procession of ills — mumps, measles, chickenpox, bronchitis, malaria, 'flu, asthma, nose-bleeds and more. His father insists on giving him the best education possible, and all his childhood is spent in poring over books. He is able to fulfil his father's dream by winning a place at an East Coast College in the US, yet he is drained of all feelings.

> She [Uma] watched and searched for an expression, of relief, of joy, doubt, fear, anything at all. But there was none. All the years of scholarly toil had worn down any distinguishing features Arun's face might once have had. They had left the essentials : a nose, eyes, mouth, ears.... There was nothing else — not the hint of a smile, frown, laugh or anything : These had all been ground down till they had disappeared. (12)

In the US, he has every intention of remaining aloof, alone and anonymous. It is as if he has been strangulated by the familial bonds, by the concern, affection and attention showered upon him.

> ...he had at last experienced the total freedom of anonymity, the total absence of relations, of demands, needs, requests, ties, responsibilities, commitments. He was Arun. He had no past, no family and no country. (172)

But his sense of relief is strikingly short-lived. When he is looking out for a place to stay during summer, it is Papa once again who takes the decision for him. Mrs. Patton, the sister of Mrs. O'Henry has offered a room for him in their house. "He was to telephone her and 'finalise it' (Papas term); it was a kind offer, generously made, and not to be rejected''. (175)

> Arun was overcome by the sensation of his family laying its hands upon him, pushing him down into a chair at his desk, showing a textbook under his nose, catching that nose and making him swallow cod liver oil, spooning food into him, telling him; Arun, this, Arun, that, Arun, nothing but....(175)

Once again, he is suffocated by kindness and concern : ''So much kindness, so much goodness, how was he to defend himself?''. (178)

> No, he had not escaped. He had travelled and he had stumbled into what was like a plastic representation of what he had known at home; not the real thing which was plain, unbeautiful, misshapen, fraught and compromised — but the unreal thing — clean, bright, gleaming, without taste, savour or nourishment. (185)

The Pattons, as described by Gabriele Annan, are 'a cartoon family' (35). The father lives in a world of steak, hamburger, ribs and chops, broiled, grilled, fried and roasted. His expression when thwarted, reminds Arun of "...his father's very expression, walking off, denying any opposition, any challenge to his authority..." (186). The son Rod, a loutish health freak, whose only interests are fitness, games, exercise and jogging, offers a stark contrast to Arun.

> There is no way that a small, underdeveloped and asthmatic boy from the Gangetic plains, nourished on curried vegetables and stewed lentils, could compete with or even keep up with this gladiatorial species of northern power. (191)

The bulimic daughter Melanie, is as desperate as the pathetically incompetent Uma. Arun sees in her

> ...a resemblance to the contorted face of an enraged sister, who, failing to express her outrage against neglect, against misunderstanding, against in attention to her unique and singular being and its hungers, merely spits and froths in ineffectual protest. (214)

Mrs. Patton is a shopaholic for food. She makes Arun accompany her on her daily expeditions to the overpowering supermarket and stocks up her overflowing freezers. She takes extra efforts to make Arun feel at home, to the extent of herself turning vegetarian for his sake.

> She smiles a bright plastic copy of a mother-smile that Arun remembers from another world and another time, a smile that is tight at the corners with pressure, the pressure to perform a role, to

> make him eat, make him grow, make him worth all the trouble and effort and expense.... On the other side of the world, he is caught up again in the sugar-sticky web of family conflicts. (194-95)

The blurb of the text says :

> Two different ways of assuaging human hunger, desires and appetites are revealed in this subtle sharp and poignant story, which moves from the hub of a close-knit Indian household, with its traditional obligations and impositions, its overpowering warmth and sensual response, to the cool centre of an American family, with its freedoms, freezers and paradoxically self-denying self-indulgence. In both there are victims — and survivors.

Who are the victims and who the survivors? Uma's cousin Anamika is most obviously a victim of the partriachal family system. Anamika, "simply lovely as a flower is lovely, soft, petal-skinned, bumblebee-eyed, pink-lipped...with a good nature like a radiance about her" (67), one who brings about peace, contentment and well being wherever she is, "cool, poised, mannerly and graceful" (68), so brilliant and clever as to have won a scholarship to Oxford, is sacrificed on the altar of marriage. Ironically, it is her scholarship, shown around with pride, that wins for her a husband who is equally qualified and has won medals and certificates. She being a girl is not to be sent abroad for study, and Anamika "could never bring herself to contradict her parents or cause them grief" (69). The brilliant and beautiful Anamika is simply obliterated by the institution of marriage, relegated to the kitchen to toil for the family, never permitted even to attend any family gatherings, beaten, ill-treated and ultimately burnt to ashes.

Though Aruna appears to have made a successful life, she has not, as Uma discovers, escaped the tangle of family conflict with its constant demands and pressures. Arun, who is drowned "in a deep well of greyness" thinks he has made his escape with his flight to the US, but realises his inability to extricate himself from the web. He is still tethered to the same system but perhaps with a longer rope. MamaPapa and the Pattons are all caught up in the flux of family tensions finding no escape. Paradoxically, it is Uma, the disgrace of the family, an abject failure, who manages to survive through an inner life of her own. Hearing Mira-masi's stories of Lord Krishna, the poet-saint Mira and Raja Harishchandra,

> Uma, with her ears and even her fingertips tingling, felt that here was someone who could pierce through the dreary outer world to an inner world, tantalizing in its colour and romance. If only it could replace this, Uma thought hungrily. (40)

When she visits the holy river, she feels an unconscious urge to rush into the water. "It had not occurred to her that she needed to know how to swim. She had been certain the river would sustain her (43).

> ...when she had plunged into the dark water and let it close quickly and tightly over her, the flow of the river, the current, drew her along, clasping her and dragging her with it. It was not fear she felt, or danger. Or rather, these were only what edged something much darker, wilder, more thrilling, a kind of exultation — it was exactly what she had always wanted, she realised. (111)

She remembers "the subterranean feelings" stirred within her by the words intoned during prayers in the convent school where she studied.

> The Lord is my shepherd, I shall not want.
> He maketh me to lie down in green pastures.
> He leadeth me beside the still waters.
> He restoreth my soul.... (20)

Often, she feels "herself drawn by an undercurrent into a secret depth, so dark that she could see nothing at all — just the darkness" (133). It is perhaps this 'secret depth' that ultimately sustains her. Towards the close of the first part, we see her in the role of a comforter, consoling her mother thinking, "they are together still, they have the comfort of each other" (155).

In her study of Hindu women, Julia Leslie shows how "it is a small deviation from the norm which may be crucial, perhaps the way the apparently negative is transformed into something positive and powerful'' (3). Unlike Melanie, who in spite of all the freedom that she enjoys, falls victim to neglect and misunderstanding, Uma is able to transcend her disabilities and constraints. As Desai writes, ''the murky water catches the blaze of the sun and flashes fire'' (156).

WORKS CITED

1. Annan, Gabriele, ''Sugar-Sticky''. London Review of Books 21.11 (27 May 1999).
2. Chew, Shirley, ''Acting as Sita Did,'' TLS, 28 May 1999.
3. Desai, Anita, *Fasting, Feasting,* London : Chatto & Windus, 1999.
4. Leslie, Julia, ''Introduction'', *Roles and Rituals for Hindu Women,* Ed. Julia Leslie, London : Pinter, 1991.
5. Robinson, Andrew, ''Families that Don't Function'', *The Spectator,* 5 June 1999.

21

Anita Desai's Novels : A Study in Verbal Pattern and Psyche

KUNJBALA GOEL*

Anita Desai is not interested so much in registering surface realities as in the probings of inner truths lying under the surface level. In order to present this submerged psychic truth she employs various linguistic devices. Carefully chosen clusters of images, symbols and myths figure most prominently amongst the devices deployed by her. Apart from them, quite often she makes use of fresh collocations, deviations and parallelisms to render the uniqueness of the psyche of her characters. She exploits even phonological patterns like alliteration, assonance, consonance, rhyme, etc. Sometimes different levels of semantic interpretation also become significant for the presentation of her character.

In Mrs. Desai's hands imagery becomes a very powerful mode to represent the perception of a character. In the following extract she is commendably capable of objectifying the particular bent of her character's mind :

> Into this din, a tonga had driven up and disgorged a flurry of guests in their visiting saris, all to flap their palm-leaf-hand-fans as they sat in a ring about her — the wives and daughters of the lecturers and professors over whom her husband ruled ... her eyes flashed when she heard, like a pair of back blades, wanting to cut them, crawling grey bugs about her fastidious feet.
>
> (*Fire on the Mountain*, p. 18)

* Department of English, Banasthali Vidyapith (Rajasthan)

Expressions like "disgorged", "crawling grey bugs" and "eyes flashed ... like a pair of black blades" give a specific shade to the image and suggest Nanda's withdrawal which is based on hatred and awareness of meaninglessness of the so called normal routine life.

In the above quoted passage though the objects seem to be seen through a particular psyche, yet they have their own clear identity, while in the following one they are on the verge of getting lost in the subjective world of the character.

> He had been -- large or small? I cannot remember but his eyes I do; they were pale, opaque, and gave him an appearance of morbidity, as though he had lived like a sluggish white worm, indoors always; in his dark room at the temple gates, where the central 'lingam' was painted bright, vicious red, as though plumged in sacrificial blood, and light burned in a single lamp from which oil spilled into a large spreading pool.
>
> (*Cry, The Peacock*, pp. 28-29)

It is a typical Indian scene of a temple with a red painted 'lingam' at the centre, an oil lamp and a foreteller examining the horoscope of a young girl still to be married. But these referential details have been given hardly any significance in comparison to the depiction of the impression of these objects on Maya's psyche. There are a great number of adjectival and adverbial phrases portraying not so much the objects themselves as the subjective way Maya views them.

When Mrs. Desai wants to present not just the subjective world of Maya but rather her psychic disintegration, she moulds images in such a way that the objects get increasingly blurred and confused. In the beginning only the edges of the images are mixed *e.g.*, the tail of the rat gets merged with father and father's voice becomes the voice of the peacock, yet they are recognisable. Later, they all get mixed up leading to an imagistic disorder which sets forth effectively the chaos of Maya's psychic.

Symbols also have a vital role to play in displaying different states. Generally the symbols used by Mrs. Desai are a part of the circumstantial details of the narrative. They acquire significance because of the appropriate correlation between the object and its symbolical meaning. The houses in *Fire on the Mountain, Where Shall We Go This Summer*? and in *In Costody* are an essential part of the created world, giving to the world of the novel a "solidity and specification." Their symbolical meanings are only semantic extrapositions. Yet they are capable of objectifying the inner psychic layers of characters in a powerful way. In *Where Shall We Go This Summer?* The house Sita comes to live in at Manori, after a gap of twenty years, is evocative of her desertion of normal routine life and objectifies the fear that is harboured in her heart.

In Mrs. Desai's novels at times, very minor objects seem to attain symbolical overtones and effectively outlay a particular shade of mind or a psychic tension. 'Tea', generally associated with normal, practical day-to-day life and get-togetherness, is rightly associated with Gautam and not with Maya in *Cry, The Peacock*. As soon as Gautam disposes of Toto's body, "it is all over" for him, so he says to Maya : "Come and drink your tea and stop crying" (p. 6). Gautam's readiness to have tea is clearly symbolical of his getting over Toto's death which becomes an obsession for Maya. *In Bye-Bye Black Bird* this symbol is judiciously related to Sarah. When Adit for the first time announces his decision to leave England and declares that his son will be Born in India, Sarah finds herself in a psychic turmoil, but soon having overpowered the storm in heart she announces : "Let's have a cup of tea" (p. 204).

If symbols, generally through their extra semantic impositions, help Mrs. Desai to objectify the nuances of a character's subjective world, at times, also by only half revealing the truth they enable the novelist to delineate the psychological depth of the characters. For instance, in *Cry, The Peacock*, Mrs. Desai suggests the subconscious decision of Maya to murder Gautam through the dust symbol. As this decision never comes to the surface of Maya's consciousness, Mrs. Desai cannot state it in clear palpable terms. Therefore, it is through the highly cautions employment of the 'dust storm' that the novelist suggests the preceding psychic turmoil and the following peace. The decision remains only as something vaguely and dimly felt — never defined. Had the decision been explicitly stated through clear denotative terms, Maya instead of being the loved and sympathised protagonist would have been a murderous villainness, and the *tour de force* of the novel a fiasco.

Some of the traditional symbols have been reinterpreted by Mrs. Desai for the sake of rendering highly individualised psyches. In *Cry, The Peacock*, the repeated references to a peacock as a "brain fever bird," "a reminder of death" and "ill-fated lover" are contrary to the traditionally popular image of the peacock. Its dancing image in the rainy season has been associated with love, romance and beauty and not with fighting, mating and dying. By presenting the peacock in her arbitrary symbolical colours, Mrs. Desai is making an attempt to depict Maya's mental predicament -- a deep love for life with a sure knowledge of death to follow. But it is true that this identification of the peacock with Maya's psyche gives the impression of being an unsatisfactory contrivance to many readers.

Myths have also been deployed by Mrs. Desai, which with all their religious and traditional associations lay out the psychological depths of characters. They serve as powerful instruments to suggest what cannot be expressed denotatively. To take an example, the mythological Sita, though not presented directly in *Where Shall We Go This Summer?*, yet owing to the identity of her name with that of the protagonist of this novel, reveals the ironical shades of the portrayal of the protagonist who suffers in her exile not from the memories of intense love for her husband, but from alienation.

At times a gap between two semantic levels of interpretation of one statement also becomes functional in revealing the inner world. In *Where Shall We Go This Summer*?, pregnant for the fifth time, Sita declares, "I don't want to have the baby" (p. 34). It is indicative of her metaphysical desire not to commit an act of violence by giving birth to a child which is now so safely contained in her womb into a world which is full of violence and destruction. Raman interprets her declaration as her will to have an abortion. The metaphysical level at which Sita lives is far beyond Raman's reasoning which is confined to material commonsense. The difference between these two semantic levels of interpretation makes the couple stare at each other uncomprehendingly and designate each other as 'mad'.

A character's speech is highly effective in throwing light on his temperament. In Mrs. Desai's hands it becomes a powerful instrument. For example, in *Voices in the City*, when Amla comes to Calcutta she invites Jiban and Monisha to tea at her aunt's place; the few sentences that Jiban speaks at this informal, intimate gathering are highly suggestive of his formal, stolid, unfeeling personality, and of highlighting the cause of his alienation from Monisha who is a highly sensitive, emotional and sincere person. With reference to the forest laid low by the fell hand of man..." (p. 194). The use of the anticipatory 'it' in "It is a sight to sadden..." distances the subject and suggests a formal, impersonal tone that is outlandish in this informal, intimate gathering. Phrases like "sadden one's heart", "virgin forests laid low," "fell hand of man" etc. being cliche's sound insincere and artificial. While going home back he tells his niece Bun Bun, "I rust you have thanked your aunt and great aunt for this most enjoyable evening spent under their auspices" (p. 198). The highly formal tone in this informal gathering shows that Jiban has learnt only one role to play in his life and that is of the formal, rigid, apathetic officer. It is no wonder then that he miserably fails in his relationship with Monisha.

Often Mrs. Desai resorts to a skilful deployment of phonological sounds to render the inner world of her characters. Among the phonological devices used by her, alliteration, assonance, rhyme and use of harsh sounds figure most prominently. In the novel *In Custody* when Sarla, ridden by Indian social tradition, cannot utter any word to vent her anger against her husband and just sulks and retires to her kitchen, the writer says : "It was only when she had disappeared into this narrow, cluttered fastness of hers and could be heard freely rattling and clattering in there that it occurred to Deven..." (p. 127). It is through the repetition of the harsh /k/,/t, and /d/ phonemes that Mrs. Desai expresses the turmoil in the heart of Sarla — her anger and bitterness against her husband. To take one more example we can see the following extract wherein alliteration seems to lend a comic effect to Ila's character and thus, expresses Nanda's attitude to Ila, which she shares with her late husband and probably also with the novelist : "Ila Das came, bobbing and bouncing, in button boots, her umbrella wildly swirling to tea" (*Fire on the Mountain*, p. 22). By emphasizing the words involved, alliteration enhances the ludicrous nature of Ila Who has been presented as rather a ridiculous person for being too involved in life which is ultimately absurd.

Mrs. Desai is remarkably successful in portraying the psyche of her sensitive, emotional and sensuous characters. Her language runs so smoothly and expresses the inner world of her select characters so impressively that the reader's attention is rarely detracted by its few miner limitations.

REFERENCES

1. Desai, Anita, *Bye-Bye Blackbird,* 1971 : rpt. Delhi : Vision Books, 1985.
2. ——, *Cry, The Peacock.* 1963; rpt. Delhi : Orient Paperbacks, 1983.
3. ——, *Fire on the Mountain.* New Delhi : Allied Publishers Pvt. Ltd., 1977.
4. ——, *In Custody,* 1984; rpt. England ; Penguin Books, 1985.
5. ——, *Voices in the City,* 1965; rpt. New Delhi : Orient Paperbacks, 1982.
6. ——, *Where Shall We Go This Summer?* 1975; rpt. Delhi : Vision Books, 1982.

22

Anita Desai's Prose Style

F.A. INAMDAR*

I

Anita Desai does not make out a case for using English for writing novels as do Raja Rao, Mulk Raj Anand, R.K. Narayan and Manohar Malgonkar. We have Raja Rao's statement about style in his Foreword of *Kanthapura* : "We cannot write like the English. We should not. We cannot write only as Indians. We have grown to look at the large world as part of us. Our method of expression therefore has to be a dialect which will some day prove to be as distinctive and colourful as the Irish or the American."[1] Mulk Raj Anand in "The Story of My Experiments with a While Lie" makes a decision to do away with all British traits from an "instinctive preference for the simpler, more primitive, even dirty life of outcastes against the more complex ritualized sophistication of the neo-Brahmanical order of the Indian intelligentsia, which had accepted the snobbery of the British rule."[2] R.K. Narayan admits that "English has served my purpose admirably, of conveying unambigously that thoughts and acts of a set personalities who flourish in a small town located in a corner of South India."[3] Manohar Malgonkar thinks about Indian novelists writing in English "a bit of a fake, as though going about with a false caste mark, for he writes in a language not his own."[4] But against all these novelists, statements, Desai's admission on style is expressed implicitly when she says : 'I think the purpose of my writing is to discover — for myself — and then describe and convey the

* Department of English, South Gujarat University, Surat.

truth...the Dutch Old masters who could paint a loaf of bread so incomparably were not merely painting the meaning of that loaf, its significance to man, its quality, even its flavour...My writing is an effort to discover, underline and convey the significance of things."[5] To convey the significance of things, R.K. Narayan's use of irony or Raja Rao's unqualified acceptance of the Indian metaphysics is totally inadequate for Desai's fictional needs as are the doctrinaire humanism of Mulk Raj Anand and the heroic postures of Kushwant Singh and Malgonkar. Her novels probe the psychic dimensions of her characters. Her overall vision is one of morbidity. *In Cry, the Peacock* Maya's predicament is to come to terms with the astrologer's prediction and to enjoy the moments of life on earth with her practical-mined husband. But she, as a creature of "song, dance and flower" meets with the situation which is beyond her control and, consequently, goes mad. Therefore, R.S. Sharma has rightly pointed out that "most of her problems as a fiction writer begin with her insistence on too much style on too small a canvas."[6] In all her novels, Desai gives us an impression that she is fond of using words for their own sake. A mynah's call holds her back to describe not only its beautiful call, but its attractive body. The narration of events is held in abeyance as she is absorbed in describing the beauty of the bird :

> In the small silence a flock of mynahs suddenly burst out of the green domes of the trees and, in a loud commotion of yellow beaks and brown wings, disappeared into the sun. While their shrieks and cakles still rang in the air, they heard another sound...[7]

The description leads on to the further description of the cat and the dog. One feel that Anita Desai is fond of describing the animal world just for the sake of displaying her skill in using words for their music and magic.

Four of Anita Desai's novels try to forge ties "with the past and the cultural spirit." "They ought to qualify Anita Desai for stylistic distinction...If ever a writer was guilty of oververbalisation it is she."[8] Therefore, we agree with Meenakshi Mukherjee's statement about Anita Desai's style when she says, "Her language is marked by three characteristics : sensuous richness, a high-strung sensitiveness and a love for the sound of words."[9] A similar observation on her style is made by Darshan Singh Maini : "Words appear to have sensuous appeal for her, and she exults in the reach and power of her rhetoric."[10]

Here I purpose to confine myself to "the reach and power of her rhetoric," "a love for the sound of words" and her experiment in fiction. Anita Desai uses native words for items of food, dress, rituals, festivals, trees, etc. and I would note how she has attempted to evoke the typically Indian atmosphere by using Indian imagery, in finding connections in experiences, events, and objects from real life. I would also take into consideration Desai's use of parenthesis as a stylistic device and a few other minor linguistic devices to achieve artistic mode of expression in *Cry, the Peacock.*

In *Cry, the Peacock,*[11] Anita Desai's power of rhetoric consists in lyricism and its repetition of words. Here Anita Desai bursts out as a lyric poet in describing the torrid and oppressive odour of Toto through a sentence using anti-climax : "Once sweet, once loved, then suddenly, rotten and repulsive" (p. 8). Maya compares "the light in the verandah" with "an inward glow as of marble at sunset" (p. 12). Maya, as a poet, never leaves the abstract notions as abstract, but exemplifies them with concrete images. Gautama's words cut "my thoughts away like a surgeon, expertly removing a boil" (p. 20). He drew away from her "thoughts of anguish which rose, every now and then, like birds that awake from dreams and rise out of their trees admist great commotion, circle a while, then settle again, on their branches" (p. 21). Her feelings about Gautama are revealed through her words. To her his hand appears "as cool and dry as the bark of an old and shady tree" (p. 22).

Maya uses words, words, words and through them reveals her neurotic mind :

> Wild horse, white horse, galloping up paths of stone, flying away into the distance, the wild hills. The heights, the dizzying heights of my mountains, towering, tapering, edged with cliff-edges, founded on rock. Fall, fall, gloriously fall to the bed of racing rivers, foaming seas. Horrid arms, legs, tentacles thrashing, blood flowing, eyes glazing. Storm -- storm at sea, at land! Fury. Whip. Lash.

> Fly furiously. Dangers! (p. 180). This morbid sensation in Maya is the result of the fear of death psychosis. She is obsessed with Toto's death because she sees her own death in it and the prediction of the astrologer.

Death by violence is that troubles her here. The vocabulary is more abrupt and broken. There are many exclamatory and interrogatory phrases. The philosophic generalizations emerge with a personal anguish as in the case of Gautama. In *Cry, the Peacock*, Anita Desai follows indirect method or the method called interior monologue. The mental process at work in Maya and Gautama is expressed when the former tells the latter :

> Not at all, like my family or myself, Maya. We are egoists, one and all. We work for fame, name, money, all other evils put together. Yet we do have our work, our vocations each one of us, and so far, I must say, it appears to have brought us a certain amount of security. Not the complete ideal peace. *Gita* tells us about not by any means, but perhaps a larger amount of it than most people have (p. 117).

And the conflict that surges in Maya's mind is worked through the interior monologue where sentences are not logically lined as seen above. They are marked by incoherence and disjointedness and have colloquial colouring :

> "Are you always certain of your beliefs — their *rightness*? I am not. After all, what is we are wrong, we Hindus? What if there is a Christian hell? Oh, I do hate to think of it," I babbled, crazed by fear. "I should not like to die and find myself in purgatory, should you, Gautama?" (p. 174). The pets' death is for her own death and damnation.

For achieving the rhythmic beauty of a lyric, Desai employs the device of repetition which gives incantatory tone to the narration, as in "Of course you are still so young, so very young" (p. 31). Such repetition of significant words adds to the fear of prediction in Maya's mind and she cries : "take me home, away from this fearsome magician — for that is what I called him, a magician" (p. 32).

To give immediacy and dramatic effect to the scene described, Desai resorts to the third person singular narration. The past events are described as if taking place in our presence. Maya describes the Himalayan bear :

> ...he closes his eyes because he cannot bear to see the flat, flat lawn, the white, white house, the many, many people, when his heart is pounding with renewed passion for the wilderness of rain scented first and the tangled undergrowth of the Himalayan mountains that mark, in the north, a jagged line of azure blue amidst coils of silver mist and the first snowflakes of a long, quiet winter (p. 87).

Desai makes use of native words to evoke Indian atmosphere in *Cry, the Peacock* as also in other novels. As Raja Rao translates Indian words, idioms, metaphors and similes into English to build up Indian atmosphere, so does Anita Desai, as in ' "*Pia, pia'* they say. 'Lover, lover, *Mio, mio.* — I die, I die" (p. 95). She also uses Hindi words without translating them into English, *e.g.* "The soft blue twilight in the garden vibrated with rich words like *zulph* and *mehtab* " (p. 98). In his early stories like "Javani" and "Akkayya, "Raja Rao had attempted to use English equivalents for Indian ways of expressions and later on had kept Indian terms in original for typically Indian items of food, dress, rituals, festivals and objects of nature. Anita Desai too uses original words from Indian languages, such as, *paimana, tamanna, attar, sindoor, kumkum, sannyasi, yogi, raga, maidan, gulmohar salatopees* and *loo*. That is why Ann Lowry Weir considers Desai's language to be more than "uniquely Indian. It is uniquely her own. She uses the normal English vocabulary for weather, food, clothing, etc. but she heightens it by inventing interesting even shocking combinations of words. Unusual juxtapositions and arresting metaphors constantly assault the senses of readers, almost demanding that they feel the way Maya herself feels."[12] Some of the fascinating combination of words are : "flower-soft eyes" and "moth-warm, mother-soft grey and fawn" (p. 156).

The imagery in *Cry, the Peacock* is Indian in the sense that Desai evokes Indian atmosphere with the description of its fauna and flora. Maya watches "faunt mauve petunias — sentimental irresolute flowers" (p. 19) which reflect her own nature. One the contrary, Gautama is compared with a horse, symbolic of his animal blindness to the beauty of nature. Though the novel permeates with the images of animals, corpses, violence and abyss, we are concerned with Indian ones, such as, the beating of drums which evokers Maya's fear of death :

> And softly, softly the drums crept across the desert, stole through the dust. Softly, softly they began to beat. Closer and closer came the sound, louder and louder. "Ah," I cried, looking up to see if I could find ... Nothing but the sound, irrepressible, relentless sound of drums, drums beating (pp. 150-51).

One of the most outstanding things in Anita Desai, as in Raja Rao, is the use of parenthesis. It is the soul of monologue and Desai uses it for explanation, modification, comment and reflection. In the sentence "Any little set-back destoys it, leads it closer to its termination" (p. 145), it is for explanation, whereas in the next sentence it is for modification : "It was so grotesque that I pressed my face close to the mirror, close to the bizarre reflection, and grinned into its teeth then atmosphere is thin here. But it reminds us of Raja Rao's similar images in which women were "tender as April mangoes" and young boys "bright as banana trunks," while the sky was "blue as a marriage shawl." In Anita Desai, the women in Monisha's house look at Amla "with faces like freshly baked bread" (p. 159). The cousin smiles "a white coconut smile" (p. 160). People in Calcutta are compared to "gutter rats" and "apparitions seen in delirium tremens" (p. 97). The city is depicted as "a stagnant aquarium" (p. 169).

About the minor linguistic experiments in the novel, we have, like Raja Rao's appended statements to capture the nuances of Indian speech : "You talk about idealists, Bose?" "What a bloody stupid thing to do, Bose" (p. 15). Desai uses 'to be' verb at the end of a sentence to emphasize the influence of the person : "Khan, I think his name is" (p. 50). This type of usage might lend a metaphysical depth to the statement : "A proper demon that man is" (p. 13). Sometimes, Desai captures the Indian habit of using genitive in apposition as in the following : "that Khan fellow's greed" (p. 82).

Verbose style, the natural sister of rhetoric, is to be traced to Desai's heavily adjectival style. To describe Gita Devi, she uses three adjectives, two of which convey the same meaning : "Large and placid and bovine" (p. 46). She is also fond of turning an ordinary qualifier group into a compound; for example, a bus going to office becomes an "office-going bus" (p. 10). A compound word of similar nature is "the wind-wild verandah" (p. 26). But out of her excessive zeal for communication, Desai's language has defects of prolixity and dragging.

III

In Desai's third novel, *Bye-Bye, Blackbird,*[17] the language of *Cry the Peacock* recurs with a similar tenacity. The hackneyed theme of the novel, the East-West encounter adds to its drawback. The palpable alliteration, the "stilted and petrified" style is what we notice here also : Dev's slow change from Anglophobia to Anglophilia is described :

> And so he walks the streets and parks of the city, grateful for *its daffodil patches of sunshine*, loathing its *sooty*, sodden dampness. Eats toffee apples in Petticoat Lane and fishes limp sausages out of *pools of fat* in Lyons Corner House. Lies in the Grass under the green canopies of Kew Gardens, and narrowly escapes being *run over* and crushed to death twenty *times over* in Piccadilly Circus. Stands in the dark, wistfully gazing at the *peacock-blue* and *rose-red paper flowers* in a Mexican boutique, then is enthralled by the massive, *blank bulk of Battersea* power station ... It is strange summer, in which he is the *bewildered alien, the charmed observer*, the *outraged outsider* and *thrilled sight-seer* all at once and in succession (Italics mine). (pp. 95-96)

Once a reader becomes familiar with what kind of language she writes, reading her novels becomes an experience into "a senile, spinsterish sensibility lashing inanities into excitement."[18]

Desai is carried away by the music in words. The sound of words in *Bye-Bye, Blackbird* is used to echo the sense : "the drum, the trombone and the electric guitar assaulted them with its persistent beat — thrum, thrum, thrum" (p. 22). While the Indians eat, " 'Ahh, *roti* and *dal*,' said someone on the carpet, 'slurp, slurp' " (p. 24), the Pakistani watches "the blonde girls in their short, tight skirts stomp and twist and scribble about the crowded floor" (p. 24). Adit, Dev and Sarah talk about Mother Goose. Adit says, "She's beef and broth, bangers and mash, fish and chips, trips and onions to them" (p. 172). Dev "sighing, felt these droplets of sound and smell drip, drip, drip into him like drops of golden syrup" (p. 179).

Desai uses more Indian words in this novel than she did in the earlier ones. A translation of these words in English would not have brought the rich connotation attached to these words. They are; *puja, bhangra, gup-shup, nimak haram, shehnai, sitar, samadhi, toba, navab, kalapani, papadum, halwa, rotis, dal, burfee, pakoras, alutikkis, salwar-kameez, kurta*, and *pallav*.

The use of imagery to evoke Indian atmosphere is rare here, but the adjectival continues as usual. Desai doubles the adjectives for emphasis : "Oh noble noble man" (p. 18). Sometimes the adjectives clutter for the irresistible charam they have. The musician and his muse are described as "this pretty lotus of a man, this exquisite ivory figure of a musician... his painted, bejewelled, tintinnabulating muse" (p. 104).

Desai's skill in sentence construction seems to be breaking down in this novel. Shiv K. Kumar, commenting on her style, says : "the sentences meander on, as usual, in response to some inscrutable rhythm, tapering off into mere nothingless."[19] Her spent energy in sentence construction may be shown in Adit's reasons for liking London. Like a school boy writing about his liking, Adit begins his sentences with "I like" :

> "I like going into the local for a pint on my way home to Sarah. I like wearing good tweed on a foggy November day. I like the Covent Garden

> opera house. I like the girls here — I like their nylon stockings and the way their noses tilt upwards ... I like steamed pudding with treacle. I like — I like thatched cottages and British history .. — I like the pubs. I like the freedom a man has here — economic freedom ! Social freedom ! I like reading the posters in the tube ... And I like the Thames — I like the ravens there ... I like the feeling I can nip across the Channel ... I like old Ma Jenkins who cleans my room ... I like these fat old London women with faces like buns ... And I — I like strawberries in summer. I like a weekend at the seaside. I even like the BBC!'' (pp. 20-21).

IV

Where Shall We Go This Suimmer?[20] does not show any signs of her progress in style. It keeps afloat an abundance of trivia into each sentence, as she describes in the monson flowing ''now thin, now dense; now slow, now fast; now whispering, now drumming; then gushing'' or ''the roar and sigh of the tide, the moan of the casuarinas in the grove below'' and ''the clatter of palm leaves'' (p. 75).

Her lyricism appears a mere flourish of words for their alliterative potentiality :

> The earth seethed with weeds and the weed with minute wild-flowers in brilliant tints — waxy white stars, curled yellow ones, small blue eyes and clusters of vermilion and coral ixora that Sita plucked and scattered for the pleasure of smelling their sweet, tarry sap on her hands (p. 88).

But her imagery is quite picturesque. Desai describes the wind that ''bowled along cold and free. It slapped them sharply, with chilly smacks that made the women hold their hair down about their ears'' (p. 89). The image of the cold air is Keatsian in its concreteness. It reminds us of ''The Eve of St. Agnes.'' At times her imagery is imaginative. Sita is described as ''the poet, the water and the fire'' (p. 38).

Anita Desai creates Indian atmosphere in the novel by translating her ideas into English, the Indian way, such as, "you have broken all the buds!" (p. 30) or "slapped cakes of mud flat on the stand" (p. 53). She also uses Indian words, such as, *burka, sari, raga, tanpura, dervishes, bhajan, chelas, swaraj, lota, mantra.* The word *chela* is used so often in the novel that it gets on our nerves. It appears that Desai's interest in this area is on the wane.

V

Fire on the Mountain[21] has received considerable critical attention, but hardly any comment on Desai's style in it. Hence, Shiv K. Kumar's perceptive remarks on the novel that "it is just words words, in tangled sentence-structures, forcing the reader into a sort of insensateness"[22] seems significant. This novel gives one the impression that she has lowered the structure of rhetoric and raised the edifice of a style through which the description of external phenomena evokes and defines the psychic traits of her characters. Nanda Kaul wants to escape from the babble of Ila Das. This effort of hers in objectified in the effort of the worm to escape from the white hen. Nanda Kaul's waiting for the cool breeze and her determination to lie still is evoked through the images of "a charred tree trunk in the forest, a broken pillar of marble in the desert, a lizard on a stone wall" (p. 23). Of similar significance is Ila Das's umbrella imaging her "dreary past" (p. 108). It objectifies the owner : "a witch of olden times tied and readied for the fatal dip in the pond" (p. 109). She is "a little frightened spider in this vast, chilly web" (p. 141). The tongueless astonishment of Raka is conveyed through the scars and scratches on her body :

> She would return with her brown legs, scratched, her knees bruised, sucking a finger stung by nettles, her hair brown under a layer of dust, her eyes very still and thoughtful as though she had visited strange lands and seen fantastic improbable things that lingered in the mind (p. 46).

The novel exposes with what thinness of material the yarn has been spun. Even the incidents narrated by Ila Das appear to be common place and done for the sake of mere padding except for the one dealing with Preet Singh. Therefore, it is pertinently remarked by Shiv K. Kumar that "wooden sexless characters stalk across her pages, chasing dark shadows at twilight."[23]

VI

In Clear Light of Day, drab and full incidents of everyday occurrence are expressed in an equally uninteresting language. Tara's parents play cards and disappear from the earth as if they grew up only to produce children and play cards and die : these long note-books and thin pencils with which her parents had sat, day after day and year after year till their deaths, playing bridge with friends like themselves, mostly silent, heads bent so that the knobs in their neck protruded, soft stained hands shuffling the cards, now and then speaking those names and numbers that remained a mystery to the children.[24]

As there is an absence of absorbing experience to be communicated to the reader, the language of communication and the diction and the sentence structures are all mechanical. Dullness and boredom are in store for the reader rather than something quite gripping and exciting.

Anita Desai as a novelist is morbid. She does not have a sense of humour and irony, and as a result of these things, her style which began with rhetorical flourish ends in stereotyped cliches. But her early novels have a good flavour of the soil in the description of flora of India. A few of the earlier novels have good images and metaphorical expressions. In them, she has artistically used Indian terms. As there are no deep emotions arising out of the characters, the prose style also degenerates from the rhetoric of sentimentality and romantic cliches into "the banality of the narrative." About the use of Desai's English prose style in her novels one may sadly remark that she found it marble but left it stone.

REFERENCES

1. Raja Rao, *Kanthapura* (New Delhi : Oxford University Press, 1974), p. v.
2. Mulk Raj Anand, "The Story of My Experiment with a White Lie," *Indian Literature*, X, 3, 1974.
3. R.K. Narayan, "English in India" in *Commonwealth Literature*, ed. by John Press (London : Heinemann, 1965), p. 123.
4. Quoted by G.S. Amur, *Manohar Malgonkar* (New Delhi : Arnold-Heinemann, 1973), p. 18.
5. Anita Desai, "Replies to the Questinnaire," *Kakatiya Journal of English Studies*, Vol. III, No. 1, 1-2.
6. R.S. Sharma, *Anita Desai* (New Delhi : Arnold-Heinemann, 1981), p. 167.

7. Anita Desai, *Clear Light of Day* (New Delhi : Allied Publishers, 1980), p. 6. Further references are to this edition.
8. Raji Narasimhan, *Sensibility Under Stress : Aspects of Indo-English Fiction* (New Delhi : Ashajanak Publications, 1976), p. 74.
9. Meenakshi Mukherjee, *The Twice-Born Fiction* (New Delhi : Arnold-Heinemann, 1974), p. 189.
10. Darshan Singh Maini, "The Achievement of Anita Desai," *Indo-English Literature : A Collection of Critical Essays*, ed. K.K. Sharma (Ghaziabad : Vimal Prakashan, 1977), p. 229.
11. Anita Desai, *Cry, the Peacock* (Delhi : Orient Paperbacks, 1980).
12. Ann Lowry Weir, "The Illusion of Maya : Feminine Consciousness in Anita Desai's *Cry, the Peacock,*" *Journal of South Asian Literature*, Vol. XVI, No. 2, summer 1981, 4.
13. Anita Desai, *Voices in the City* (Delhi : Hind Pocket Books, 1965).
14. Darshan Singh Maini, "*Cry, the Peacock as a poetic novel*" in *Indian Literature of the Past Fifty Years*, ed. by C.D. Narasimhaiah (Mysore : University of Mysore, 1970), p. 230.
15. Shiv K. Kumar, "Art and Experience : A Note on Anita Desai as a Short Story Writer," in *The Twofold Voice : Essay in Honour of Ramesh Mohan*, ed. by Rizvi (Austria : Institute for Anglistik and Amerikanastik, 1982), pp. 191-92.
16. Madhusudan Prasad, *Anita Desai : The Novelist* (Allahabad : New Horizon, 1981), p. 30.
17. Anita Desai, *Bye-Bye, Blackbird* (Delhi : Hind Pocket Books, 1971).
18. Shiv K. Kumar, p. 193.
19. Ibid, p. 191.
20. Anita Desai, *Where Shall We Go This Summer*? (Delhi : Vikas Publishing House, 1975).
21. Anita Desai, *Fire on the Mountain* (New Delhi : Allied Publishing Pvt. Ltd., 1977).
22. Shiv K. Kumar, p. 194.
23. *Ibid.*
24. Anita Desai, *Clear Light of Day* (New Delhi : Allied Publishing Pvt. Ltd., 1980), p. 22.

23

The Concept of 'New Woman' in Anita Desai's "Clear Light of Day"

RAMESH KUMAR GUPTA*

A common contemporary issue facing every country is the question of woman whether in Western or Indian literary tradition, the women are seen as launching themselves for their identity. The 'new woman' today challenges the traditional notions of 'Angel in the house' and 'sexually voracious' image. The 'new woman' is essentially a woman of awareness and consciousness of her low position in the family and society. The feminist literary criticism has developed as a component of women's movement and its impact has brought about a revolution in literary studies.

Anita Desai's emerging 'new woman' is contemplative about her predicament and chooses to protest and fight against the general, accepted norms and currents. What is different about these women is that they are prepared to face the consequences of their choices. Anita Desai asserts that her protagonists are new and different : "I'm interested in characters who are not average but have retreated or been driven into some extremity of despair and so turned against, ... the general current."[1] It is for them a challenge to better their own personal existence.

Anita Desai's protagonists, brought up to be diffident, meek and quiet in the face of exploitation, are yet highly sensitive and intelligent and are desperate to find an outlet to their pangs. Their extreme sensitivity, however, channelises their mode of liberation in various directions. "Clear Light of Day" is chosen to evince and

* Research Scholar (English), Jai Prakash University, Chapra-841 301 (Bihar).

examine the wide space that divides the two types of women hailing from the same family — the women who do not act but surrender and so keep the tradition alive and next the women who choose not to surrender and be meek but break the convention to face their situation and take up a new road where no one can dictate to them.

Bim is the chief and simplest protagonist of Anita Desai. Her ambition was two-fold : to be emotionally and economically independent. She never wanted to marry : "I can think of hundred things to do instead. I won't marry, ... I shall earn my own living — and look after Mira Masi and Baba and be independent"(140). She would not depend on anyone, not even on her father. Had she depend on her father for education she would have been an illiterate : "for all father cared, I could have grown up illiterate — and cooked for my living or swept. So I had to teach myself history and teach myself to teach." (155) She gets education in history, a subject which has immense significance for her. The past is important as the progenitor of the present. Bimla has confidence much like her creator that "both the past and the future exist always in time present."[2] In an interview, Anita Desai points out clearly "time is presented as the fourth dimension of human existence."[3] The whole novel revolves round 'Time' drawing different impressions from the characters. Mr. Desai herself says :

> My novel is about time as a destroyer, as a preserver and about what the bondage of time does to people. I have tried to tunnel under the mundane surface of domesticity."[4]

It is her opinion of present as the important section of past and future that makes her pursue her ambitions, despite the gloomy atmosphere at home, and the burden of responsibility.

Bim's desire to be independent, to be courageous, and to dress and smoke like a man enables her to grow up both strong and confident. It is only because she has trained herself to be different that the much eulogized characteristics of women *i.e.*, weakwill, dependence and shyness are alien to her perception. Bim refuses to confine herself to her role as a traditional woman, showing an insignificant victim or object for others use and pleasure. "Women in our society are still trained from infancy to entertain, to please and to serve men."[5] But Bim was fortunate in her family. Her father was only known by his arrivals and exists and the mother through her diabetes and the cards, there was virtually no one to instruct the young girls the expected conducting patterns of weaker sex. The free will and the lack of training in meekness enables Bimla to pursue her ambitions.

Bim has confidence in herself that she could withstand the shock of the sudden death of her parents, the alcoholic Mira Masi, the tubercular Raja and the mentally retarded Baba without drawing back at any stage. Bimla alone is left to carry the family away from its perturbed atmosphere. Tara, being meek and weak willed, has no help. She has no courage to face the innumerable problems that the family all of a sudden starts to face. This sort of problem and her own business with insecurity and fear drive her towards Bakul. Tara with matrimony succeeds in getting away from the family which had suddenly gone out of control. With the death of Mira Masi and unexpected sudden departure of Raja Bim became only disappointed but she never became bitter and angry upon them.

The confused condition of Bim's mind disappears, and she is able to consider her inner psyche "by the Clear light of day." (65). Her calmness of mind is the emblem of the quiet before the storm, which is to overtake her soon as she does not know how to conquer her psychic contrast between accepting her sister and brothers and not accepting them. The growth of Bim's self is not yet to complete and this way her mind starts thinking about the past and the present. In spite of this, she begins to study a book which turns out to be the life of Aurangzeb. After perusal of the emperor's death, she is highly impressed by two sentences :

> "Many were around me when I was born. But now I am going alone..."and"... Strange that I came with nothing into the world, and now go away with this stupendous caravan of sin."

Bim thinks her life again in the light of these two sentences and explores its meaning. The image of birds, animals and insects are indications of the landscape of the house. They depict the atmosphere, participate in the emotional tumults of the chief characters, and throw their mental states into sharp relief. The novelist starts with the call of the Koel presenting the soul of the day-break :

> "The Koel began to call before day light. Their voices rang out from the dark trees like an arrangement of bells, calling and echoing each other's call, mocking and enticing each other into ever higher and shriller calls." (165)

Bimla is an educated unmarried working woman, enjoys financial freedom. Mrs. Desai appears indirectly to demonstrate that violence and oppression against women which can be diminished if women are financially self-sufficient and self-assured. R.K. Srivastava has rightly said that "The man-woman relationship becomes more important due to rapid industralization, growing awareness among women of their rights and individualities, and westernization of attitudes and lives of the people."[6] D.H. Lawrence has also pointed out that "The great relationship for humanity will always be the relation between man and man, woman and woman, parent and child, will always be subsidiary."[7]

Bimla, eldest of all, incurs upon her all the burden of the family. During his days her father passed his time in the office, and in the evening at the Club. But after his death Bim accepts the role of a father care of her sisters and brothers and later marrying them. Due to the responsibilities she has no time for her own love and life. Even though she has an affair with a doctor who becomes her family doctor. In this present novel she appears as a middle aged woman teaching history in a college, living an ascetic life, the only luxury she affords is to buy books. She explores her solace and refuge to buy books and reading of them. Bim is fairly representative of a new woman of contemporary Indian urban woman-single, independent, self-assured. At a superficial level, such woman may be seen as "westernized". Madhusudan Prasad, commenting on this image points out, "This image combined with the image of Sisyphus, is replete with deeper symbolic significance. A momentus image, it is connected with the theme of the novel illuminating the real character of Bim."[8]

It is her extreme sense of responsibility for the family and for Baba which makes her feel strong, and in control of herself. She does not lose her courage with the burden of responsibility. She appears to show that a woman can look after the family much better than any man. Bim is careful and conscious enough not to think the need of protection or love of anyone. She hates Mira Masi who craves for love and protection and is elated to receive it from the children if not from anyone else :

> "They crowded about her so that they formed a ring, a protective railing about her. Now no one could approach, no threat, no menace ... They owned her and yes, she wanted to be owned." (109)

The novelty in Bim is that she had no desire to be owned. She doesn't want anyone to feel either kindness or responsibility for her.

In spite of all the odds Bim gets success in building up her ambition, is triumphant in being independent, and it is Tara and Bakul who realizes this :

> "Bim had found everything she wanted in life. It seemed so incredible that she hadn't had to go anywhere to find it, that she had stayed on in the old house, taught in the old college, and yet it had given her everything she wanted. Isn't that strange Bakul... . She did not find it — she made it, she made what she wanted." (158)

Bim appears as new woman of the coming years. She is independent and liberated and yet there is no mark of arrogance or superiority in her. Bim is very clear about her aspirations urges an expectations, yet she is not the one to roll in pity about her alienation. If she felt cheated and stranded and thought Raja and Tara to be selfish. She was ready to forgive them. She was ready to see every flaw of others in the light of understanding. She would have to forgive her parents too, towards whom she was resentful because she could not grasp the disturbed atmosphere of their lives. Bim is able to obtain everything in life without the help of the masculine forces due to her confidence in herself. It is in Bim that we recognize the emerging new and independent woman that Simon de Beauvoir delineates :

> "Once she ceases to be a parasite, the system based on her dependence crumbles; between her

> and the universe there is no longer any need for a masculine mediator."[9]

Bimla and Tara in their quest for identity, liberty and individuality act and react in radical ways to the set conventional construct. Tara was certainly not unhappy in obeying her husband, but the question which finally perturbs her is 'how long'? She realizes that she does something that she never likes :

> "She felt she had followed him enough, it has been such an enormous strain, always pushing against her grain, it had drained her of too much strength, now she could only collapse, inevitably collapse."(18)

Tara analyses her position as a young and hopeful girl :

> "I must have used him as an instrument of escape. The completest escape I could have made — right out of the country." (157)

The used him as the direct track of escape because :

> "Bakul was so much older; and so impressive, wan't he? And then he picked me, paid me attention — it seemed too wonderful, and I was overwhelmed."(156).

The attention he used to pay her was something she always craved for but never received from anyone at home. So she became meek and her submissiveness and deference were used to keep her at the level of a docile and unquestioning wife. Tara feels that it is time for her to stop being submissive. She does not want to make Bakul stoop to come to her level, rather she would stretch out and reach over to his position.

In comparison, Bim has everything that Tara has not. And in that she has all this, and not what the society and tradition expect her to be, she is mostly misunderstood :

> "Now I understand why you do not wish to marry. You have dedicated your life to others — to your sick brother and aged aunt and your little brother who will be dependent on you all his life. You have sacrificed your own life for them." (97)

But Bim concedes to carry the burden of responsibility in spite of the dismal atmosphere of the house. She uses to do manly duties and breaks the traditional norms and currents. Here Mrs. Desai seems to suggest the significant sign of new woman.

Anita Desai's women are all reflective about their condition. Their protest is not for equality but for the right to be acknowledge as individuals — capable of intelligence and feeling. They do not look for freedom outside the house but within, without painting their lives in various artificial shades of sentiments.

Thus, this leads us to the very concept of 'new woman'. The new woman that has been explored in the book reveals that she (Bim) is not the 'ideal' or the 'best' woman. She is new in the dimension of time by being a rebel against the general current of the patriarchal society, and in exploring her true potential, along with the struggle to fulfil her urges and needs.

REFERENCES

1. Dalmia, Yashodhara, 'An Interview with Anita Desai', *The Times of India,* April 29, 1999, 13 Quoted in 'Introduction' Perspectives on Anita Desai, ed. Ramesh K. Srivastava, Vimal Prakashan, Ghaziabad, 1984, p. XXXIII.
2. Desai, 'Anita at Work : 'An Interview' Ramesh K. Srivastava, Perspectives on Anita Desai, Vimal Prakashan, Ghaziabad, 1984, p. 225.
3. Desai, Anita, Tremendous Changes, Interview by Sunil Sethi, *India Today* (December 1-5, 1980), p. 142.
4. *Ibid.*
5. Cooke, Joanne, 'Here's to you, Mrs. Robinson : An Introduction' The New Woman : A Motive Anthology on Women's Libers (ed. Joanne Cooke, Robin Morgan *et al.*, Fawcett Book, 1970), p. 16.
6. Srivastava, Ramesh Kr., "Perspectives on Anita Desai" published by Vimal Prakashan, Ghaziabad, 1984, P. XXVI.
7. Lawrence, D.H. Morality and the Novel in David Lodge, ed. 20th Century Literature Criticism, London : *Longman Group Ltd.*, 1972, p. 138.
8. Prasad, Madhusudan, "The Novels of Anita Desai : A Study in Imagery, p. 75."
9. Beauvoir, Simon de, The Second Sex, p. 412.